D1565849

Choice Contemporary
Stories and Illustrations

Choice Contemporary Stories and Illustrations

For Preachers, Teachers, and Writers

Craig Brian Larson

Baker Books
A Division of Baker Book House Co
Grand Rapids, Michigan 49516

Published by Baker Books
a division of Baker Book House Company
P.O. Box 6287, Grand Rapids, MI 49516-6287

Printed in the United States of America

Library of Congress Cataloging-in-Publication Data

Larson, Craig Brian.
    Choice contemporary stories and illustrations : for preachers, teachers, and writers / Craig Brian Larson.
        p.   cm.
    Includes bibliographical references and index.
    ISBN 0-8010-9064-4
    1. Homiletical illustrations. I. Title.
BV4225.2.L365   1999
252'.08—dc21   98-31829

For current information about all releases from Baker Book House, visit our web site:
                        http://www.bakerbooks.com

Contents

Introduction

I am a pastor who preaches weekly, and I have molded this book to meet the needs I myself sense.

I need contemporary illustrations from the world we live in. While I illustrate from my own life, I also want to illustrate from the world at large, from our common culture. Contemporary illustrations are relevant and interesting to our media-engaged listeners.

I need an illustration book to have an extensive index. I put the bulk of my work and time into studying the biblical text, so I need to be able to access illustrations quickly. Therefore, if anything, I have gone overboard with the alternative subjects that accompany each illustration and are indexed in the endnotes. I have done that for several reasons. First because we all use different handles to lay hold of the same idea. One person might look for an illustration with the word *faith* and another with the word *belief;* or you might look for the opposite, *doubt.* So the alternative subjects often cover the waterfront of synonyms to make it easier to find what you need through the index. In addition, illustrations can be applied in numerous ways, and so the major heading at the top of each illustration indicates how I have applied each one, while alternative subjects at the end of the illustration give other slants that you could take with the same story. For example, a story of an argument between husband and wife could be used to illustrate marriage or anger or conflict or reconciliation or the power of the tongue. Therefore, although this book has 254 illustrations, it in effect has many times that.

I need believable illustrations that have specific places, dates, and people's names, as well as documented sources. In this book, sources are usually mentioned in the illustration itself, and the endnotes typically contain full references that not only allow you to quote the date that an article appeared if you desire but also to research the story for further details at the library or online.

I need variety and balance. In my selection of material I used an editorial grid that calls for a roughly equal number of illustrations that are positive or negative, figurative or literal, and from Christian or secular sources.

The copyright law of the United States allows for the "fair use" of a limited number of words from other sources, and I have made frequent use of that liberty. Hence my thanks for the talented writers who have contributed unawares. For longer excerpts I have secured the permission of authors and publishers, and for their gracious permission I am deeply grateful.

This book is not intended to make a pastor's life easier; its purpose is to make your sermons more effective. May the Lord Jesus Christ use these illustrations to advance his truth, bring his lost sheep into the fold, strengthen his precious people, and build his glorious church.

Craig Brian Larson

Acceptance 1

In the *Atlanta Journal-Constitution*, Doug Cumming writes:

Lonnie J. Edwards, a physical-education instructor . . . was explaining square-dancing to his fifth-grade class at Hooper Alexander Elementary School in DeKalb County, Georgia. As he called the children to their places, boy-girl, boy-girl, Nancy, a little redheaded girl, said she was not coming. She started to cry and walked away, carrying a towel over her hands.

Edwards approached the twelve-year-old child cautiously. With her back to the other students, Nancy privately revealed why she couldn't possibly hold hands with boys: she had been born with only her pinkies and two partial fingers. Amazingly, she had hidden her deformity from teachers—she was able to hold a pencil—but the students knew about it and were cruel to her.

Gathering himself, Edwards said, "Nancy, we can't do anything about this problem, but I can help you overcome it and become the best you can be. Now I want you to hold your head up. From this moment on, you will no longer use this as a limitation."

Slowly, Nancy gave him the towel, which he never returned. Four days later Edwards began the square dance as Nancy's partner. Soon all the children seemed willing—even eager—to touch Nancy's hands.

That was in 1971. Over the next two years, Edwards continued to encourage her.

Today, Nancy Miller, thirty-eight, can do almost anything she sets her mind to, including play the piano and type about sixty-five words a minute. Married, she lives in Orlando with her husband and four children. . . .

"I grew up because of one man," Miller says.

Do you know someone crippled by shame? In the presence of others, be the first to show you accept that person. Acceptance is a precious gift we all can give others.

Community, Love, Shame
Matt. 8:1–4; Rom. 15:7

Date used _____ Place _____

Acceptance

According to the *Chicago Tribune,* on Monday, August 26, 1996, tragedy struck a Fort Lauderdale, Florida, family. Two boys found their twelve-year-old brother Samuel dead in their yard. He had hanged himself from a tree. Beneath the tree were a step stool and a flashlight.

There was little mystery about what had provoked Samuel to end his life. Samuel had a weight problem, and this would have been his first day at a new school. He had told his family that he was nervous about going to school because he was afraid of the teasing that would likely come from the other children.

There are few things more painful than shame. One of the great kindnesses we can do for others is to take away their false shame through acceptance and affirmation.

Affirmation, Appearance, Cruelty, Fear, Humiliation, Insults, Mocking, Peer Pressure, Shame, Suicide, Youth
Ps. 34:4–5; Rom. 15:1–7; 1 Thess. 5:11; Heb. 12:2

Date used _____ Place _____

Adultery   3

A study published in the *Journal of the National Cancer Institute* confirmed what God has always known. Adultery is bad for you. One of the many ways it harms people is by increasing a woman's risk of cervical cancer.

According to the Associated Press, the study found that women are five to eleven times more likely to develop cervical cancer if they or their husbands have numerous sexual partners. Cervical cancer is directly linked to HPV, a virus commonly spread by sexual intercourse.

"Male behavior is the important thing in this cancer," said Dr. Keerti Shah, a professor at Johns Hopkins University School of Medicine and the coauthor of the study. "In effect, the husband takes cancer home to his wife." Dr. Shah explains that men who have many sexual partners are very likely to carry HPV home and that up to 97 percent of cervical cancers are infected with that virus.

In the study group, wives whose husbands had twenty-one or more sexual partners were eleven times more likely to develop cervical cancer. Wives whose husbands frequented prostitutes were eight times more likely to develop cervical cancer.

As always, God commands what is moral because he is looking out for our welfare. Nothing is more healthful than righteousness.

Health, Immorality, Righteousness, Sex,
Ten Commandments, Unfaithfulness
Exod. 20:14

Date used _____ Place _____

Anger 4

What does it take to turn a person into a Judas? What motivates someone to betray deep-seated loyalties?

Unresolved anger and resentment, for one thing. Consider the story of Earl Pitts, FBI agent turned Soviet spy.

According to Evan Thomas in *Newsweek*, Pitts was raised on a farm in Missouri and was recognized as a Future Farmer of America. His parents said they disciplined him firmly but fairly. He was a captain in the army who regarded himself as a patriot. Even today he is described by his wife as a "good man." So what happened?

After getting his law degree and serving as a military policeman for six years, in 1983 Pitts realized a lifelong ambition by going to work for the FBI. In 1987 he was assigned to the New York office, and there his troubles began. He did not see how he could afford to live in the Big Apple on his $25,000 salary.

Thomas writes, "Morale in the office was poor, and petty cheating on expense accounts was rampant. Burdened with debt from student loans, Pitts had to ask his father . . . for a loan. He felt humiliated. Pitts later told a psychiatrist that he was 'overwhelmed' by a sense of rage at the FBI."

One morning he came up with the idea of spying for the KGB. That way he could kill two birds with one stone: he could solve his money problems and get back at his bosses. He later told a psychiatrist, "I was shoved by the bureaucracy, and I shoved back."

Over the next seven years Pitts worked as a Soviet spy and for his services received $224,000. When he was finally caught and convicted, the judge sentenced him to twenty-seven years in prison. At his sentencing the judge asked him point-blank why he had become a traitor. Earl Pitts replied, "I gave in to an unreasonable anger."

Never allow anger to fester. Deal with anger as God prescribes.

Betrayal, Greed, Malice, Resentment
Jon. 4; Matt. 5:21–22; Mark 14:3–11;
John 12:4–8; Eph. 4:26–27

Date used _____ Place _____

Anger 5

In *Scope* Shirley Belleranti shows the negative impact of anger on our most important relationships:

I remember one summer day when my ten-year-old son and a friend were getting a pitcher of lemonade from the refrigerator. I'd spent hours that morning scrubbing, waxing, and polishing the kitchen floor, so I warned the boys not to spill anything. They tried so hard to be careful that they innocently bumped a tray of eggs on the door shelf. Of course, it fell, splattering eggs all over my clean floor.

The boys' eyes widened with alarm as I exploded angrily. "Get out of here—now!" I shouted, while they headed for the door.

By the time I'd finished cleaning up the mess, I had calmed down. To make amends, I set a tray of cookies on the table, along with the pitcher of lemonade and some glasses. But when I called the boys, there was no answer—they'd gone somewhere else to play, somewhere where my angry voice wouldn't reach them.

Anger separates us from those we want to be near. Anger shatters intimacy.

> Child Rearing, Family, Home,
> Perfectionism, Self-Control, Temper
> Eph. 6:4; Col. 3:8; James 1:19–20

Date used _____ Place _____

Apology   6

Thomas "Hollywood" Henderson played football for the Dallas Cowboys from 1975 to 1979. On the field the first-round draft pick starred at middle linebacker. Off the field, according to the *New York Times*, he led a life of which he is now ashamed, the life of a crack cocaine addict. Coach Tom Landry eventually found out about Henderson's habit, and a few days before Thanksgiving 1979 he fired him.

Unfortunately, Henderson didn't learn his lesson. He moved to California to pursue an acting career and continued his drug habit. Finally in November 1983 the law caught up with him, and he went to prison for more than two years.

That was a turning point for Thomas "Hollywood" Henderson. He overcame his cocaine addiction and eventually moved back to Austin, Texas, where he began working as a drug and alcohol counselor. He was clean of drugs and helping others get clean, but something deep within his conscience still troubled him. He was haunted by what the fans of the Dallas Cowboys remembered of him.

He knew he had to do one more difficult thing, and thirteen years after being arrested he finally mustered the courage. He wrote an open letter to Cowboy fans and sent it to the *Dallas Morning News*, where it was published on Sunday, January 5, 1997.

"I had arrived in Dallas," he wrote, "as a 21-year-old, wide-eyed, big-mouth rookie from Langston University as the Cowboys' No. 1 draft choice. I had a covert life in the fast lane of stardom, cocaine and sex. . . . I want to apologize to Dallas, the Cowboys, fans of football, fans of Thomas Henderson, and the kids then and now for what I did thirteen years ago. I take full responsibility and have paid the dues. . . . I wanted to commit suicide on many, many occasions. What you thought of me haunted me."

Time cannot heal the conscience. Only a sincere apology can do that.

> Community, Confession, Conscience, Guilt, Repentance
> Luke 18:9–14; 1 John 1:8–10

Date used _____ Place _____

14

Appearance 7

In the *Pentecostal Evangel,* church leader T. Ray Rachels writes:

Most of the famous people photographed by Yousuf Karsh and included in his book, *The Faces of Greatness,* were not physically attractive. Somebody studied the faces of the 90 people in the book and determined that 35 had moles or warts; 13 had noticeable freckles or liver spots; 20 had obvious traces of acne or other pimples; and 2 had highly visible scars.

But the blemishes did not deter these people. Thornton Wilder, the playwright; Richard Rodgers, the composer; Picasso, the painter; and many others had obvious imperfections. But what might have embarrassed some just added character when they posed before the truthful lens of the great photographer.

Weaknesses do not deter those whom God has gifted.

Blemishes, Character, Faults, Gifts, Greatness,
Ministry, Talents, Weakness
1 Sam. 16:7; 2 Cor. 12:7–10

Date used _____ Place _____

Assumptions   8

Colin Rizzio, a seventeen-year-old high school senior—and a member of the school math club—from Peterborough, New Hampshire, took the SAT in October 1996 in preparation for college. As he took the test, one math question caught his attention. He blackened the circle for answer "D," but he thought it just might be that the testmakers viewed the problem differently, and that as a result they would mark his answer wrong. So he made a mental note of the problem and afterward went to his math teacher for his opinion. The math teacher agreed with Colin.

Colin then sent an e-mail letter to the Educational Testing Service. The ETS receives numerous letters of this sort, but no one had found an error in the SAT since 1982. Proposed questions for the test are tried out on a battery of thousands of students and dozens of math teachers before they ever make it to the actual SAT. Nevertheless, to their embarrassment, this time the testmakers were wrong, and Colin was right.

The error was based on an assumption. Those who had written the question assumed the numerical value for the letter "a" in one equation was positive. Colin saw that the equation was such that the numerical value for "a" could be positive or negative, which would affect the answer.

False assumptions on an SAT can lead to error. False assumptions about life and reality are far more harmful. They are especially dangerous because they are rarely questioned.

False assumptions are what keep many people from believing in Christ.

Beliefs, Creation, Evolution, Knowledge, Theology, Truth, Unbelievers
    Matt. 11:2–6; John 7:45–52; 9:1–41; 1 Cor. 1:18–25; 2 Cor. 10–11

Date used _____ Place _____

16

General Ron Griffith served in the U.S. Army during the Desert Storm War in Iraq. As the battle neared, Griffith was apprehensive about how many casualties the 24,000 troops he commanded would suffer. In *New Man* magazine, Gene Bradley and Wes Pippert write:

Griffith had estimated between 1,000 and 2,000 casualties during a war that might last between four and six months. After all, the Iraqis—on paper—probably outnumbered the American forces 2- or even 3-to-1. Worse, the intelligence showed the Iraqis had moved chemical weapons into position and Hussein had given his commanders authority to use them.

A Christian, Griffith spoke about his concerns with chaplain Dan Davis. "Let me tell you something," Davis said. "Before we left Germany, we had a prayer group that met every morning in Stuttgart as the war drew near. We prayed there would be no war. But once it became certain there would be war, we prayed that the air war might be successful and that we would not have to put our ground forces into this potential cauldron.

"We prayed that God's will be done, whatever it was.

"Now, I want to tell you something that is not an instinct. This is not intuition. It is a full assurance from God. I can tell you the attack will be hugely successful, more successful than anybody has envisioned. The war will be short, very short, and the casualties will be few, very, very few."

Until this conversation, Griffith had not finished his work before 1:30 A.M. each night. Even when he went to bed, he couldn't sleep.

"I kept thinking about casualties," he recalls. "Am I doing everything I can to assure they have the best chance possible to get through this thing? Have we thought of everything? I thought about the number of people I would have to send back in body bags to their mothers and fathers and spouses."

But after his talk with Davis, Griffith went back to his van, zipped up his sleeping bag and slept for five hours—the best night's sleep he had in six weeks. A great sense of calm fell over him.

"I felt God's presence with me. I took Dan's words as absolute truth. More important, that great calm stayed with me."

Gen. Norman Schwarzkopf wanted the Iraqis to believe that the Americans would attack straight ahead into Kuwait. So, the decision was made for Griffith's 1st Armored Division, as part of the U.S. 7th Corps, to move far to the west, then sweep north and then east in a big "hooking" movement that would catch the Republican Guard from the rear.

The Americans attacked on February 24, 1991. The war was over in four days. Thousands were not killed, nor were hundreds. Only four soldiers were killed. Was it a miracle? Griffith says yes.

Assurance, even in the most trying circumstances, is one of God's great gifts to his children.

Confidence, Faith, Leading, Peace, Prayer,
Revelation, Word of Knowledge, Worry
Heb. 11:1; 1 Peter 5:7

Date used _____ Place _____

Atonement

How can we atone for our sins?

A Canadian Press photo shows how one man from Havana, Cuba, tried to appease God's wrath. The man is lying on his back on a dirt road. Attached to his ankle is a chain several feet long. The other end of the chain is wrapped around a rock. The caption explains that the bearded man is inch by inch pulling the rock on a pilgrimage to a sanctuary dedicated to St. Lazarus.

This man's devotion is misguided, for we can do nothing—absolutely nothing—to atone for our sins. God has provided instead the free gift of forgiveness through faith in Jesus Christ.

Cross, Redemption, Salvation
Rom. 3–4; Eph. 2:8–9; 1 John 1:8–2:2

Date used _____ Place _____

Attitude

On January 13, 1997, reports Richard Conniff in *National Geographic,* adventurer Steve Fossett climbed into the cockpit of a hot-air balloon in St. Louis, Missouri, and rose into the sky with the ambition of being the first to circle the globe in a balloon. After three days he had crossed the Atlantic and was flying at 24,500 feet eastward over Africa.

The prevailing wind carried him on a direct course for the country of Libya, and that was a problem. Libya had refused him permission to fly in its air space, which meant he could be shot down. Of course, hot-air balloons cannot turn. When a change of direction is called for, what they must do is change altitude. At a higher or lower altitude a balloonist can usually find a crosswind blowing in a different direction.

Fossett vented helium, and the balloon dropped 6,300 feet, where it came under the control of a wind blowing southeast. Fossett skirted safely south of Libya, then heated the balloon, rose almost 10,000 feet and caught an easterly wind, which carried him back on course.

Although Fossett got only as far as India, he set dual records for the longest distance (10,360 miles) and duration (6 days, 2 hours, 44 minutes) in balloon flight.

Bertrand Piccard, another man seeking to sail around the world in a balloon, sees a similarity between balloon flight and daily life. "In the balloon," says Piccard, "you are prisoners of the wind, and you go only in the direction of the wind. In life people think they are prisoners of circumstance. But in the balloon, as in life, you can change altitude, and when you change altitude, you change direction. You are not a prisoner anymore."

A person changes altitude by changing attitude.

Faith, Humility, Praise, Submission, Thanksgiving, Trust
Eph. 4:23–24; Phil. 2:5; 1 Thess. 5:16–18;
James 4:1–10; 1 Peter 5:5–7

Date used _____ Place _____

Authority

In *Christian Reader* Erma Landis writes:

For decades, anyone living within five or six miles of the hat factory in Denver, Pennsylvania, set their clocks and watches by the sirens the factory set off five days a week. At 5:30 A.M., the wake-up siren would begin the day followed by the starting, lunchtime, and quitting sirens at the designated times.

When the siren system was eventually disbanded, a friend of mine was reminiscing with the timekeeper about his job. "What did you use to determine the exact time?"

With a twinkle in his eye, the man reached in his pocket and pulled out a child's Mickey Mouse watch.

Some experts are not as authoritative as they seem.

Evolution, False Prophets, False Teachers, Inspiration, Truth
Mark 13:22; 1 Cor. 4:20; 2 Cor. 11:4–6; 2 Tim. 3:16–17

Date used _____ Place _____

Belief # 13

Athletes illustrate what it means to truly believe in a person in authority.

A high school basketball player, for example, who believes in his coach because that coach is a former NBA champion, will do whatever that coach says. He believes the coach is right. If the coach says to change his technique in his shooting motion, he will do it even if it feels awkward and initially causes him to shoot worse. If the coach says to run four miles a day or lift weights thirty minutes each day, he will do it even though it hurts. If the coach says to pass the ball more and shoot less for the sake of the team, he will accept that role.

Why? Because the athlete believes the coach knows better than he does what makes a winner. When you truly believe in a person in authority, you follow that person in complete obedience.

The athlete who does not truly believe *in* the coach will not fully follow. He may believe things *about* the coach—that he is a former NBA champion, that he is honest, that his name is Michael—but believing certain information and believing in someone's authority are two different things.

Those who believe in Jesus not only believe the facts about his deity, atoning death, and resurrection, they believe in his right to direct their lives. True believers follow.

Faith, Lordship of Christ, Obedience,
Repentance, Submission, Surrender
John 3:16; 6:29; Rom. 1:5

Date used _____ Place _____

Beliefs

Lynette Holloway writes in the *New York Times* of a woman who unknowingly moved into a "sick building." Randi Armstrong moved from California to Staten Island in 1996 with her two daughters. Soon she and her girls began suffering recurring itching, fatigue, headaches, and cold and flu symptoms. Family members would spend days at a time in bed, missing school and work. Randi talked to the landlord and her doctor, but no one could help her or identify the problem.

After suffering for months, one day she saw a television news program describing maladies caused by a noxious mold called *Stachybotrys atra* (pronounced stock-e-BAH-trus AH-tra) that grows in dark, warm, moist conditions. It had become a problem in some buildings on Staten Island because of the borough's high water table. A library and a day-care center had been closed because of the mold. Instantly Armstrong recognized the streaky patches of black, slimy mold on some of the walls and ceilings of her apartment. As quickly as she could, she moved out of the apartment.

Sick buildings make a person physically ill. Like sick buildings there are belief systems and worldviews and religions that make a person spiritually and emotionally sick. If you live in that belief system, you cannot help but be hurt by it.

Error, Existentialism, Ideas, Myths, Naturalism, New Age, Nihilism, Pantheism, Philosophy, Postmodernism, Religion, Values, Worldview
Acts 17:16–34; 1 Cor. 1:20–21; Col. 2:8;
1 Tim. 1:4; 4:7; 6:20–21; 2 Tim. 3:7

Date used _____ Place _____

Beliefs

According to the *Chicago Tribune*, a British psychiatrist named Giles Croft, of the University of Leeds, did an experiment to find out whether people who believe in the reality of the Monday blues are more likely to feel bad on Monday.

Croft divided volunteers into three groups. He gave one group a report that said Monday blues are for real. He gave the second group a report that denied their existence. The third group received nothing to read. What Croft found was that the first group, which had received the report substantiating Monday blues, was more likely to rate Monday as the worst day in the week. From his research Croft concluded that how people expect to feel affects how they do feel.

What you believe is crucial! Beliefs affect not only what you expect and feel, but what you think and do and become. Beliefs are the grid we use to interpret life.

> Depression, Emotions, Expectations,
> Feelings, Reality, Truth
> Prov. 4:23; John 8:31–32; Rom. 12:1–2;
> Eph. 4:23; Phil. 4:4; 2 Thess. 2:10

Date used _____ Place _____

According to V. Dion Haynes and Jim Mateja in the *Chicago Tribune,* some astonishing news came forth in the aftermath of the tragic auto accident that killed Princess Diana in 1997. The chauffeur of the car had three times the legal limit of alcohol in his bloodstream. Furthermore, police estimated the car had been going as fast as 120 miles per hour when the crash occurred in the Paris tunnel. Clearly the wrong man was at the wheel of the princess's car.

But that is not unusual for celebrities, reported one security expert. Jerry Hoffman, president of a Cincinnati-based company that builds armored cars and trains drivers, said, "My experience is that a person will spend $150,000 to $200,000 on a limo and then spend no money on training the person to drive it. The driver is hired based on how friendly he is."

No doubt after Diana's death many celebrities began to pay more attention to whether their chauffeur could get them safely to their destination than whether he could carry on a charming conversation.

The same wisdom must be used when we choose the religious beliefs that steer our lives. The issue is not whether our religion makes us feel good. The only question is whether it is trustworthy and thus able to bring us to our hoped-for destination of eternal life with God.

> Cults, Deception, Error, False Religions,
> False Teachers, Gospel, Idols, Purpose, Salvation,
> Truth, Uniqueness of Christ
> John 14:6; 20:31; Acts 4:12; 1 John 5:12

Date used _____ Place _____

In January 1997, according to Moira Hodgson in the *New York Times*, Sam Sebastiani Jr., a member of one of California's most prominent winemaking families, died from eating poisonous mushrooms that he had gathered near his home in Santa Rosa, California.

"The mushroom Mr. Sebastiani is thought to have eaten," writes Hodgson, "was an *Amanita phalloides*, also known as the death-cap mushroom. It is the cause of 95 percent of lethal mushroom poisoning worldwide and is fatal more than 35 percent of the time; toxins in its cap destroy the victim's liver by rupturing the cells.

"Experts . . . are warning inexperienced mushroom enthusiasts to leave the picking to trained mycologists, who will not be fooled by poisonous varieties that closely resemble their nonpoisonous cousins."

Roseanne Soloway, a poison-control-center administrator, says, "A level of presumed expertise is not enough to save your life."

"One of the most sinister aspects of deadly mushroom poisoning," writes Hodgson, "is the delay between ingestion and onset of symptoms. The stronger the poison, the longer it takes to show itself, and by the time a patient is aware of the problem, it may be too late."

Some things you shouldn't attempt to learn by trial and error, for the price of a mistake is far too high. That's the way it is with our beliefs about the meaning of life and our choices about right and wrong. Much is at stake, and the full consequences of our actions may not be seen until it is too late. The only expert you can fully trust is the Bible.

Authority, Beliefs, Choices, Ethics, Guidance,
Knowledge, Lifestyle, Morality, Scripture, Sex
Prov. 14:12; Hos. 4:6; Matt. 7:24–27;
2 Tim. 3:16–17; Heb. 5:11–14

Date used _____ Place _____

Bitterness 18

In the early years of the Promise Keepers organization, it exploded in size and impact, and the demands of the ministry put tremendous strain on the marriage of its leader Bill McCartney. In *From Ashes to Glory* Lyndi McCartney candidly describes how she struggled with bitterness and what terrible destruction it brought into her life:

I never enjoyed sharing my husband. I always felt cheated. So many times Christians would send me cards or flowers, writing lovely letters saying how much they appreciated me sharing my husband with them. Sometimes my unChristian spirit would take over and I'd want to tell them to "quit borrowing my husband." I really did not like sharing him so much, and I began to resent it. People were always poking into our lives, stealing Bill's time, and I was so angry with him because he would let them do it. . . .

I spent about a year in isolation. The kids were out and on their own, and it was just the two of us in the house. I didn't answer the telephone, and I shut the door on all outsiders. I even shut out friends who loved me. I thought I needed time to myself. . . . I realized we had run amok, and even though thirty years together had generated many great, loving memories, I had to confront my own bitterness. I was hopelessly caught, eyebrow deep, in pain, and I was blind to all the good. I was a wounded, ugly woman. I had made my husband my god and my Savior my sidekick. My life was bleeding profusely. . . . I lost seventy pounds that year—thirty of them in January alone. It was a very scary time. . . . I was totally and completely withdrawn.

Coach McCartney eventually reordered his priorities, and God restored Lyndi McCartney's heart and marriage. The lingering lesson that she has courageously shared with others is that bitterness and isolation are spiritually deadly.

Community, Isolation, Marriage, Resentment
Heb. 10:25; 12:15

Date used _____ Place _____

Blaming God   19

In *Christianity Today* Philip Yancey writes:

When Princess Diana died, I got a phone call from a television producer. "Can you appear on our show?" he asked. "We want you to explain how God could possibly allow such a terrible accident." . . .

At the 1994 Winter Olympics, when speed skater Dan Jansen's hand scraped the ice, causing him to lose the 500-meter race, his wife, Robin, cried out, "Why, God, again? God can't be that cruel!"

A young woman wrote James Dobson this letter: "Four years ago, I was dating a man and became pregnant. I was devastated! I asked God, 'Why have You allowed this to happen to me?'"

In a professional bout, boxer Ray "Boom-Boom" Mancini slammed his Korean opponent with a hard right, causing a massive cerebral hemorrhage. At a press conference after the Korean's death, Mancini said, "Sometimes I wonder why God does the things he does."

Susan Smith, who pushed her two sons into a lake to drown and then blamed a black carjacker for the deed, wrote in her official confession: "I dropped to the lowest point when I allowed my children to go down that ramp into the water without me. I took off running and screaming, 'Oh God! Oh God, no! What have I done? Why did you let this happen?'"

I once watched a television interview with a famous Hollywood actress whose lover had rolled off a yacht in a drunken stupor and drowned. The actress, who probably had not thought about God in months, looked at the camera, her lovely face contorted by grief, and asked, bizarrely, "How could a loving God let this happen?" Perhaps something similar lay behind the television producer's question. . . . Exposed as frail and mortal, we lash out against someone who is not: God.

Free Will, Goodness of God, Love of God, Problem of Evil,
Questions, Responsibility, Sowing and Reaping
Gal. 6:7–8

Date used _____ Place _____

Calling

In *Discipleship Journal* author and editor Kevin Miller writes:

Jesus had a specific, narrowly defined ministry. He didn't try to do everything. . . . Jesus poured Himself out for people, but within the limits of the calling God the Father had given Him. He focused. . . .

Let me share how this works in my life. . . . One thing I know: God has called me to be a husband. That means He's not going to call me to something that destroys my ability to lovingly care for my wife and my children.

For example, a few years ago, I was invited to join the board of a Christian organization. I really believed in the work, and I wanted to help. To me, even being asked felt like a dream come true. I was ready to start the day before yesterday.

But as I talked with my wife Karen, she pointed out all the Saturday meetings and the evening phone calls that would come with the position. With her in graduate school, the family already felt stretched, and time for just the two of us was at a premium. She didn't think I should join the board.

I did not want to hear that. I grumped at her and felt irritable inside. How could I say no to something that would please God and perfectly match my interests? For three days, I went back and forth between yes and no, not sure what to do.

What helped me finally make this grueling decision was to pray, "God, what specific things have You called me to do?" One answer was, "Love your wife and children. Support them and help develop their gifts." If I joined the board, I realized, I couldn't fulfill that very well. As much as it hurt to say no, I had to turn the opportunity down. My specific calling as a husband became a protective boundary.

Balance, Boundaries, Burnout, Decisions,
Fathers, Focus, God's Will, Guidance, Love, Men,
Ministry, Mission, Priorities, Sacrifice, Servanthood
Matt. 14:22–23; 15:24; John 13:34–35; Rom. 12:1–2; Eph. 5:21–33; 6:4

Date used _____ Place _____

Character   21

When you think of someone buying a luxury home with a price tag of more than $300,000, you expect the new home to be of high quality. Such is not always the case, writes Julie Iovine in the *Chicago Tribune*. The preliminary designs for the new home of Michael Eisner, the head of Disney, included one wall that was so thin it would have buckled under its own weight. The $40 million new home of one billionaire software developer had pine siding so vulnerable to decay it started to rot before the home was even completed. It is easy for buyers to mistake luxury for quality. Experts in the home building industry say that "most buyers agonize over the wrong things."

Tom Kligerman, a Manhattan architect, says many buyers "find it boring to spend money on foundations and stud walls. They'd rather spend it on what they can see."

A builder of luxury homes said, "It appears that what sells houses depends on having a tub large enough for at least two people, and probably more; flashy stairs . . . and other glitzy, totally unnecessary elements, as opposed to spatial or constructional quality."

As it is with homes, so it is with people. Too many people put all their effort into image and appearance and pay no attention to the quality of their character.

Appearances, Excellence, Image, Integrity,
Ministry, Quality, Soul, Style
1 Sam. 16:7; Ps. 19:14

Date used _____ Place _____

In a story that shows the power of character, Oseola McCarty became something of an American legend in 1995.

Until that year, she had lived in obscurity in the Deep South. She dropped out of school in the sixth grade to help care for an ailing family member and to help her mother with the laundry. After a time she began to do laundry for the business people in the town of Hattiesburg, Mississippi, for fifty cents a load, which amounted to one week of laundry for a family. That's not a lot of money, but Oseola was thrifty and content, and after paying bills each week she deposited what was left in a savings account at the bank.

Year after year Oseola lived a quiet life of integrity. She cared for her grandmother, her aunt, and her mother. She traveled outside of Mississippi only once. She never had an education beyond the sixth grade. She read her Bible each day and kneeled each night to pray to her God. She regularly attended Friendship Baptist Church. She worked and saved.

And then when she was eighty-six years old, the banker sat down with her to talk about what she wanted done with the money in her savings account if she should die. To her astonishment she learned she had a quarter of a million dollars in the bank.

Oseola had lived simply in the past, and she wasn't about to change. She decided to donate some of her money to help other African Americans get what she had had to do without: an education. And so in the summer of 1995 Oseola quietly gave $150,000 to a scholarship fund at the University of Southern Mississippi, not asking that a single brick be named in her honor.

But word of her gift became known, and Oseola's name soon had greater prominence than if the university had named every building on campus after her. She was invited to appear on a spate of TV programs, including interviews with Barbara Walters, *Good Morning America,* and each of the major network news programs. She received numerous honors, including a trip to the White House for the Presidential Citizenship Award and a stop at Harvard for an honorary doctorate of humane letters. Her story was featured on the front page of the *New York Times*, in *Ebony, Jet, People, Guideposts, Christian Reader*, and *Glamour*. She traveled from one end of the country to another to be honored by people who longed to meet the modern-day saint.

Oseola McCarty proves that greatness is measured not by birth or wealth or fame, but by character. We all have the resources to be great in the kingdom, for we all can give ourselves away.

Generosity, Giving, Greatness, Humility,
Money, Persistence, Sacrifice, Saving, Servanthood
Matt. 20:24–28; 2 Cor. 8:9; 9:6–15

Date used _____ Place _____

Child Rearing

In *New Man*, a pastor tells how on one occasion his firm discipline helped his wayward daughter. His daughter Cori, who had given birth out of wedlock, was chafing at the house rules now put on her by her parents. She was warned that their evening curfew had strict consequences. The pastor writes:

Once, in the middle of the night, I awoke to the sound of the doorbell ringing. I rushed downstairs and peered through the window. It was Cori, standing on the porch, begging me, "Daddy, Daddy, let me in."

I saw Michael, my grandson, bundled up in a baby carrier next to Cori. I pointed to my watch and closed the curtain. She continued to bang and ring, waking up the neighbors, my wife and my youngest daughter, Sharryl.

"Daddy, let her in," Sharryl pleaded.

"Haman, the baby is out there," my wife pleaded.

"No," I said. "If we hold the line now, we won't have to do this again."

I wondered about the risk I was taking. I might wound my daughter permanently. My tiny grandson was out there. I might be blamed forever.

For twenty minutes my wife, Sharryl and Cori begged me to reconsider. "No," I said. "I'm going to bed. You should all do the same."

Cori gave up and spent the night at a friend's house. The next morning she repented, deciding to submit to the house rules and the values of the church. We warmly welcomed her back.

Parents know that at times real love feels unloving.

Consequences, Decisions, Discipline, Fathers, Love, Rules, Tough Love
Pss. 94:12; 119:67–71; Prov. 13:24; 23:13–14; 1 Cor. 11:32; Heb. 12:5–11

Date used _____ Place _____

Child Rearing 24

After an interview with singer CeCe Winans, *People Weekly* reported:

Gospel singer CeCe Winans, who was raised in a Christian home and who didn't wear makeup until she was 18, says she isn't about to embrace pop rock——professionally or personally.

"I don't listen to secular music at home," says Winans, 31, who lives in Nashville with her husband and manager, Alvin Love, and their kids Alvin III, 10, and Ashley, 8. "Very seldom do you find a mainstream artist who does only clean music. It's hard for me to wonder whether my children are going to listen to just the clean songs, so it's better to eliminate that music altogether."

CeCe Winans understands that parents are responsible for the environment their children have in the home. And often that means parents must give up something themselves.

Entertainment, Family, Holiness, Home, Music, Purity
Prov. 22:6; Matt. 18:6–9; Eph. 6:4

Date used _____ Place _____

Children of God

In our entertainment-oriented culture, it's easy to imagine that performing on stage in front of thousands of people would make life complete. Someone who ought to know is Dallas Holm, who has sung on the contemporary Christian music scene for decades. In *Contemporary Christian Magazine*, he tells Devlin Donaldson:

"I have young artists who come up to me and say, 'If I don't get to do what you are doing, then I will never be happy.'

"I have to say to them, 'Then you will never be happy. Happiness isn't based on what you do for him; it's based on who you are in him.'"

Happiness truly is being a child of our Father in heaven.

Happiness, Identity, Performance, Relationship, Works
Rom. 8:28–39; Gal. 2:20–21; Eph. 1:3–14; 1 John 3:1

Date used _____ Place _____

In the *New York Times* Barnaby J. Feder reports that in 1994 the Quaker Oats Company, which had posted strong financial earnings for several years, purchased the Snapple drinks business. Although in late 1994 Snapple had been the leader in beverages like fruit drinks and iced teas, the purchase turned out to be a debacle for Quaker Oats and for numerous executives in the company.

In late 1994 Quaker paid $1.7 billion to buy Snapple. A few years later they could sell the company for only $300 million—a loss of $1.4 billion! In the first quarter of 1997 Quaker announced an overall net loss of $1.1 billion owing to its sale of Snapple.

In April 1997 the chairman and chief executive of Quaker, who had promoted the purchase of Snapple, resigned.

Like large corporations choosing what businesses to buy, Christians need to choose their commitments and involvements wisely. Some activities are nothing but a drain.

Busyness, Commitments, Distractions, Habits, Involvements, Money, Priorities, Sin, Thoughts
1 Cor. 10:23; 2 Cor. 7:1; Eph. 5:8–17; Heb. 12:1–2

Date used _____ Place _____

David Huxley owns a world record in an unusual category: he pulls jetliners.

On October 15, 1997, for example, he broke his own record at Mascot Airport in Sydney, Australia. He strapped around his upper torso a harness that was attached to a steel cable some fifteen yards long. The other end of the steel cable was attached to the front-wheel strut of a 747 jetliner that weighed 187 tons. With his tennis shoes firmly planted on the runway, Huxley leaned forward, pulled with all his might, and remarkably was able to get the jetliner rolling down the runway. In fact, he pulled the 747 one hundred yards in one minute and twenty-one seconds. A superhuman feat indeed.

The church resembles that 747 jetliner. The strength of a few extraordinary humans can pull the institution of the church for very short distances. Or we can pray until God starts up powerful engines that enable his church to fly thousands of miles on the wings of the Holy Spirit.

> Dependence, Evangelism, Fruitfulness, Holy Spirit,
> Leadership, Power, Prayer, Revival, Self-Reliance, Strength
> Zech. 4:6; Luke 5:4–7; John 21:1–6; Acts 1:4–8; 2:1–47;
> Rom. 8:1–14; 2 Cor. 12:7–10

Date used _____ Place _____

Church   28

In her teens, Pulitzer Prize–winning author Annie Dillard went through a season of disillusionment with the church. In *Books & Culture* Philip Yancey writes:

She got fed up with the hypocrisy of people coming to church mainly to show off their clothes. Wanting to make a major statement, she decided to confront the authority of the church head-on. The senior minister . . . terrified her, so she marched into the assistant minister's office and delivered her spiel about hypocrisy.

"He was an experienced, calm man in a three-piece suit," says Dillard. "He had a mustache and wore glasses. He heard me out and then said, 'You're right, honey, there is a lot of hypocrisy.'"

Annie felt her arguments dissolve. Then the minister proceeded to load her down with books by C. S. Lewis, which, he suggested, she might find useful for a senior class paper. "This is rather early of you, to be quitting the church," he remarked as they shook hands in parting. "I suppose you'll be back soon."

To Annie's consternation, he was right. After plowing through four of the Lewis volumes she fell right back in the arms of the church. Her rebellion had lasted one month.

People should no more assess the church or the gospel by looking at hypocrites than they should test the value of diamonds by looking at a counterfeit. The question is, What is true? not, How have people failed to live up to the truth?

Belief, Church, Disillusionment, Doubt, Gospel, Hypocrites, Rebellion
Matt. 16:18; Eph. 2:19–22; 1 Peter 2:9–10

Date used _____ Place _____

On September 15, 1995, Canadian-born pastor Jim Bradford became an American citizen. In the *Pentecostal Evangel* he writes:

In the process of becoming an American citizen I learned that, since the mid–1970s, Canada has recognized the citizenship of any Canadian who has taken out citizenship in another country. I am technically the citizen of two countries—the United States and Canada. It's called dual citizenship.

Jesus described His followers as being part of two kingdoms or two worlds (John 17). Physically, they were a part of this present world and therefore under the rule of human kingdoms. Spiritually, they were also part of a heavenly kingdom, representing a greater allegiance. . . .

By virtue of natural birth, I am a Canadian citizen. To become a citizen of the United States, I had to choose to embrace that privilege and responsibility. And because I am not "naturally" an American by birth, I needed to be naturalized.

By physical birth, I am a citizen of this world; but, as a boy, I met Christ personally and was born again. This rebirth was the result of a choice—to put my faith in Jesus and to turn my primary allegiance over to Him.

Governments, Heaven, Kingdom of God
Matt. 22:21; John 17; Rom. 13:1–7; Eph. 2:19; Phil. 3:20

Date used _____ Place _____

Cleansing 30

The American Society for Microbiology studied the hand-washing habits of Americans and found some disturbing results.

According to the Associated Press, the researchers hid in stalls or pretended to comb their hair as they observed 6,333 men and women in restrooms in five cities.

The results: In New York's Penn Station only 60 percent of those using restrooms washed up. At a Braves game in Atlanta 64 percent washed. The study found that women wash their hands more than do men, with 74 percent of women washing their hands after using the toilet versus only 61 percent of men.

"Hand washing in this country has become all but a lost art," said Dr. Michael Osterholm, a Minnesota state epidemiologist.

And that's not good. The Center for Disease Control and Prevention says that hand washing is one of the "most important means of preventing the spread of infection."

To prevent disease, the American Society for Microbiology recommends you wash your hands in the following manner:

—Use warm or hot running water.

—Use soap, preferably antibacterial soap.

—Wash all surfaces thoroughly, including under the fingernails.

—Rub hands together for at least ten to fifteen seconds.

God also has advice on how to be clean—that is, how to be clean within—for our spiritual health likewise depends on it. We can only come clean through Christ.

Blood of Christ, Confession, Conscience, Forgiveness, Guilt, Holiness, Justification by Faith, Purity, Salvation, Shame, Washing, Works
John 13:8; 2 Cor. 7:1; Heb. 10:22; James 4:8; 2 Peter 1:9; 1 John 3:2–3

Date used _____ Place _____

Closure

Former president George Bush was a Navy pilot during World War II. On one mission, after being hit by Japanese gunfire, he had to bail out of his burning torpedo bomber. That did not go smoothly. As he bailed, he slammed his head against part of the plane, cutting and bruising himself badly, and partially tearing his parachute. He plummeted swiftly to the earth and might have been killed if he had not landed in the ocean.

Mr. Bush received a Distinguished Flying Cross for his troubles, but before he left the Navy he promised himself he would jump out of an airplane again someday and this time get it right.

It took five decades and a stint as president of the United States before he got around to it, but on March 25, 1997, George Bush, age seventy-two, jumped from a plane at 12,500 feet above an army testing base in the desert of Arizona. With him were several professional jumpers from the Parachute Industry Association and the Army's Golden Knights demonstration team. The former president and his "shepherds" sailed without a hitch to the ground, and Mr. Bush made a feather-soft landing just forty yards from the target X.

"It was wonderful," he told onlookers enthusiastically. "I'm a new man. I go home exhilarated."

It took fifty years, but in what had been termed Operation Second Look George Bush had closed the book on a bad memory.

Bringing closure takes many forms. Sometimes it means a long overdue apology, or the fulfillment of a promise, or finally taking on a frightening spiritual challenge. Sometimes it means handling unfinished business with God himself. Closure is usually difficult, but to be right with ourselves and right with God it needs to be done. God can help us in our own Operation Second Look.

> Amends, Challenge, Danger, Fear, Perseverance,
> Promises, Reconciliation, Regrets, Risk
> John 20:24–29; Acts 15:37–38; 2 Cor. 6:1–2

Date used _____ Place _____

Community

In *Leadership* pastor and author John Ortberg writes:

Psychologist Milton Rokeach once wrote a book called *The Three Christs of Ypsilanti.* He described his attempts to treat three patients at a psychiatric hospital in Ypsilanti, Michigan, who suffered from delusions of grandeur. Each believed he was unique among humankind; he had been called to save the world; he was the messiah. They were full-blown cases of grandiosity, in its pure form.

Rokeach found it difficult to break through, to help the patients accept the truth about their identity. So he decided to put the three into a little community, to see if rubbing against people who also claimed to be the messiah might dent their delusion. A kind of messianic, 12-step recovery group.

This led to some interesting conversations. One would claim, "I'm the messiah, the Son of God. I was sent here to save the earth."

"How do you know?" Rokeach would ask.

"God told me."

One of the other patients would counter, "I never told you any such thing."

Every once in a while, one got a glimmer of reality—never deep or for long. Deeply ingrained was the messiah complex. But what progress Rokeach made was pretty much made by putting them together.

Church, Sanctification, Truth
Prov. 27:17; Eph. 4:15; Heb. 10:24–25

Date used _____ Place _____

To live in community with others benefits one's health significantly. That is a finding reported in *The Journal of the American Medical Association.*

"Building on a dozen studies correlating friendship and fellowship with health, a new study has found that people with a broad array of social ties are significantly less likely to catch colds than those with sparse social networks," reported *The New York Times* News Service.

"The incidence of infection among people who knew many different kinds of people was nearly half that among those who were relatively isolated, the researchers reported. The lack of diverse social contacts was the strongest of the risk factors for colds that were examined, including smoking, low vitamin C intake and stress."

Researchers have found similar health benefits from community for heart disease patients. In one study Dr. Redford Williams, director of the behavioral medicine research center at Duke University Medical Center, "found that heart disease patients with few social ties are six times as likely to die within six months as those with many relatives, friends and acquaintances."

Reportedly, one of the main beneficiaries of a broadened network of relationships is our immune system. In another study, Dr. Janice Kiecolt-Glaser, director of health psychology at the Ohio State University College of Medicine, and her husband, Dr. Ronald Glaser, a virologist at Ohio State, "have reported that a person's immune response to vaccines increases with the strength of his or her social support."

As always, when God tells us how to live, those guidelines are for our own good. Church involvement contributes to our health!

Church, Health, Isolation, Relationships
Acts 2:42–47; Rom. 12:10; Heb. 10:24–25

Date used _____ Place _____

Community   34

According to Bill Jauss and Steve Rosenbloom in the *Chicago Tribune*, on July 19, 1996, Chad Kreuter, a reserve catcher for the Chicago White Sox, severely dislocated and fractured his left shoulder on a play at home. He underwent surgery, and the Sox placed him on the sixty-day disabled list. That's the kind of thing that makes a backup player feel even less like a part of the team.

But quite the opposite happened. Apparently Chad's teammates had a strong liking for him; each player put Chad's number 12 on his ball cap to show support. Chad was a member of the team whether he played or not.

As you can imagine, that meant a lot to Chad. Later in the season when he was able to suit up again, he showed his appreciation by, you guessed it, putting the numbers of each of his teammates on his ball cap.

All devoted to one. One devoted to all. That is what makes a team, and that is what makes the community of Christ.

Body of Christ, Church, Devotion, Loyalty, Team
Acts 2:42–47; Rom. 12:10; 2 Tim. 1:16–18

Date used _____ Place _____

While working in the 1980s on the computing staff of the University of Illinois, computer programmer Steve Dorner created the Eudora e-mail system that in 1997 was used by some 18 million people. To know that so many people are benefiting from his work has to make a programmer feel good. No doubt, millions of these users can't thank Dorner enough for using his skill and sweat to make their communication easier. But not everyone feels that way, and Dorner hears about it, because he now works for the company that owns the program.

Jo Thomas writes in the *New York Times:*

He gets about 100 e-mail messages a day and says that having 18 million users "is very gratifying, but it can also make me feel a little hunted sometimes.

"I'm the one who has to, in the final analysis, deal with every single problem, and I tend to concentrate on what's wrong," Mr. Dorner said. "There are days when I think that every one of those 18 million people thinks I'm wrong, stupid, and out to get them."

God must feel something like this computer programmer. As the Creator, he takes all kinds of blame from people who don't like his program for their lives. Often these people blame him for their own mistakes. Often they blame him for situations that are for the best, though they cannot begin to understand.

Worst of all, people think God is out to get them, when in fact the opposite is true. God has employed his infinite genius to program goodness into every person's life.

Creator, Goodness of God, Love of God, Pain,
Prayer, Providence, Suffering, Trust, Will of God
Prov. 3:5–6; Hab. 1:2–4; Rom. 8:28, 31; 11:33–36; James 1:5

Date used _____ Place _____

Confessing Christ

In his autobiography, *Standing Firm,* Dan Quayle, former vice president under George Bush, writes:

Although I had been raised a Presbyterian, my personal acceptance of Christ occurred in a Methodist church on a Sunday afternoon in 1964, when I was seventeen years old. With about fifteen or twenty other young people, I'd gone through an ecumenical Bible study course, one that alternated between the local Methodist and Presbyterian churches. We talked about Christ having died for our sins and the importance of accepting him as our personal Savior. On this particular Sunday afternoon, our group leader urged each of us to make a personal, open statement about accepting Christ. And in a quiet, peaceful way most of us did. Almost as much as the moment itself, I can still remember how the next day at school we nodded to one another as brother and sister Christians who had publicly professed our faith.

When Jesus ministered on the earth, he called people in public to follow him. Our decision to follow Christ must not remain a secret. Jesus calls us to make a public stand for him.

Born Again, Community, Conversion, Decision,
Family of God, Receiving Christ, Testimony
Matt. 5:14–16; 10:32–33; John 1:12; Rom. 10:8–10

Date used _____ Place _____

Confession

An article by Carolyn Hagan in *Child* includes a first-person account by Pulitzer Prize–winning author Alice Walker:

When I was a little girl, I accidentally broke a fruit jar. Several brothers and a sister were nearby who could have done it. But my father turned to me and asked, "Did you break the jar, Alice?"

Looking into his large, brown eyes, I knew he wanted me to tell the truth. I also knew he might punish me if I did. But the truth inside of me wanted badly to be expressed. "I broke the jar," I said.

The love in his eyes rewarded and embraced me. Suddenly I felt an inner peace that I still recall with gratitude to this day.

In the same way, we find that confessing our sins to our heavenly Father brings us closer to him.

Forgiveness, Guilt, Honesty, Repentance, Truth
Ps. 51; 1 John 1:8–10

Date used _____ Place _____

Conflict

In the *Chicago Tribune Magazine* writer William Palmer tells a story of conflict that will inspire a knowing nod from anyone who has had a difficult neighbor.

When Mr. Palmer moved into his new house, he and his new neighbor got along just fine. They would smile broadly and wave when they saw each other in the driveway. There was no fence between their yards, and it appeared they would never need one.

The problems began when Palmer's children began stepping in dog droppings in their yard, though they themselves didn't own a dog. The neighbor had two poodles, and Palmer was sure they were the culprits, so one day Palmer brought up the delicate subject. The neighbor denied the poodles were the problem, and before long the two neighbors descended into a messy spiral of antagonism. Droppings were thrown from lot to lot. Angry words were exchanged. Signs were posted.

Eventually the dogs disappeared, but the damage had been done.

In Palmer's mind, the conflict reached its low point when another issue surfaced. One day he received a note from his hostile neighbor suggesting that the dead elm tree that stood squarely on the lot line between them should be cut down. Palmer didn't like the idea of splitting the costs involved and ignored the letter. A few months later he and his wife suddenly heard the sound of a chain saw outside. They looked out their window and watched the dead elm on the lot line as it was sawn vertically down the middle, leaving half of a grotesque dead elm standing on his property. He left it standing for a few years as a conversation piece, then finally cut it down.

What a price we pay for hostility! This tree sawn in half vertically, standing on the lot line between two antagonistic neighbors, is a symbol of the pettiness, craziness, and desolation that so often accompany unresolved conflict.

Anger, Bitterness, Divorce, Hatred, Litigation,
Malice, Neighbors, Property, Revenge
Gal. 5:15; Heb. 12:15

Date used _____ Place _____

In *Inside Sports* John Feinstein writes:

In 1994 golfer Davis Love III called a one-stroke penalty on himself during the second round of the Western Open. He had moved his marker on a green to get it out of another player's putting line. One or two holes later, he couldn't remember if he had moved his ball back to its original spot. Unsure, Love gave himself an extra stroke.

As it turned out, that one stroke caused him to miss the cut and get knocked out of the tournament. If he had made the cut and then finished dead last, he would have earned $2,000 for the week. When the year was over, Love was $590 short of automatically qualifying for the following year's Masters. Love began 1995 needing to win a tournament to get into the event.

When someone asked how much it would bother him if he missed the Masters for calling a penalty on himself, Love's answer was simple: "How would I feel if I won the Masters and wondered for the rest of my life if I cheated to get in?"

The story has a happy ending. The week before the 1995 Masters, Love qualified by winning a tournament in New Orleans. Then in the Masters he finished second, earning $237,600.

The only truly satisfying reward is one gained honestly, for a guilty conscience can spoil any gain.

Character, Cheating, Guilt, Honesty, Integrity, Truth
Ps. 15:4; 1 Tim. 1:19; Heb. 13:18

Date used _____ Place _____

Conversion

In *Discipleship Journal* author Jean Fleming writes:

Recently something rapturous happened a few spaces down the church pew from me. The pastor announced that a young boy in our congregation named Crockett had given his heart to Christ that week. Another boy, about four years of age, jumped up on the seat of our pew, thrust his fist into the air, and yelled, "Yeah, Crockett!"

His response was totally unself-conscious; his joy and exuberance exhilarated and rebuked me. His mother had him sitting again in a second. Too bad. The entire congregation should have been standing on the pews.

In the life of any church, history is made when a person receives Christ. These are moments so great they must be celebrated in heaven—and on earth.

Celebration, Community, Enthusiasm,
Expressiveness, Rejoicing, Reserve
Luke 15:1–32; Rom. 12:15

Date used _____ Place _____

40

Conversion

In his book *The Moral Intelligence of Children*, Harvard professor and Pulitzer Prize-winning author Robert Coles writes:

Ralph Waldo Emerson once said, "Character is higher than intellect." Marian, a student of mine several years ago, much admired Emerson. She had arrived at Harvard from the Midwest and was trying hard to work her way through college by cleaning the rooms of her fellow students. Again and again she met classmates who had forgotten the meaning of please, of thank you, no matter their high SAT scores. They did not hesitate to be rude, even crude toward her. One day she was not so subtly propositioned by a young man she knew to be very bright. She quit her job, and was preparing to quit going to school. Full of anxiety and anger, she came to see me. "I've been taking all these philosophy courses," she said to me at one point, "and we talk about what's true, what's important, what's good. Well, how do you teach people to be good?"

The answer to that question, according to the Bible, is not education but conversion. No one can learn to be truly good, for only God is perfectly good. The light of true goodness dawns in the heart only when God shines there.

Born Again, Character, Depravity, Education, Ethics,
Evil, Flesh, Goodness, Intelligence, Morality,
Philosophy, Regeneration, Righteousness, Sin, Sinful Nature
Jer. 31:33; John 3:1–8; Rom. 3:23; 10:3–4;
2 Cor. 5:17; Eph. 2:1–10; Titus 3:3–7

Date used _____ Place _____

Conviction

When babies are born prematurely, one of the most common critical problems is with their underdeveloped lungs. In September 1996, the *New England Journal of Medicine* reported the results of a pilot study that offered hopeful treatment. The treatment is surprising. In the study, doctors filled the lungs of critically ill premature babies with liquid—an oxygen-rich liquid. Through this liquid the babies actually "breathe."

Normally, when fluid fills the lungs, people drown. But this special oxygen-filled fluid actually saves lives.

In a similar way, there is a sorrow that kills and another sort of sorrow that brings life. Normally, sorrow and depression drown a person's spirit. But like oxygen-filled fluid, sorrow that comes from God brings repentance and life.

Grief, Mourning, Repentance, Sorrow
Matt. 5:4; John 16:8–11; 2 Cor. 7:8–11; James 4:7–10

Date used _____ Place _____

Ken Walker writes in *Christian Reader* that in the 1995 college football season 6-foot–2-inch, 280-pound Clay Shiver, who played center for the Florida State Seminoles, was regarded as one of the best in the nation. In fact, one magazine wanted to name him to their preseason All-America football team. But that was a problem, because the magazine was *Playboy*, and Clay Shiver is a dedicated Christian.

Shiver and the team chaplain suspected that *Playboy* would select him, and so he had time to prepare his response. Shiver knew well what a boon this could be for his career. Being chosen for this All-America team meant that sportswriters regarded him as the best in the nation at his position. Such publicity never hurts athletes who aspire to the pros and to multimillion-dollar contracts.

But Shiver had higher values and priorities. When informed that *Playboy* had made him their selection, Clay Shiver simply said, "No thanks." That's right, he flatly turned down the honor. "Clay didn't want to embarrass his mother and grandmother by appearing in the magazine or give old high school friends an excuse to buy that issue," writes Walker. Shiver further explained by quoting Luke 12:48: "To whom much is given, of him much is required."

"I don't want to let anyone down," said Shiver, "and number one on that list is God."

Compromise, Example, Honor, Leadership,
Purity, Stumbling Blocks, Testimony, World
Matt. 5:13–16; 7:13–14; Rom. 14:13–23; James 4:4; 1 John 2:15–17

Date used _____ Place _____

Creation   44

Consider the power and greatness of the One who created the universe and inhabits every square inch.

Begin with our solar system. At the speed of light, 186,000 miles a second, sunlight takes eight minutes to reach the earth. That same light takes five more hours to reach the farthest planet in our solar system, Pluto. After leaving our solar system that same sunlight must travel for four years and four months to reach the next star in the universe. That is a distance of 40 trillion kilometers—mere shoutin' distance in the universe!

The sun resides in the Milky Way Galaxy, which is shaped like a flying saucer, flat and with a bulge in the center. Our sun is roughly 3/4 of the way to the edge of the galaxy. To get a feel for that distance, if our solar system were one inch across, the distance to the center of the Milky Way Galaxy would be 379 miles. Our galaxy contains hundreds of billions of stars.

Yet the Milky Way is but one of roughly one trillion galaxies in the universe. Says astronomer Allan Sandage, "Galaxies are to astronomy what atoms are to physics."

There are twenty galaxies in what is called our local group. The next sort of grouping in the universe is called a supercluster of galaxies. Within our supercluster, the nearest cluster of galaxies, called Virgo, is 50 million light years away. (A light year is the distance light travels in one year. To get a feel for the distance of one light year, if you drove your car at 55 miles per hour, it would take you 12.2 million years to travel one light year.)

Astronomers estimate that the distance across the universe is roughly 40 billion light years and that there are roughly 100 billion trillion stars.

And the Lord Almighty is the Creator of it all. Not a bad day's work.

God's Greatness, God's Power, Omnipresence
Gen. 1; Ps. 33:6–9; John 1:3; Acts 4:24;
Col. 1:16–17; Rev. 4:11

Date used _____ Place _____

The more scientists learn about the solar system, the more we see God's hand.

Writing in the journal *Nature*, Benjamin Zuckerman, a professor of astronomy at the University of California at Los Angeles, says that one factor contributing to Earth's ability to sustain life is the size of the largest planet in our solar system: Jupiter. Jupiter, the next neighbor to Earth after Mars, is a giant gaseous planet, with a mass that is 318 times greater than that of Earth and thus a much greater gravitational force.

It is that gravitational force that benefits Planet Earth. When massive objects that could do great harm to our planet hurl through our solar system, Jupiter acts as a sort of vacuum cleaner, sucking comets and asteroids into itself or causing them to veer away from Earth. Without Jupiter, says Zuckerman, Earth would be a sitting duck.

Zuckerman says massive gaseous planets like Jupiter are rare in the universe.

Once again we see God's design in creation. Having a planet like Jupiter nearby may be rare, but it is no coincidence.

God's Wisdom
Gen. 1; Ps. 136:5

Date used _____ Place _____

Cross

In *Leadership*, pastor and author Tim Keller writes:

Unless we come to grips with the terrible doctrine of hell, we will never even begin to understand the depths of what Jesus did for us on the cross. His body was being destroyed in the worst possible way, but that was a flea bite compared to what was happening to his soul. When he cried out that his God had forsaken him, he was experiencing hell itself.

If an acquaintance denounces you and rejects you—that hurts. If a good friend does the same—the hurt's far worse. However, if your spouse walks out on you, saying, "I never want to see you again," that is far more devastating still. The longer, deeper, and more intimate the relationship, the more torturous is any separation.

But the Son's relationship with the Father was beginningless and infinitely greater than the most intimate and passionate human relationship. When Jesus was cut off from God, he went into the deepest pit and most powerful furnace, beyond all imagining. And he did it voluntarily, for us.

Atonement, Christ, Hell, Love of God
Isa. 53:1–12; Matt. 27:46; Mark 15:34; Rom. 3:25;
2 Cor. 5:21; 1 Peter 2:24

Date used _____ Place _____

Cross

According to the *Chicago Tribune*, on June 22, 1997, parachute instructor Michael Costello, forty-two, of Mt. Dora, Florida, jumped out of an airplane at 12,000 feet altitude with a novice skydiver named Gareth Griffith, age twenty-one.

The novice would soon discover just how good his instructor was, for when the novice pulled his rip cord, his parachute failed. Plummeting toward the ground, he faced certain death.

But then the instructor did an amazing thing. Just before hitting the ground, the instructor rolled over so that he would hit the ground first and the novice would land on top of him. The instructor was killed instantly. The novice fractured his spine in the fall, but he was not paralyzed.

One man takes the place of another, takes the brunt for another. One substitutes himself to die so another may live. So it was at the cross, when Jesus died for our sins so that we might live forever.

Atonement, Gratitude, Love, Sacrifice,
Substitutionary Atonement, Teaching
Isa. 53:4–6; Matt. 20:28; Rom. 4:25; 2 Cor. 5:21;
1 Peter 2:24; 1 John 3:16–18

Date used _____ Place _____

Cross

In *Christianity Today* Andrea Midgett writes:

When I think of the cross, I see the arms of Jesus. And I hear him saying, in Matthew, "O Jerusalem, Jerusalem, you who kill the prophets and stone those sent to you, how often I have longed to gather your children together, as a hen gathers her chicks under her wings."

One cold night years ago in North Carolina I went outside to check on some animals then housed in my father's small barn. There was a full moon shining down in bright, brittle light above the pines. It was so cold that the water in the horses' trough had frozen over, unusual for the coastal counties. As I went to get an axe to chop through the ice, I noticed a yard chicken, a hen, perched near the trough, with several biddies tucked under her wings. I was impressed with how she had turned her face and frail body of fluff into the icy wind, her wings outstretched and, it seemed to me, surely tired, for the sake of her children. And I was uplifted by what I took to be a gift and encouragement to my faith, this visual depiction of Jesus' care for me.

But it struck me that those chicks had come to the hen. I don't know if she chased them around the yard first, if some came more willingly than others, or if some were still out there half-frozen. (There were a few late arrivals perched on top of her wings.) I only know the chicks I could see had allowed themselves to be gathered up and protected. They had quit fighting what they had no control over in the first place and said, "You do it, Mom."

And there is Jesus, dying a slow and terrible death, with his arms pulled wide.

The cross is God's passionate invitation to us to come in from the cold.

Good Friday, Invitation, Protection, Receiving Christ
Matt. 23:37; 27:32–50; John 1:12; Eph. 2:16–18

Date used _____ Place _____

Cults

In March 1997 police came to a Rancho Santa Fe, California, mansion and found the corpses of thirty-nine people who had said yes to the wrong thing. They were members of the Heaven's Gate cult, impressionable people who had left homes, friends, and families all across America to follow cult leader Marshall Applewhite. The police found their bodies clothed in black and shrouded in purple. They had committed mass suicide, believing that their souls would leave their bodies and join up with a spaceship that they hoped was trailing behind a comet passing near earth.

In the aftermath of the suicides, journalists talked with individuals who had at one time been proselytized by the cult and had seriously considered joining. Writers Jeff Zeleny and Susan Kuczka reported in the *Chicago Tribune* that a young man named Donald had heard about the cult while he was at the University of Wisconsin. His roommate became a believer. Donald put the cult out of his mind until a few months later when he received a phone call from a representative of Heaven's Gate who offered to send him a videotape entitled "Beyond Human—The Last Call."

"At that time in my life I decided I needed something to grasp on to," he said. Donald responded to the offer and watched the videotape. A few weeks later the cult representative phoned again and offered to send Donald a bus ticket to join the group. Donald thought about it, but eventually he declined, he said, because his girlfriend got upset about it. When the suicides later became public, Donald and his family shuddered with relief.

Just as it is vital to say yes to what is right, it is equally important to say a firm no to what is wrong. The word no can save you.

Deception, False Prophets, False Teaching, Spirit of Error
Mark 13:21–23; Eph. 4:14–15; 2 Peter 2:1; 1 John 4:1–3

Date used _____ Place _____

Death   50

According to the Associated Press and the *Chicago Tribune*, in the span of one year tragedy struck twice in one family. In 1994 Ali Pierce, the fourteen-year-old daughter of John and Anna Pierce of Massachusetts, was diagnosed with liver cancer. She fought the disease bravely for two years, but in November 1996 she succumbed.

Her parents of course were grief-stricken. To deal with his loss, the father sought a constructive way to help others. He started running and set the goal of entering the 1998 Boston Marathon. He intended to take pledges for his run in support of the cancer center where his daughter had died.

On October 11, 1997, Pierce entered a half marathon of thirteen miles in Hollis, New Hampshire. It was the longest race he had ever run. He was fifty-one years old, and so before the race he had a medical exam and was given a clean bill of health.

He almost finished the race. Just ten feet short of the finish line, wearing a baseball cap that said, "In Memory of Ali Pierce," John Pierce crumpled to the pavement, dead of a heart attack.

Death—what a terrible enemy!

Cross, Easter, Grave, Resurrection
Mark 5:35–43; John 11:25; Rom. 6:23;
1 Cor. 15; Heb. 2:14–15; Rev. 21:4

Date used _____ Place _____

In *Living with Uncertainty* author and church leader John Wimber writes:

Margie Morton was a woman of wonderful faith. Over the years I had watched her exercise that faith in many different situations. She and her husband were committed members of the church from the very first day.

Margie suffered from brain tumors for a number of years. She had surgery that was somewhat successful, but continued on the long, long journey of this condition.

I was praying for her one day when I sensed the Lord speaking to me. It wasn't an audible voice. Rather, I felt that he gave me some guidelines for ministering to Margie while I sat before him quietly. He said, "You taught Margie how to live. Now you must teach her how to die."

I started sweating immediately. I was not happy to hear those words. I loved Margie greatly and did not want to see her life come to an end.

At the time, her doctors wanted to send her to a hospital in Los Angeles with no real prospect of being healed. They recommended a treatment that might prolong Margie's life but without much quality. She would suffer tremendously, even with the treatment. I shared with her that I thought her remaining weeks could be better spent at home with her children, husband, and loved ones. I told her to share her heart and life with them, and that I thought she would know when it was time to go be with the Lord. I didn't think that Margie would agree, because she was not one to give up without a fight.

However, the next eight weeks she chose to stay home, sharing her life with her family and friends while conscious of her impending death. She did not spend her energies simply fighting cancer.

When it was time, she told her husband that she needed to go to the hospital. When she was in the hospital, her children and husband gathered around the bed and prayed for her. As they left they said, "Well, we'll see you tomorrow, Mom." She responded by saying, "You won't find much."

As soon as they left, she took a shower, and put on her brand-new nightgown. The nurse happened to come in just as she was getting back in bed, and said, "My, how pretty you look! You're all dressed up to go someplace. Where are you going?"

"I'm going to meet my King," Margie replied. Then she died, and did meet her King. That's victory! That's death that has no sting!

Hearing God's Voice, Prayer, Revelation,
Spiritual Gifts, Word of Wisdom
1 Cor. 15

Date used _____ Place _____

Deception 52

The Portia spider is a master predator whose chief weapon is deception. To begin with, says Robert R. Jackson in *National Geographic*, the spider looks like a piece of dried leaf or foliage blown into the web. When it attacks other species of spiders, it uses a variety of methods to lure the host spider into striking range.

Sometimes it crawls onto the web and taps the silken threads in a manner that mimics the vibrations of a mosquito caught in the web. The host spider marches up for dinner and instead becomes a meal itself.

The Portia spider can actually tailor its deception for its prey. With a type of spider that maintains its home inside a rolled-up leaf, the Portia dances on the outside of the leaf, imitating a mating ritual.

Jackson writes, "Portia can find a signal for just about any spider by trial and error. It makes different signals until the victim spider finally responds appropriately—then keeps making the signal that works."

Like the Portia spider, Satan's weapon of choice is deception.

Lies, Satan, Stumbling, Temptation
Matt. 4:1–11; John 8:42–45; 2 Cor. 11:14–15

Date used _____ Place _____

Deliverance

Jeffrey Bils and Stacey Singer reported in the *Chicago Tribune* that on Friday, August 16, 1996, a group of nine children and three adults were enjoying the animals of the Tropic World exhibit at Brookfield Zoo in Chicago. They walked to the large gorilla pit where seven western lowland gorillas live in an environment that resembles their native home, with flowing water, trees, and grass. Then what every mother fears actually happened. Somehow as the group viewed the gorillas from the highest point overlooking the pen, a three-year-old boy climbed up the railing without his mother seeing him. He then tumbled over the railing and fell some twenty-four feet to the concrete floor of the gorilla pit. As he fell his face struck the wall, and when he landed he lay completely still.

At the sight of a toddler at the mercy of gorillas, the crowd immediately began screaming and calling for help. One gorilla, named Binti-Jua, quickly moved toward the boy. Binti-Jua reached down with one arm and picked up the little boy. With him in one arm and her own baby gorilla on her back, she carried the boy some forty feet to the door where the zookeepers enter. When another gorilla moved toward her, Binti-Jua turned away, shielding the boy. Then she gently laid him down at the door of the gorilla pit and waited with him until zookeepers arrived to take him away.

Meanwhile other staff were spraying water at the other gorillas to keep them away. The boy was rushed to the hospital in critical condition, but he soon recovered and returned home.

That the gorilla Binti-Jua saved rather than mauled the little boy was a surprising outcome to a menacing situation. Like Binti-Jua, many things we fear are actually used by God to rescue us. Our God is the God of surprising outcomes, the God who sends astonishing deliverance, the God of Binti-Jua.

Miracles, Prayer, Redemption, Rescue, Salvation, Surprising Outcomes
Exod. 14; Matt. 27–28; Acts 12:1–19; 2 Cor. 1:3–11

Date used _____ Place _____

Diligence

According to the Associated Press, on December 14, 1996, a 763-foot grain freighter, the *Bright Field*, was heading down the Mississippi at New Orleans, Louisiana, when it lost control, veered toward the shore, and crashed into a riverside shopping mall. At the time the Riverwalk Mall was crowded with some 1,000 shoppers, and 116 people were injured. The impact of the freighter demolished parts of the wharf, which is the site of two hundred shops and restaurants as well as the adjoining Hilton Hotel.

The ship had lost control at the stretch in the Mississippi that is considered the most dangerous to navigate. After investigating the accident for a year, the Coast Guard reported that the freighter had lost control because the engine had shut down. The engine had shut down because of low oil pressure. The oil pressure was low because of a clogged oil filter. And the oil filter was clogged because the ship's crew had failed to maintain the engine properly.

Furthermore, this failure was not out of character. According to the lead Coast Guard investigator, the ship's owner and crew had failed to test the ship's equipment and to repair long-standing engine problems.

Sudden disasters frequently have a long history behind them.

Caretaking, Consequences, Laziness, Maintenance, Management, Responsibility, Shipwreck, Sluggards, Sowing and Reaping, Stewardship
Gal. 6:7–8; 1 Tim. 4:15–16

Date used _____ Place _____

When Andy Griffith, star of the classic television program that bore his name, entered his fifties, he found it increasingly difficult to find work in Hollywood, and his personal finances became tighter and tighter. He wrote in *Guideposts* that finally he and his wife Cindi decided things would be easier if they moved from Los Angeles back to Andy's home state of North Carolina; so they put their home up for sale and waited for a buyer. Unfortunately the real estate market was down, and no one gave them a decent offer for their home. Months passed, and Andy grew depressed.

Then one day the Lord gave Cindi an insight. "Maybe it's a good thing we couldn't sell the house," she said. "Maybe it was God showing us grace. If we moved to North Carolina now, you might indeed never work again. What we need to do is stay here and stoke the fire."

And stoke the fire they did. Day after day they went together to the office of the talent agency that represented Andy. They sat in the lobby, chatted with agents, and went with them to lunch. Eventually the work started to come in: four TV movies that year, including the pilot for *Matlock*, a show that ended up running for nine years.

Sometimes a closed door is a signpost from God. He has a better way for us to go.

Obstacles, Will of God
Acts 16:6–10; Rev. 3:7

Date used _____ Place _____

According to the Associated Press, a Dallas, Texas, man had a disagreement with a bank. His home sat adjacent to a tract of land on which the bank planned to build a new facility. The bank wanted to buy his home and knock it down.

The man said no deal. His property was appraised at $86,350, and he claimed the bank had offered only $68,000. The bank claimed it had offered more than that.

Ninety years old, the man had lived in his house for some fifty years. He didn't have to sell his home, and so he decided he wouldn't. The bank wanted to build, and so it decided it would. The result is a new bank building shaped like a horseshoe around the man's home. An automatic teller machine dispenses cash fifteen feet from where he sleeps. The cars of drive-through customers idle in front of his kitchen window.

These two parties may be adjacent to one another, but can scarcely be called neighbors. Those who walk in love do more than coexist; they cooperate.

Church, Community, Cooperation, Fellowship,
Flexibility, Harmony, Love, Marriage, Negotiation,
Neighbors, Relationships, Stubbornness, Submission
Matt. 22:39; Eph. 5:21; Phil. 2:4; 1 Peter 3:8

Date used _____ Place _____

On March 1, 1997, a series of tornadoes swept through Arkansas, killing twenty-six people and resulting in hundreds of millions of dollars in damage. To protect disaster victims, the Arkansas legislature passed a bill that would bar insurance companies from canceling the coverage of storm victims, and sent the bill to Governor Mike Huckabee for his signature. To the surprise of the legislators, however, the governor refused to sign it, objecting to one phrase in the bill.

The *New York Times* reported, "Mr. Huckabee said that signing the legislation 'would be violating my own conscience' inasmuch as it described a destructive and deadly force as being 'an act of God.' . . . He suggested that the phrase 'acts of God' be changed to 'natural disasters.'"

In a letter to the legislators who drafted the bill, Governor Huckabee, a former Baptist minister, explained, "I feel that I have indeed witnessed many 'acts of God,' but I see His actions in the miraculous sparing of life, the sacrifice and selfless spirit in which so many responded to the pain of others."

Insurance companies have traditionally referred to any natural disaster as an act of God. Who is right?

Such disasters highlight one of the central dilemmas of this life. The Bible portrays God as perfect both in love and in power, yet bad things happen. From our finite and limited perspective, this is a mystery we may never understand in this life.

Acts of God, Death, Love of God, Problem of Evil,
Providence, Questions, Sovereignty of God
Exod. 4:11; Deut. 29:29; Job 1; Isa. 45:7; Matt. 6:13;
John 9:1–7; Rom. 11:33–36

Date used _____ Place _____

Discipline

In *Returning to Your First Love,* author and pastor Tony Evans writes:

I'll never forget the time my younger brother rebelled against my father. He didn't like my father's rules. . . . Now, little brother was the Maryland state wrestling champion in the unlimited weight class. At 250 pounds, he was big and strong. . . .

My father told my brother to do something. I don't remember what it was, but my brother didn't think he should have to do it. So he frowned, shook his head, and said, "No!"

Dad said, "Oh yes!"

Little brother said, "No!"

My father . . . took him upstairs, and helped him pack his suitcase. My brother jumped bad and said, "Yeah, I'm leaving! I don't have to take this!"

And he walked out of the house. But he forgot a few things. He forgot he didn't have a job. He forgot it was snowing outside. He forgot he didn't have a car. He jumped bad, but he forgot that when you don't have anything, you don't jump bad.

So twenty minutes later . . . knock, knock! Brother was at the door wanting to come home. My father delivered him to the elements that he might be taught respect. . . .

When he was put out, my brother was no longer under the protective custody of our home. He had to fend for himself.

So it is with those who come under church discipline.

Chastisement, Church Discipline, Punishment
Matt. 18:15–18; 1 Cor. 5:1–13; Heb. 12:5–13

Date used _____ Place _____

Distractions

According to Jeff Gammage in the *Chicago Tribune*, in the summer of 1996 several thoroughbred racehorses in Kentucky developed foul nasal odors and bloody noses followed by infections in their nostrils. When veterinarians examined the horses, to their astonishment they found small egg-shaped sponges deep in the horses' nasal passages.

Where did the sponges come from?

Authorities determined that someone wanting to fix races had tampered with the horses, inserting the sponges to interfere with the horses' breathing, cut down their oxygen intake, and slow them down. Ten instances of such "sponging" were reported within a nine-month period, and the FBI was called in to investigate.

Like sponges in a thoroughbred's nostrils, sins and distractions weaken a Christian. They take away from what God wants us to be and do. They diminish our ability to breathe of the Holy Spirit.

Commitment, Compromise, Devotion, Entertainment, Habits,
Performance, Preoccupations, Priorities, Sins, Strength
Luke 14:15–24; Eph. 5:18; 6:10; Heb. 10:24–25; 12:1–2; 1 Peter 2:2

Date used _____ Place _____

Doubt

Richard Conniff writes in *National Geographic* that on January 12, 1997, two Swiss men, Bertrand Piccard and Wim Verstraeten, set out to be the first to circle the earth in a balloon. Their aircraft was called the *Breitling Orbiter*, and it was a high-tech masterpiece, complete with solar power panels and an airtight capsule for pressurized flight at high altitudes that would enable them to fly the jet stream at two hundred miles an hour. Price tag: $1.5 million.

Shortly after liftoff, however, calamity struck. With the cabin sealed tight and pressurized, the pilots suddenly noticed strong kerosene fumes.

Soon they e-mailed their control center: "Kerosene's coming through each pipe on both inside tanks and we cannot tighten them anymore. It is a nightmare. . . . Answer quick."

They were advised to lower their altitude, open the capsule, and hold on until they could reach the coast of Algeria. The fumes proved overwhelming, however, and they were forced to ditch in the Mediterranean.

The cause of the kerosene leak? A clamp, like those used on an automobile radiator hose, had failed. Price tag: $1.16.

It doesn't take much to undermine a great enterprise.

God intends that the Christian life be a triumphant journey, but often we allow small things like doubt or fear to scuttle God's grand plan for us.

Details, Fear, Sin, Small Things, Thoughts, Tongue, Trivialities, Words
Matt. 12:33–37; Mark 11:23; James 1:6; 3:1–12

Date used _____ Place _____

Jonathan Melvoin was a backup keyboard player for the rock group Smashing Pumpkins. On the night of July 11, 1996, he died of a drug overdose. The drug that killed him is a brand of heroin known on the streets as Red Rum—that's murder spelled backwards.

When news of his death hit the media, it caused an astounding reaction among other drug users on Manhattan's Lower East Side. The demand for Red Rum skyrocketed. "When people die from something or nearly die," explained one police official, "all of a sudden, there's this rush to get it because it must be more powerful and deliver a better high."

This is but one more example of how drugs produce their own peculiar brand of insanity.

Addiction, Death, Fear, Pleasure, Self-Deception, Sin
Rom. 6:23; 2 Tim. 3:4; Titus 3:3

Date used _____ Place _____

Duty

Jimmy Carter, the thirty-ninth president of the United States, did not retire to a life of ease when he left the White House in 1981. A committed Christian and longtime Sunday school teacher, Carter began working with Habitat for Humanity and busied himself in many diplomatic peacekeeping missions.

In *The New Yorker*, Carter said:

When Rosalynn and I left the White House, we decided since I was one of the youngest survivors of the office and we had a lot of years ahead of us, and I was deeply interested in human rights, and I didn't want to just build a library and go back to farming— we would do things that others wouldn't or couldn't do.

To me, this is part of my duty as a human being. It is part of my duty to capitalize on my reputation and fame and influence as a former President of a great nation. And it's exciting. It's unpredictable. It's gratifying. It's adventurous. I just enjoy it.

Whether a former president or a teenager working at McDonald's, we all have a sacred duty to use to the fullest what God has given us. But thankfully it is not a grim duty! God intends that our duties bring us joy.

Human Rights, Responsibility,
Service, Spiritual Gifts
Luke 12:48

Date used _____ Place _____

According to Lisbeth Levine in the *Chicago Tribune,* for several years TV talk-show host Oprah Winfrey carried on a running public battle against excess pounds that many people can identify with. Having tipped the scales as high as 237 pounds, she tried one diet after another. The weight would come off but then later come right back on.

Then in 1993 Oprah found a new personal trainer named Bob Greene. Greene gave Oprah a ten-step program that included guidelines such as (1) exercise aerobically five to seven days a week, preferably in the morning; (2) exercise at an intensity level of 7 or 8 on a scale of 1 to 10; and (3) work out for twenty to sixty minutes each session.

But Greene's ten steps were not the most important bit of coaching he gave Oprah. He turned the tide for Oprah by helping her understand why she wanted to eat so much. In *People* magazine Oprah said, "For me, food was comfort, pleasure, love, a friend, everything. I consciously work every day at not letting food be a substitute for my emotions."

When we're sad, lonely, feeling empty, eating is one way we can try to fill the void.

Similar to the substitution of excess food for love, we often use things in this world to try to satisfy our true need for God. God designed us to live in relationship with him. Therefore we will feel empty until we love him and walk with him. To substitute things like sex, money, success, and family is to fight a losing battle.

Conversion, Fulfillment, Gospel, Happiness,
Idolatry, Relationship with Christ, Salvation
Exod. 20:3; Isa. 55:1–3; John 4:10–14;
6:35; 7:37–39; Rom. 1:22–25

Date used _____ Place _____

Chris Edwardson, a medical doctor who practices in Dallas, Oregon, writes in the *Pentecostal Evangel:*

One day a judge came to my office. I asked him what he was really in for because his leg cast didn't need to be checked.

He said, "I just thought maybe you could give me a reason to live." He broke down and cried. I led him to the Lord.

I asked him what prompted him to tell me that. He said, "When you walked into the room, I saw something in your eyes that told me you had what I wanted. Something told me you knew the answer to life. I look in men's faces all day long, judging the truth. I could see that you believed with all your heart that what you were telling me was true. It was enough to convince me I needed it."

Sincere faith is in itself a powerful witness.

Divine Appointments, Light, Salt, Sincerity, Truth, Witnessing
Matt. 5:13–16; 2 Cor. 2:14–17; 1 Peter 3:15

Date used _____ Place _____

Evangelism   65

When Jeff Van Gundy, coach of the New York Knicks basketball team, was attending Yale University, he learned an important lesson the hard way. In the *New York Times* Ira Berkow writes:

Living in a dorm across the quad from Van Gundy in New Haven was the actress Jodie Foster, also a Yale freshman. The twelve students on Van Gundy's floor had put up $100 each and the total would go to the one who got a legitimate date with her.

"I had seen her around," Van Gundy said, "but was too shy to go engage her in conversation and then ask her out."

One evening on his way back to the dorm he was walking by a store that made popcorn, and a voice behind him said, "Geez, that popcorn smells really good." Young Van Gundy turned around, and it was Jodie Foster. "Yeah, it does," he said. And that was it!

"Finally one guy had the guts to ask her out, and she went with him," said Van Gundy, shaking his head in sorrow after all these years. "He got the $1,200.

"But I vowed that I would never be that flustered, or that unprepared, again."

Many opportunities come suddenly, including the chance to tell others the good news of Jesus Christ. We need to be prepared.

Ministry, Opportunity, Preparation, Readiness
1 Peter 3:15

Date used _____ Place _____

Evangelism

In *Today's Christian Woman*, contemporary Christian singer Susan Ashton tells how God arranged for her to sing about Christ in a setting she never would have dreamed of:

Garth Brooks's brother Kelly dates a woman who likes my music. One day, after she played my recordings for Kelly, he called Garth and told him he should take me on the road. So he did!

When I got to know Garth better, he admitted he hadn't heard me sing until I stepped on stage in Spain. That night, he was floored—he said he loved my voice and found my song lyrics moving.

But I was scared! I was afraid I might be booed off the stage while the audience screamed, "Garth! Garth!" But incredibly, I received a standing ovation. I was overwhelmed with how open the audience was to me talking about what it means to be a Christian.

While very few of us will bear witness for Christ on a country music stage, God will put each of us in situations we never would have imagined to shine forth his glory and gospel. Your stage may be the cafeteria at work, or a PTA meeting at school, or a conversation with a solitary stranger on a bus. The God who arranged the situation will also empower you to speak. When it happens, be bold!

Boldness, Fear, Witness
Matt. 10; Acts 1:8; 8:26–40; 23:11;
1 Cor. 16:9; Phil. 1:20; 1 Peter 3:15–16

Date used _____ Place _____

On Monday, December 8, 1997, tragedy struck Heath High School in Paducah, Kentucky. According to Roy Maynard in *World* magazine, a small group of students, who conducted a daily prayer meeting in a hallway near the administrative offices, finished their morning prayers and were about to head off to classes. Shortly after the final amen, it is alleged that a freshman named Michael, whom the prayer group leader had befriended earlier in the year, opened fire on the students with a .22-caliber automatic.

The group's leader, Ben Strong, called out, "Mike, what are you doing?" and walked toward him. After firing ten rounds, Michael finally dropped his gun. Ben Strong walked up and put his arms around the gunman, urging him to calm down.

Three students were killed in the shooting spree, and five were wounded, including one paralyzed.

In the aftermath of the tragedy, pastors and youth ministers were called in to counsel the students. According to one counselor, "The thing the kids are asking most is 'Why?' And all I can tell them is that what Satan means for evil, God can bring good out of. And it's already happening."

"The morning prayer meetings," writes Maynard, "usually attract 25 to 30 kids; on Tuesday morning, nearly half the school—more than 250 students—attended. A number of the youth ministers who have compared notes all say that they've led kids to Christ in the aftermath of the shooting."

Said Ben Strong, "God's the only one we can turn to in something like this, and a lot of people are turning to him. I believe God can bring revival out of this."

Whatever happens, one thing is sure: good can overcome evil. Fifteen-year-old Melissa Jenkins, paralyzed in the shootings, was one of the first victims to send a message to the assailant: "Tell Michael I forgive him."

Forgiveness, Goodness, Murder, Tragedy
Gen. 50:20; Rom. 8:28; 12:21

Date used _____ Place _____

Example   68

On September 19, 1997, a drivers-ed teacher from Durham, North Carolina, gave a lesson he would like to forget. According to the Associated Press, police said the teacher, age thirty-six, had one student driver at the wheel and another in the car when another car cut them off. At that the teacher apparently went into road rage. It is alleged that he ordered the student driver to pursue the other car. When the other car pulled over, the drivers-ed teacher got out of his car and punched the other driver in the face, giving him a bloody nose. The bloodied driver then pulled away.

Amazingly, that wasn't enough for the angry teacher. He again ordered the student to pursue the other car. Eventually the police pulled over the drivers-ed car for speeding, and the motorist with the bloody nose circled back to report to the police what had happened.

The drivers-ed teacher was arrested and charged with simple assault, punishable by up to sixty days in jail. He was released on $400 bail. Later he was suspended from his job and then resigned.

When teachers are the problem, we really have a problem.

Anger, Self-Control, Teachers, Temper
1 Cor. 11:1; James 3:1

Date used _____ Place _____

Example

69

In *Everyone's a Coach*, Don Shula, the winningest coach in National Football League history, writes:

A lot of leaders want to tell people what to do, but they don't provide the example. "Do as I say, not as I do," doesn't cut it. Of course, I'm not about to show players how to run or pass or block or tackle by doing these things myself. My example is in things like my high standards of performance, my attention to detail, and—above all—how hard I work. . . .

During the 1994–95 season, I had what I thought was a calcium spur on my heel. It became so painful to move around on the practice field every day that I began to wear something like a ski boot at practice to reduce some of the pain. I didn't want to take the time to correct the problem until after the season. I can't ask my players to play hurt if I wimp out when I'm hurting a little bit. Finally I had no choice. One day in early December, when I was heading off the field after a practice, I felt something pop. It turned out I'd ruptured my Achilles tendon. . . . The day I had the operation was the first regular-season practice I had missed in my twenty-five years with the Dolphins.

The next day Shula was back at practice getting around in a golf cart.

The pin in the hinge of leadership is our example.

Consistency, Dedication, Devotion, Leadership, Sacrifice
1 Cor. 11:1; 1 Tim. 4:12; Titus 2:7; 1 Peter 5:3

Date used ＿＿＿＿＿＿＿＿ Place ＿＿＿＿＿＿＿＿＿＿＿＿＿＿＿＿

Author Marshall Shelley, who suffered the deaths of two of his children, writes in *Leadership:*

Even as a child, I loved to read, and I quickly learned that I would most likely be confused during the opening chapters of a novel. New characters were introduced. Disparate, seemingly random events took place. Subplots were complicated and didn't seem to make any sense in relation to the main plot.

But I learned to keep reading. Why? Because you know that the author, if he or she is good, will weave them all together by the end of the book. Eventually, each element will be meaningful.

At times, such faith has to be a conscious choice.

Even when I can't explain why a chromosomal abnormality develops in my son, which prevents him from living on earth more than two minutes. . . .

Even when I can't fathom why our daughter has to endure two years of severe and profound retardation and continual seizures. . . .

I choose to trust that before the book closes, the Author will make things clear.

Confusion, Death, Mourning, Trials, Trust
Prov. 3:5–6; Mark 4:35–41; 2 Cor. 5:7; Heb. 11

Date used _____ Place _____

In 1972 NASA launched the exploratory space probe Pioneer 10. According to Leon Jaroff in *Time,* its primary mission was to reach Jupiter, photograph the planet and its moons, and beam data to Earth about Jupiter's magnetic field, radiation belts, and atmosphere. Scientists regarded this as a bold plan, for at this time no probe had ever gone beyond Mars, and they feared the asteroid belt would destroy Pioneer 10 before it could reach its target.

But Pioneer 10 accomplished its mission and much more. Swinging past the giant planet in November 1973, Pioneer 10 was then hurled by Jupiter's immense gravity at a higher rate of speed toward the edge of the solar system. At 1 billion miles from the sun Pioneer 10 passed Saturn, then swept past Uranus at some 2 billion miles, Neptune at nearly 3 billion miles, Pluto at almost 4 billion miles. By 1997, twenty-five years after its launch, Pioneer 10 was more than 6 billion miles from the sun. (Not bad for a device that was designed to have a useful life of only three years.)

And despite that immense distance, Pioneer 10 was still beaming back radio signals that scientists on Earth could decipher. "Perhaps most remarkable," writes Jaroff, "those signals emanate from an 8-watt transmitter, which radiates about as much power as a bedroom night light, and take more than nine hours to reach Earth."

Even a faint message can travel a long way. Similarly, even prayers with small faith can reach the heart of God, whose great strength can work the impossible.

Expectations, Mustard Seed, Perseverance,
Persistence, Prayer, Weakness
Matt. 17:20–21; Luke 17:5–6

Date used _____ Place _____

Falsehoods have a way of taking on an air of truth the more they're quoted. Consider one commonly quoted statistical falsehood. In *Better Families,* J. Allan Petersen writes:

Pollster Louis Harris has written, "The idea that half of American marriages are doomed is one of the most specious pieces of statistical nonsense ever perpetuated in modern times.

"It all began when the Census Bureau noted that during one year, there were 2.4 million marriages and 1.2 million divorces. Someone did the math without calculating the 54 million marriages already in existence, and presto, a ridiculous but quotable statistic was born."

Harris concludes, "Only one out of eight marriages will end in divorce. In any single year, only about 2 percent of existing marriages will break up."

As this statistical example shows, falsehoods are tenacious. Just because it's said doesn't mean it's so.

Divorce, Marriage, Statistics, Truth
Prov. 30:8; 1 John 4:6

Date used _____ Place _____

Where do all these computer viruses come from anyway? What sort of a sick mind would intentionally mess up the computer data of others?

John Norstad, a Northwestern University systems engineer and computer guru who invented "Disinfect," a software program that protects computers from viruses, once discovered the source of many of the computer viruses. In an interview with writer Peter Gorner, Norstad said:

I went to a conference in Europe in 1992 and met most of my counterparts in the PC anti-viral community. One fellow was a Bulgarian who told us about the Bulgarian virus-writing factory.

Evidently, during the Communist heyday, the KGB trained and paid PC programmers to break Western copy-protection schemes. It was an official piracy program. Then, when the government fell in Bulgaria, all these people were out of work and bitter. So they formed virus-writing clubs and set about infecting the PC community worldwide. A significant percentage of the PC viruses came out of a group of disaffected hackers who had formerly worked for the Communists.

Computer viruses are a lot like false teachings about God and morality: they destroy what is valuable. Where do all the false teachings come from? According to the apostle Paul, many come from a group of malicious spirits called demons. They intentionally pump error into the world to deceive and destroy people.

Deceiving Spirits, Deception, Demons, Satan
John 8:44; 1 Tim. 4:1

Date used _____ Place _____

Family   74

Families don't grow strong unless parents invest precious time in them. In *New Man* Gary Oliver writes about a difficult decision made by professional baseball player Tim Burke concerning his family:

From the time Burke can first remember, his dream was to be a professional baseball player. Through years of sacrifice and hard work he achieved that goal.

While a successful pitcher for the Montreal Expos, he and his wife wanted to start a family but discovered they were unable to have children. After much prayer, they decided to adopt four special-needs international children. This led to one of the most difficult decisions of Tim's life.

He discovered that his life on the road conflicted with his ability to be a quality husband and dad. Over time it became clear that he couldn't do a good job at both. After more prayer and soul-searching, he made what many considered an unbelievable decision: he decided to give up professional baseball.

When he left the stadium for the last time, reporters wanted to know why he was retiring. "Baseball is going to do just fine without me," he said. "It's not going to miss a beat. But I'm the only father my children have. I'm the only husband my wife has. And they need me a lot more than baseball does."

Choices, Decisions, Devotion, Marriage,
Parenting, Priorities, Sacrifice
Eph. 5:25; 6:4

Date used _____ Place _____

According to the Associated Press, in June 1997 an employee at a Massachusetts store found a $20 bill on the washroom floor with a note folded inside.

"HELP KIDNAPPED CALL HIGHWAY PATROL," the note said on one side, and listed two Oklahoma phone numbers. "MY FORD VAN CREAM & BLUE OKLA," it said on the other side.

The police were notified, and after they determined the names of the elderly couple registered at those phone numbers, Floyd and Rita Rupp, they put out an all-points bulletin. The media published photos and descriptions of the missing couple. The two daughters of the couple sat anxiously by their phones waiting for news as the interstate police search lasted twenty-four hours.

Then a phone call was received at the office of Mr. Rupp. The office manager heard a familiar voice report, "I'm sitting here enjoying the view of the ocean."

It was none other than the missing man.

"You have no idea what's going on, do you?" said the office manager.

No, he didn't, but when he found out, he and his wife were quite embarrassed. It turned out his wife had been feeling insecure about the drive back to Oklahoma, which she would be making alone. She had written the kidnap note and kept it in her purse just in case she needed it. It had accidentally fallen out of her purse in the store washroom.

When our fears—and our elaborate efforts to find security—are brought into the open, what once terrified us can seem silly. The basis for a strong sense of security is a deep trust in God.

Danger, Fear, Peace, Security, Trust
Ps. 46:1–3

Date used _____ Place _____

Fear

An aerosol propellant called 1,1,1 trichloroethane, which has been used in spray cans of household cleaners, is toxic when the product is used improperly. John Broder writes in the *New York Times:*

In the early 1980's, teen-agers discovered they could get high by spraying the cleaner into a plastic bag and breathing the propellant fumes.

The label on the can clearly warned of death or serious injury if the product was inhaled, said Victor E. Schwartz, a Washington lawyer, but some young people ignored it, leading to at least one death. The company wanted to make the warning larger, but Mr. Schwartz argued against it, saying that teen-agers would then assume that there was more of the propellant in the product.

"What do kids worry about more than death or injury?" Mr. Schwartz asked his clients. "How they look, of course. So we wrote the warning to say that sniffing the stuff could cause hair loss or facial disfigurement. It doesn't, but it scared the target audience and we haven't had a liability claim since then."

What we fear controls us. What we fear results from our values. What is most important to you?

Warnings, Worry
Matt. 6:25–34; 1 Peter 3:14

Date used _____ Place _____

At 7:00 on Thursday night, December 5, 1996, at a dinner in Washington sponsored by the American Enterprise Institute, Alan Greenspan, the chairman of the Federal Reserve Board, gave a speech that to the average person would be nothing more than boring, economic mumbo jumbo. But not to investors with thousands, millions, or billions of dollars in the stock and bond markets.

In that speech Greenspan uttered ten sentences that in less than an hour began to shake markets around the financial world. The stock market in Australia, which was trading at the time, suddenly took a nose dive when news of Greenspan's comments came over the newswires; a whopping 2.91 percent of its total value was lost by the end of the trading day. Japan's markets tumbled 3.19 percent in value, Germany 4.05 percent. "A little over 14 hours after Mr. Greenspan rose to give his speech," wrote Richard Stevenson in the *New York Times*, "the New York Stock Exchange opened, and the Dow-Jones industrial average was soon down more than 144 points."

What did Greenspan say in those ten sentences that shook the financial world? For one thing, he used the word *bubble,* suggesting that the stock market at the time may have been overheated and overvalued by speculation. "In financial markets, one of the nastiest things that can be said about a rising market," wrote Floyd Norris, "is that it is a 'bubble,' conjuring images of a burst that would wipe out most of the gains in an instant."

As this episode shows, when the chairman of the Federal Reserve Board talks, investors listen. Their money is at stake. The chairman has the power to adjust interest rates, which dramatically affect the economy and investments.

In a similar way, when God talks, the wise person listens, for far more than money is at stake.

Obedience, Reverence, Word of God
Exod. 19–20; Isa. 66:2; Phil. 2:12–13; 1 Peter 1:17

Date used _____ Place _____

Fear of God 78

In 1996 U.S. astronaut Shannon Lucid spent 188 days in space along with two cosmonauts from the former Soviet Union. One night after supper she and the two cosmonauts began talking about their childhoods and what life was like for them during the Cold War between the United States and the Soviet Union.

Lucid and the cosmonauts surprised each other. She told them she had grown up fearful of the Soviet Union, and most American adults would have felt the same way. But the cosmonauts said they had been equally afraid of the United States.

What? Afraid of the United States? The idea that Russians would think we wanted to destroy them is incredible to Americans.

These Russian cosmonauts resemble those who do not know God. They think that God wants to harm them, but nothing could be farther from the truth. Although there is a spiritual cold war going on, in which those who do not know Christ are indeed God's enemies because of their sins, they are not enemies that God wants to destroy. They are enemies that God dearly wants to make his friends.

Fear, Love of God, Peace, Reconciliation
John 3:16; Eph. 2:1–9

Date used ______________ Place ______________________________

According to Tim Franklin in the *Chicago Tribune,* in the 1996 summer Olympics in Atlanta, the U.S. women's softball team lost only one game, and it was a game they should have won. Here's why.

In the fifth inning, with the score tied 0–0, U.S. player Dani Tyler clubbed a home run over the fence. She took her home run trot around the bases, and when she reached home, amid the excitement and congratulations and high-fives from her teammates, she failed to tag home plate. When she reached the dugout, the opposing team of Australians tagged home, and the umpire at first base agreed that she had stepped right over the plate.

Tyler had to return to third base, where she was stranded. The score remained 0–0 until the end of regulation play.

The U.S. scored a run in the top half of the tenth inning. Then in the bottom of the inning, one strike away from defeat, an Australian player hit a two-run homer to win the game for Australia. The loss was an emotional blow to the American team, and especially to Dani Tyler. "I just can't believe I missed it," she said after the game. "I didn't know anything about it until I was in the dugout."

How easy it is to feel that if we have started well, the job is done. We knock the ball over the fence and assume the rest will take care of itself. Not so! How we finish is crucial.

Carelessness, Completeness, Details, Law,
Obedience, Perseverance, Persistence, Righteousness
Matt. 10:22; 2 Tim. 4:7; James 2:10

Date used _____ Place _____

Forgiveness

In 1982 would-be assassin John Hinckley shot President Ronald Reagan. Reagan underwent surgery and recovered, and through the entire ordeal Reagan's daughter Patti Davis saw God at work. In *Angels Don't Die* she writes:

I give endless prayers of thanks to whatever angels circled my father, because a Devastator bullet, which miraculously had not exploded, was found a quarter inch from his heart. The following day my father said he knew his physical healing was directly dependent on his ability to forgive John Hinckley. By showing me that forgiveness is the key to everything, including physical health and healing, he gave me an example of Christ-like thinking.

The same grace of God that protects and heals us also calls us to forgive those who hurt us the most.

Christ-likeness, Grace, Mercy, Protection, Providence
Matt. 6:12; 18:21–35

Date used _____ Place _____

Forgiveness

Jimmy Carter ran for president of the United States against Ronald Reagan in 1980. According to David Wallis in the *New York Times Magazine*, prior to a televised debate between the two candidates, columnist George Will came upon Carter's debate notes and sneaked them to the Reagan camp. Many pundits felt that Reagan won that debate, and he went on to win the election. Carter did not forget what George Will had done to him.

In a 1997 interview with Wallis, Carter said:

I was teaching forgiveness one day in Sunday school, and I tried to go through my memory about people for whom I had a resentment. George Will was one of those people, so I wrote him a note. I asked myself, What do we have in common, and I had known that he had written a book about baseball, which I had refused to read. I went to a bookstore and found a remaindered copy. Paid a dollar for it. So I wrote him a note and told him the facts: that I had a feeling of resentment toward him, that I had found his book delightful and I hoped that we would be permanently reconciled.

He wrote me back a nice, humorous note. He said his only regret was that I didn't pay full price for his book.

Anyone can hold a grudge. It takes character to initiate reconciliation.

Grudges, Reconciliation, Resentment
Matt. 5:23–26; 18:15–35; Col. 3:13

Date used _____ Place _____

In *Running on Empty*, Jill Briscoe writes:

A woman I met at a conference told me how she was sexually abused as a small child by her father. She grew up, overcame the emotional damage that had been done, and eventually married a missionary. Years later, after her children were fully grown, she received a letter from her father telling her he had become a Christian and had asked God for forgiveness and received it. He had, moreover, realized he had sinned dreadfully against her, and was writing to ask for her pardon.

Feelings she didn't know were there suddenly surfaced. It wasn't fair! He should pay for what he had done, she thought bitterly. It was all too easy. And now he was going to be part of the family! She was sure her home church was busy killing the fattened calf for him and that she would be invited to the party! She was angry, resentful. . . .

Then she had a dream. She saw her father standing on an empty stage. Above him appeared the hands of God holding a white robe of righteousness. She recognized it at once, for she was wearing one just like it! As the robe began to descend toward her father, she woke up crying out, "No! It isn't fair! What about me?"

The only way she could finally rejoice, as her heavenly Father pleaded with her to do, was to realize that her earthly father was now wearing the same robe that she was. They were the same in God's sight. It had cost his Son's life to provide both those robes. As she began to see her father clothed with the garments of grace, she was able to begin to rejoice.

Bitterness, Family, Grace, Mercy,
Righteousness, Sexual Abuse
Matt. 18:21–35; Luke 15:11–32

Date used _____ Place _____

In August 1995 a scene occurred in Burma, now called Myanmar, that fifty years earlier no one could ever have imagined. It happened at the bridge over the Kwai River. During World War II the Japanese army had forced Allied prisoners of war from Britain, Australia, and the Netherlands to build a railroad. The Japanese soldiers committed many atrocities, and some sixteen thousand Allied POWs died building what has been called Death Railway.

But after the war, a former Japanese army officer named Nagase Takashi went on a personal campaign to urge his government to admit the atrocities committed.

After many years of effort, the result of his crusade was a brief ceremony in 1995 at the infamous bridge. On one side of the bridge were fifty Japanese, including five war veterans, and Mr. Takashi. Eighteen schoolteachers from Japan carried two hundred letters written by children expressing sadness for what had happened during the war.

At the other side of the bridge were representatives of Allied soldiers: Two old soldiers from Britain who declared the business of fifty years ago finished at last. A young woman from Australia who came to deliver, posthumously, her father's forgiveness. A son of a POW who came to do the same. And there was 73-year-old Australian David Barrett, who said he made the pilgrimage because he felt that to continue hating would destroy him.

The two groups began to walk the narrow planks of the black iron bridge toward one another. When they met in the center, they shook hands, embraced, shed tears. Yuko Ikebuchi, a schoolteacher, handed the letters from the Japanese children to the veterans, and in tears turned and ran without a word.

Forgiveness can transform the very place where atrocities have occurred into something beautiful—a display of God's mercy.

Confession, Peacemakers, Reconciliation
Matt. 5:9, 23–26; 18:21–35

Date used _____ Place _____

Fruitfulness

According to Julie Iovine in the *New York Times*, in the 1990s many owners of small farms in America began to reduce their wholesale farming to a mere sideline and instead started using their property for another purpose: entertainment farming. Other terms for this new way to make a living on the farm are agritainment and agritourism.

Entertainment farmers attract paying customers to their property with country bands, hay-bale mazes, petting corrals, and tricycle courses. City-dwelling families eager for a feel of life on the farm can pay $12 for admission, food, and amusements. It can cost a child $1 to frolic in a pile of straw or pick a flower. Some farms have mazes cut into their cornfields that can take a person forty-five minutes to navigate. Iovine reports that one farmer in Arizona makes up to $15,000 on a good weekend.

In 1994 Alaska and Oklahoma introduced agritourism as official parts of their state tourism policies.

The catalyst for many of these farmers to take up agritainment was economic pressure.

Sometimes a Christian, or a church, can resemble an entertainment farmer. For whatever reason, we are diverted from the central purpose of producing a crop. Fruitfulness is God's will for every Christian and every church.

Complacency, Discipleship, Evangelism, Growth,
Maturation, Missions, Outreach, Repentance
Matt. 3:8; 28:18–20; John 4:34–38; 15:1–17;
Rom. 12:1–2; Gal. 5:22–26; 6:9–10; Heb. 5:11–6:3

Date used _____ Place _____

According to *National Wildlife*, each week people in the United States generate four million tons of trash. During the holiday season between Thanksgiving and Christmas, though, we throw out even more—five million tons per week—and a high percentage of that trash is simply wasteful.

For example, if each person in America throws away just one bite of Thanksgiving turkey, that comes out to 8.1 million pounds of edible turkey in the trash can. If each person throws away one tablespoon of stuffing, 16.1 million pounds of edible stuffing is wasted.

And then, of course, there's all that wrapping paper. The average U.S. consumer gift-wraps twenty packages during the holidays. If each person wrapped just three of those packages with recycled wrap, the amount of paper saved would cover 45,000 football fields.

New Year celebrations add to the trash heap. After the Times Square New Year's Eve celebration, for example, the New York sanitation department cleans up forty-two tons of extra garbage.

Environmentalists aren't the only ones bothered by the waste of valuable resources. God, too, hates waste. He doesn't want to see valuable resources he bestows on individuals—such as spiritual gifts, time, money, ability, and vitality—lost and unused. The Lord commands that we bear fruit in this life.

Excess, Giving, Money, Spiritual Gifts, Stewardship, Waste
Matt. 25:14–30; Luke 12:48; 13:6–9; John 6:12; 15:1–8

Date used _____ Place _____

For decades various universities, hospitals, and other charitable organizations had received huge financial gifts—as high as $30 million to one recipient—from an anonymous donor. The gifts came in cashier's checks so that the recipient could not trace the source. But in 1997 this secret giver was forced to reveal himself when he sold his company, and a lawsuit over the sale disclosed his anonymous donations.

His name is Charles F. Feeney, one of the cofounders of a company called Duty Free Shoppes, which sells luxury items in airports and in the mid-nineties had sales of more than $3 billion annually. According to writer Judith Miller in the *New York Times,* over a fifteen-year period Feeney's two charitable foundations gave away some $600 million, leaving himself some $5 million. In 1997 the proceeds from the sale of Duty Free Shoppes and other business assets—some $3.5 billion—also went into Feeney's charitable foundations.

Mr. Feeney reluctantly explained his generosity. "I simply decided I had enough money," he said. "It doesn't drive my life. I'm a what-you-see-is-what-you-get kind of guy."

Indeed, the lawyer who advised him in the setting up of his charitable foundations said, "He doesn't own a house. He doesn't own a car. He flies economy. And I think his watch cost about $15."

But the most extraordinary part of Feeney's giving was his absolute commitment to secrecy. Said one doctor associated with a school of medicine, "Anonymous giving, giving that is not dependent on ego, is just really rare."

It is important both to give and to give in the right way. According to Jesus, the right way to give is in secrecy.

Generosity, Money, Secrecy, Simplicity
Matt. 6:3–4

Date used _____ Place _____

According to David Dunlap in the *New York Times*, in 1997 during the construction of a new $6 million children's zoo in New York's Central Park, the administrators received some very bad news. The couple that had agreed to donate half of the money for the project decided to rescind their gift of $3 million.

The problem was the plaque that would acknowledge their gift. The commission that decided on such things said it would be just two inches tall and be placed on a center pier in the gateway of the zoo. Flanking the gateway would be two piers that acknowledged another couple who had donated $500,000 for the original zoo and the gateway itself thirty-six years earlier.

It was proposed that the names of these original donors be eradicated from the gateway and replaced by the names of the new donors. When the commission refused, the couple rescinded their gift.

"We were not talking about neon lights," the couple told the *New York Times*. "We were talking about a very modest plaque that would give acknowledgment to a very sizable gift by anybody's standard."

Although this donation certainly turned sour, in the secular arena it is not frowned upon to donate to a cause with the expectation of some sort of recognition. Not so when we give to God. Those who want rewards in heaven should seek no plaques on earth.

Credit, Motives, Recognition
Matt. 6:1–4; 1 Cor. 4:5

Date used _____ Place _____

In 1976 six men took over a Nebraska-based company called Bethesda Care Centers, which administered fifteen nursing homes and two acute-care centers. The company had recently lost $3 million and was facing bankruptcy. These six unlikely men were about to turn this ailing company into a showcase of God's grace.

Previously the six had been, respectively, a biology teacher, a math teacher, a rancher, a used-car salesman, a construction worker, and an accountant—not exactly Harvard Business School graduates! But these men were Christians, and they had the gifts of faith and giving. Despite the company's dire financial picture, one of the first things the six did was donate $5,000 to a missionary in Calcutta, India.

Four years later the company was in the black. "And by 1988," writes Ron Barefield in the *Pentecostal Evangel*, "the company had grown to 34 successful nursing homes in seven states. They were so successful that a lucrative offer to sell the homes was received.

"The offer was accepted, but the sixsome had a decision to make. They could take the funds and build personal estates. It is done every business day. If they did that, however, Uncle Sam would have taken a $25 million bite out of the proceeds.

"So, they opted for a corporate not-for-profit restructuring which put the $25 million to work for Father God instead of Uncle Sam—a separation of church funds from state that has greatly benefited the cause of world evangelism. The proceeds of the 1988 sale are invested in stocks, buildings, shopping centers, assisted-living facilities, radio stations, and land development, generating funds that are invested in the Kingdom."

These six men turned themselves and their company into financiers of God's work. Their personal and business goals are to give as much to missions as they can—to bankroll the work of the gospel. From 1976 to 1996 they gave away $35 million. In 1995 alone they gave $5 million to ministries in their denomination.

Says Dave Burdine, who is one of the six, "We're just common people who like to work and play but have a passion for the lost and want to reach as many people as we can with the gospel."

They have definitely put their money where their hearts are. They have allowed their story to be told for one reason: to encourage others to follow their example. At whatever level, large or small, each of us has the opportunity to be a part of financing the work of God.

Business, Generosity, Gospel, Missions, Money, Vocation, Work
Hag. 1:2–15; Luke 8:1–3; 12:16–21; Rom. 12:8; 2 Cor. 9:6–11; Eph. 4:28

Date used _____ Place _____

During his championship years with the Chicago Bulls, Michael Jordan was motivated by many things. One motivation most people did not hear about was his desire to win for the sake of the new players and coaches who had never been on a championship team.

So it was in 1997 when the Bulls pursued their fifth championship. Assistant coach Frank Hamblen was new to the team that season. Before coming to the Bulls he had been an assistant coach on various teams for twenty-five years, but did not own a championship ring. He was now fifty years old.

Jordan told writer Melissa Isaacson of the *Chicago Tribune,* "He's been around the league for so long, on a lot of teams and made some great contributions . . . and then not to be on a championship team. . . . That will be my gift to Hamblen. That's part of my motivation."

Hamblen said, "Michael came to me early in the season and told me it was a big motivation for him to win so that I can get a ring. When the best basketball player in the world tells you that, well, it certainly made me feel special."

The Bulls did win it all in 1997, and Frank Hamblen got his ring.

Jesus Christ has a similar desire for us. He is determined to carry us to victory. He wants to see us glorified with him. He wants us to share the glory of his triumphant kingdom. When the Lord of heaven and earth tells us that, well, it certainly makes us feel special.

Goodness, Grace, Heaven, Kingdom,
Overcomers, Victory, Winning
Rom. 8:30, 37, 1 Cor. 3:21–23; 2 Cor. 2:14;
Eph. 1:3–14; 2:6–7; 1 Peter 1:13

Date used _____ Place _____

Pete Rose, one-time star of baseball's Cincinnati Reds, holds the record for the most hits by a player: 4,256. He is better remembered, though, for his style of play. On every single pitch Rose gave it 110 percent, no matter whether his team was winning or losing by ten runs, or whether it was the World Series or the preseason. Pete Rose's nickname was Charlie Hustle.

Rose's son, Pete Rose, Jr., played minor league baseball for the South Bend Silver Hawks. One of the owners of the team, Stuart N. Robinson, told *Sports Illustrated*, "Last year I saw Big Pete. . . . I fell in step with him, identified myself and my South Bend connection, and gave Big Pete my observations of Pete Jr. He never looked at me, or smiled, or broke stride. All he said was, 'Did he hustle?'"

We learn a lot about a father by what he looks for in his son. Our heavenly Father asks one question about his children: Are they walking in love? By that question we see the values of God himself.

Fathers, Imitating God, Love
John 13:34–35; 15:9–17; 1 John 4:7–12

Date used _____ Place _____

Gospel

In *Christianity Today*, Wendy Murray Zoba says that one of the more effective evangelistic tools that Campus Crusade for Christ has developed is the *Jesus* film. She writes:

Several years ago in Peru, during the insurgence of the Sendero Luminoso (Shining Path), a Wycliffe couple was traveling to show the film in a village. Their vehicle was intercepted by the Senderos, and they feared for their lives (with just cause). Instead of killing them, however, the terrorists decided to seize their equipment, including the film projector. The husband boldly suggested that they might as well take the film reels too.

Some time later, a man contacted them to say that he had been among the Senderos who had robbed them. He told them they watched the film seven times (out of sheer boredom), and some had been converted through it. He came to apologize and to tell of his ministry in preaching and evangelism.

Not even a cold-blooded terrorist can withstand the white-hot power of the gospel.

Evangelism
Rom. 1:16

Date used _____ Place _____

According to the Associated Press, on a windy day in March 1997 a father and his son came to Valley Forge National Historical Park, where George Washington stationed the Revolutionary Army during the difficult winter of 1777–1778. The father and son had something much less historic in mind: they wanted to launch a model rocket. At first they tried using electric ignition wires to light the fuse, but to no avail. So they tried lighting the fuse with a common sparkler, the kind seen on the Fourth of July.

That's when the trouble began. Sparks ignited a grass fire, and the winds quickly spread the blaze, burning one field where Revolutionary War soldiers had trained, and coming within a half mile of George Washington's headquarters. Thirty units from twelve fire departments fought the blaze for an hour before bringing it under control, and in the end over thirty acres were charred. The man with the sparkler was charged with destruction of government property and use of fireworks.

Like that sparkler, gossip never seems as dangerous as it really is.

Criticism, Slander, Tongue
Prov. 26:20; Eph. 4:29; James 3:3–12

Date used _____ Place _____

Grace

In his book *In the Grip of Grace*, Max Lucado writes:

In my first church, we had more than our share of southern ladies who loved to cook. I fit in well because I was a single guy who loved to eat. Our potlucks were major events.

I counted on those potluck dinners for my survival. While others were planning what to cook, I was studying my kitchen shelves to see what I could offer. The result was pitiful: one of my better offerings was an unopened sack of chips, another time I took a half-empty jar of peanuts.

Wasn't much, but no one ever complained. Those ladies would take my jar of peanuts and set it on the long table with the rest of the food and hand me a plate. "Go ahead. Don't be bashful. Fill up your plate." And I would! Mashed potatoes and gravy. Roast beef. Fried chicken. I came like a pauper and ate like a king!

The apostle Paul would have loved the symbolism of those potlucks. He would say that Christ does for us precisely what those women did for me.

Community, Salvation, Works
Isa. 64:6; Rom. 3–5; Eph. 2:8–10

Date used _____ Place _____

In his sermon "Why Christ Had to Die," author and pastor Stuart Briscoe says:

Many years ago when the children were small, we went for a little drive in the lovely English countryside, and there was some fresh snow. I saw a lovely field with not a single blemish on the virgin snow. I stopped the car, and I vaulted over the gate, and I ran around in a great big circle striding as wide as I could. Then I came back to the kids, and I said, "Now, children, I want you to follow in my footsteps. So I want you to run around that circle in the snow, and I want you to put your feet where your father put his feet."

Well, David tried and couldn't quite make it. Judy, our overachiever, was certain she would make it; she couldn't make it. Pete, the little kid, took a great run at it, put his foot in my first footprint and then strode out as far as he could and fell on his face. His mother picked him up as he cried.

She said to me, "What are you trying to do?"

I said, "I'm trying to get a sermon illustration."

I said, "Pete, come here." I picked up little Peter and put his left foot on my foot, and I put his right foot on my foot. I said, "Okay, Pete, let's go." I began to stride one big stride at a time with my hands under his armpits and his feet lightly on mine.

Well, who was doing it? In a sense, he was doing it because I was doing it. In a sense there was a commitment of the little boy to the big dad, and some of the properties of the big dad were working through the little boy.

In exactly the same way, in our powerlessness we can't stride as wide as we should. We don't walk the way we should. We don't hit the target the way we ought. It isn't that at every point we are as bad as we could be. It's just that at no point are we as good as we should be. Something's got to be done.

The message of Easter is it has been done. You can be justified. You can be saved from wrath. You can be saved by his life.

All that is the message of grace—God offering you what you don't deserve.

Depravity, Easter, Faith, Justification,
Original Sin, Powerlessness, Righteousness, Sin
Jer. 33:16; Rom. 3:10–26; 4:1–25; Eph. 2:8–10

Date used _____ Place _____

In *Pursuit* author and evangelist Luis Palau writes:

Thank God His grace isn't "fair." A couple of years ago, one of my nephews (I'll call him Kenneth) was near death. He had AIDS. During a family reunion in the hills of northern California, Kenneth and I broke away for a short walk. He was a hollow shell, laboring for breath.

"Kenneth, you know you're going to die any day," I said. "Do you have eternal life? Your parents agonize. I must know."

"Luis, I know God has forgiven me and I'm going to heaven."

For several years, since his early teens, Kenneth had practiced homosexuality. More than that, in rebellion against God and his parents, he flaunted his lifestyle.

"Kenneth, how can you say that?" I replied. "You rebelled against God, you made fun of the Bible, you hurt your family terribly. And now you say you've got eternal life, just like that?"

"Luis, when the doctor said I had AIDS, I realized what a fool I'd been."

"We know that," I said bluntly, but deliberately, because Kenneth knew full well that the Bible teaches that homosexual behavior is sin. "But did you really repent?"

"I did repent, and I know God has had mercy on me. But my dad won't believe me."

"You've rebelled in his face all your life," I said. "You've broken his heart."

Kenneth looked me straight in the eye. "I know the Lord has forgiven me."

"Did you open your heart to Jesus?"

"Yes. Luis! Yes!"

As we put our arms around each other and prayed and talked some more, I became convinced that Jesus had forgiven all of Kenneth's rebellion and washed away all his sin. Several short months later, he went to be with the Lord at age twenty-five.

My nephew, like the repentant thief on the cross, did not deserve God's grace. I don't either. None of us do. That's why grace is grace—unmerited favor.

AIDS, Conversion, Forgiveness,
Homosexuality, Rebellion
Luke 23:43

Date used _____ Place _____

Gratitude

In 1997 *Fortune* magazine said Bill Gates, CEO of Microsoft, was the richest American in history, with personal wealth of some $35 billion. According to Carey Goldberg in the *New York Times*, in February of 1997 Mr. Gates spoke to 1,500 people in Seattle at the annual convention of the American Association for the Advancement of Science. After Mr. Gates's speech, Dr. John Cantwell Kiley, a medical doctor with a Ph.D. in philosophy, stood up and asked a question. If Bill Gates were blind, Kiley asked, would he trade all of his billions to have his sight restored?

The reply of Bill Gates shows where true value lies. He said that he would trade all his money for his sight, and then he offered his e-mail address for further discussion.

If we have nothing else, if we have our sight, our hearing, our mobility, our hands and fingers—our health, we have much to be grateful for, because they are a priceless gift from God.

Contentment, Goodness of God, Money, Thanksgiving, Values
Prov. 20:12; Luke 17:11–19; Rom. 11:36; 1 Thess. 5:18

Date used _____ Place _____

110

Guidance

Author Gary Thomas, founder of the Center for Evangelical Spirituality, writes in *Discipleship Journal:*

When my wife and I prayed extensively about buying a house, we gave God many opportunities to close the door. God appeared to bless the move. Five years later, our house is worth considerably less than what we paid for it.

"Why didn't God stop us?" my wife and I kept wondering. After all, we had given Him plenty of opportunities. But one day as my wife was praying, she sensed God asking her, "Have you ever considered the possibility that I wanted you in that neighborhood to minister there rather than to bolster your financial equity?"

We thought of the people we have been able to reach, and then asked ourselves, are we willing to surrender to a God who would lead us to make a decision that turned out to be undesirable financially but profitable spiritually? Does obedience obligate God to bless us, or can obedience call us to sacrifice? Think about the cross before you answer that one.

Availability, Blessing, Cross, Evangelism, God's Leading, God's Will, Loss, Money, Outreach, Prosperity, Sacrifice, Surrender
Gen. 12:1–10; Exod. 5:1–23; Rom. 12:2; 2 Cor. 6:3–10

Date used _____ Place _____

Guilt

According to the Casper, Wyoming, *Star-Tribune,* Charles Taylor was brought into the courtroom of Judge James Fleetwood. Taylor was accused of robbing a shoe store at knifepoint, taking a pair of tan hiking boots and $69. During the trial Taylor propped his feet up on the defense table. The judge looked over and did a double take. Taylor was wearing a pair of tan hiking boots. Surely, nobody would be so stupid as to wear the boots he stole to his trial, the judge thought.

Nevertheless, as the jury deliberated, the judge had an FBI agent call the shoe store. He learned that the stolen boots were size 10 1/2 from Lot 1046. They checked the boots that Taylor wore to trial and found that they were size 10 1/2 from Lot 1046.

The jury found Taylor guilty, and the judge sent him back to jail in his stocking feet.

Some transgressors are either very stupid or very brazen about their crimes. Before God their judge, defiant sinners oftentimes are both.

Brazenness, Conscience, Defiance,
Judgment, Lawlessness, Rebelliousness
Rom. 1:18–3:8; Rev. 9:20–21; 16:8–21

Date used _____ Place _____

You just can't deny the obvious. That's what a man named Daron discovered, according to Mitchell May in the *Chicago Tribune*.

Police had a warrant out on Daron for possession of a controlled substance with intent to deliver. On August 4, 1997, in Champaign, Illinois, police stopped Daron as he left an apartment in an area of town known for drug trafficking. The police asked his name. Daron claimed his name was John Henry Jones.

The police didn't believe him. Like Sherlock Holmes, they were observant. They pointed to a tattoo on his arm. The tattoo said, "Daron."

Oops!

Thinking fast, Daron claimed it was the name of his girlfriend.

Needless to say, the police could not be snookered, and they took him into custody.

Often we do not want to own up to who we are or what we have done. But the truth cannot be denied forever. Like Daron's tattoo, the guilt of our sins cannot be hidden. Sooner or later our identity will come into the open.

> Accountability, Blame, Deception, Denial,
> Identity, Name, Responsibility, Shame, Sin
> Ps. 51; Isa. 59:12; John 4:16–19;
> Rom. 5:12–14; 1 Tim. 5:24–25; Heb. 4:13

Date used _____ Place _____

Is money the key to happiness? Consider what it did for Buddy Post, of Oil City, Pennsylvania. According to the Associated Press and *Chicago Tribune*, in 1988 he won a jackpot of $16.2 million in the Pennsylvania Lottery. That was the beginning of his misery.

His landlady claimed that she shared the winning ticket with Post and successfully sued him for one-third of the money.

Post started an assortment of business ventures with his siblings, all of which failed.

In 1991 he was sentenced to six months to two years in prison for assault. Post claimed that he had simply fired a gun into his garage ceiling to scare off his stepdaughter's boyfriend, who was arguing with him over business and ownership of Post's pickup.

In 1993 Post's brother was convicted of plotting to kill Buddy and his wife to gain access to the lottery money.

In 1994 Post filed for bankruptcy.

Post's wife left him, and the court ordered that Post pay $40,000 a year in support payments.

Post finally had enough. To pay off a mountain of legal fees, he tried in September 1996 to sell off the rights to the seventeen future payments from his jackpot, valued at some $5 million. But the Pennsylvania Lottery tried to block the sale.

"Money didn't change me," says Post. "It changed people around me that I knew, that I thought cared a little bit about me. But they only cared about the money."

Greed, Money
1 Tim. 6:6–10

Date used _____ Place _____

In November 1996 *Sports Illustrated* reported a bizarre story of competitiveness gone too far. According to the magazine, in a New Mexico high school football game between Albuquerque Academy and St. Pius X on October 12, 1996, several of the Academy players found themselves with strange cuts, slashes, and scratches on their arms and hands. One boy was bleeding freely from three cuts that later required ten stitches to close. Another boy told his coaches, "It feels like they've got razor blades out there."

Well, almost. Referee Steve Fuller inspected the equipment of the opposing team. What he found on the helmet of the offensive center were two chin-strap buckles sharpened to a razor's edge. In the investigation that followed, the offending player's father, a pediatric dentist, admitted to milling the buckles. He had been angered in the previous game by what he thought was excessive head-slapping against his son by opposing linemen. This was his solution.

Sports Illustrated reported, "Several observers describe the father, who was working on the sideline chain gang during the Albuquerque Academy–St. Pius game, as a hothead. He was so vocal in his criticism of the officiating during St. Pius's game against Capital High on Sept. 28 that he was asked to leave the sideline crew."

Hatred and anger—they're as ugly and violent as those razor-sharp buckles.

Aggression, Anger, Competition, Revenge
Gal. 5:20; James 1:20; 1 John 2:11; 3:12–15

Date used _____ Place _____

In the *Pentecostal Evangel* church leader George O. Wood writes:

Have you ever heard a healing take place? I have. I listened to an audiotape of Duane Miller teaching his Sunday school class from the text of Psalm 103 at the First Baptist Church in Brenham, Texas, on January 17, 1993. Duane prematurely retired from pastoring three years earlier because of a virus which penetrated the myelin sheath around the nerves in his vocal cords, reducing his speech to a raspy whisper. . . .

Teaching his class that day with a special microphone resting on his lips, he reaffirmed his belief in divine healing and that miracles had not ended with the Book of Acts. Listening to the tape, at times you can barely understand his weakly spoken wheezy words of faith. The miracle happened at verse 4 when he said, "I have had and you have had in times past pit experiences."

On the word *pit* his life changed—the word was as clear as a bell, in contrast to the imperfect enunciation of the preceding word *past*. He paused, startled; began again and stopped. He said a few more words—all in a normal clear tone—and stopped again. The class erupted with shouts of joy, astonishment, and sounds of weeping. God completely healed him as he was declaring the truth in this psalm. (You can read the full account in Miller's book *Out of the Silence,* Nelson Publishers.)

Faith, Miracles
Exod. 15:26; Ps. 103:1–5; Matt. 8:17; James 5:14–16

Date used _____ Place _____

Healing   103

In 1993 the late author and church leader John Wimber found he had inoperable cancer and underwent radiation treatments. The cancer went into remission. In *Living with Uncertainty* he writes about going without a miraculous healing for himself even though he had seen others dramatically healed by God. He relates this account:

I was speaking in South Africa at a large conference. A friend, John McClure, was with me, and we were asked to go to the home of a lady of the church. She was dressed beautifully but was very emaciated, weighing only 85 pounds. She had been sent home from the hospital to die. Her body was full of cancer. Her only hope of survival was divine intervention.

We prayed for her, but not with great fervency. John had confidence that she would be healed. I felt nothing.

That night she woke up with a vibrant, tingling feeling throughout her body. For the next four hours her body was full of intense heat. She tried to call out to her husband in the next room but couldn't raise her voice loud enough for him to hear.

Alone and frightened, she crawled into the bathroom, her body racked with pain. At the time she thought, "O my God. My body is coming apart and I'm dying." Without knowing it, she eliminated from her body a number of large tumors. Finally, exhausted from the night's events, she fell back asleep. She didn't know if she'd wake up.

But half an hour later she woke up incredibly refreshed. Later her husband woke up to the smell of freshly brewed coffee. "What are you doing?" he asked, astonished to see his wife on her feet and preparing breakfast.

She replied with sudden understanding: "God has healed me."

Two days later she reported to her doctors, who gave her a clean bill of health. They couldn't find a cancer in her body. God had completely delivered her of all of it.

Without much energy to pray on our part and without any desperation or faith on her part, the Lord chose to heal this woman's cancer-infested body through divine means. That's God, and that is sometimes how he does it.

Faith, Miracles, Prayer, The Supernatural
Exod. 15:26; Ps. 103:3; Matt. 8:17; James 5:13–16

Date used_____ Place_____

In December 1995 NASA's Galileo space probe parachuted into the atmosphere of Jupiter. Paul Hoversten writes in *USA Today* that Galileo's mission was to radio data back to Earth on the nature of this gaseous planet. Through telescopes astronomers have long seen tremendous storms on the surface of Jupiter. The winds of these storms have been blowing at some four hundred miles per hour for literally hundreds of years. Scientists wondered, was sunlight driving these storms, as happens on Earth, or was there some sort of reaction going on within the planet, as happens in the stars?

Galileo found the answer to that question. It discovered temperatures ranging from a chilling minus 171 degrees at the cloud tops to a sizzling 305 degrees closer to the core. More important, it found that the super hot core of the planet is the source of the centuries-long storms. The storm winds actually swirl ten thousand miles deep into the planet.

Andrew Ingersoll of the California Institute of Technology explained, "The winds we see at the cloud tops are just the tip of the iceberg. Jupiter's whole fluid interior is in motion just as rapidly as winds at the surface. . . . This helps us explain why you can have 300-year-old storms and jet streams that last for hundreds of years. You've got so much inertia behind it, it's like a giant flywheel spinning forever."

The core of Jupiter is the engine of the planet. So it is with a person. The only way to really change a person is to change the heart.

Emotions, Habits, Motivation, New Creation,
Repentance, Sinful Nature, Tongue, Zeal
Matt. 15:18–20; Luke 6:45; John 3:3; 2 Cor. 5:17

Date used _____ Place _____

In *Preaching Today* Leith Anderson says:

My family and I have lived in the same house for seventeen years. We've lived there more than twice as long as I have lived at any other address in my entire life. I'll sometimes refer to it as "our house," but more often I refer to it as "home." What makes it home isn't the address or the lot or the garage or the architecture. What makes it home is the people.

You may live in a bigger or newer or better house than we live in, but as nice as your house may be, I would never refer to your house as home because the people who are most important to me don't live there. So what makes home home is the people in the relationships.

And what makes heaven heaven is not streets made out of gold, great fountains, lots of fun, and no smog. That all may well be. Actually, I think that heaven is far greater than our wildest imagination. The same God who designed the best of everything in this world, also designed heaven, only he took it to a far greater extent than anything we've ever seen. Yet, that's still not what makes heaven heaven.

What makes heaven heaven is God. It is being there with him.

Death, Home, Hope, Inheritance, Love for God
John 17:24; 1 Thess. 4:17; Rev. 21:1–4

Date used _____ Place _____

In *Preaching Today* writer Joni Eareckson Tada recalls the comment of one boy at the end of a retreat for the handicapped when participants were asked to tell what the week had meant to them:

Little freckle-faced, red-haired Jeff raised his hand. We were so excited to see what Jeff would say, because Jeff had won the hearts of us all at family retreat. Jeff has Down's syndrome. He took the microphone, put it right up to his mouth, and said, "Let's go home."

Later, his mother told me, "Jeff really missed his dad back home. His dad couldn't come to family retreat because he had to work." Even though Jeff had had a great time, a fun-filled week, he was ready to go home because he missed his daddy.

This world is pleasant enough. But would we really want it to go on forever as a family retreat? I don't think so. I'm with Jeff. I miss my Daddy, my Abba Father. My heart is longing to go home.

The hope of being with God in heaven is one of the strong pillars of the Christian life.

Death, Father God, Hope
Rom. 8:15–16; 1 Cor. 13:13; 1 John 2:15

Date used _____ Place _____

U.S. astronaut Shannon Lucid desperately wanted to go home. She had spent six months on the Russian Mir space station, from March to September 1996. Her ride home was delayed six weeks by two hurricanes and assorted mechanical problems with the shuttle booster rockets, making her stay in space the longest of any American astronaut, man or woman. Nevertheless she faced each setback with patient good cheer and a stiff upper lip.

But as the days wore on, she knew where she would rather be. Eventually she admitted she wanted to return home to see her family, to feel the sun and wind on her face, and to check out the new books published in the last six months. Prior to being picked up for her return to Earth by the space shuttle Atlantis, Shannon Lucid quipped, "You can rest assured I am not going to be on the wrong side of the hatch when they close it."

There is another important door in Shannon Lucid's future—and in each of ours as well. It is the door of heaven. If our heart is set on going home to heaven, we will do whatever is necessary to ensure we are on the right side of heaven's door when it shuts for the last time.

Door, Repentance, Treasures
Matt. 6:19–21; Luke 13:22–30

Date used _____ Place _____

Holy Spirit 108

In the *Pentecostal Evangel* Paul Grabill, a pastor in State College, Pennsylvania, interviewed Eric Harrah, a recent convert to Christ. Harrah had previously been the owner and partner in twenty-six abortion clinics, making him the second largest abortion provider in the United States. He received Christ late in 1997, and the supernatural working of the Holy Spirit through a believer named Steve Stupar played a part in his decision. Harrah recalls:

A week before I gave my life back to Christ, we were sitting at a restaurant and Steve said the Holy Spirit had revealed three things to him and he wanted to confirm them. He said, "The name John keeps coming up. What does that name mean to you?"

I said, "That's my grandfather's name. He is dying with lung cancer."

He said, "I saw a girl in a plaid outfit and a white shirt. Do you know who that would have been?"

As soon as he said that I knew it was my sister. I remember the picture explicitly because my grandfather has her school picture in which she is wearing a plaid outfit and a white shirt. I wasn't too impressed because people knew I had a sister and everybody knew who my grandfather was.

Then he said, "The Holy Spirit revealed to me a plate that had blue pills on it with white bands. Does that mean anything to you?"

I denied it at first, but later called him and told him what the significance was. About a week before, I had come home with some joint pains. I went to my kitchen to get some pain medication. One of the bottles contained the blue pills with the white band. I went to take one, and just said to myself, Enough is enough—tonight is a good night to die. I reached up into my cabinet and got a plate out and dumped all the blue pills onto the plate. I got my other medication and dumped them all out on the plate too. When I went to put the first pill in my mouth, my dog barked and looked up at me as if to say, What about me?

123

Who's going to take care of me? I knew nobody would, so I put the pills back in their containers. . . .

It was amazing to me that the Holy Ghost revealed that to him. That is when I knew it was time to give in.

One reason God gives us the power of the Holy Spirit is to help us win lost people to Christ.

Evangelism, Power, Spiritual Gifts,
The Supernatural, Word of Knowledge
Acts 1:8; 1 Cor. 2:4–5; 12:1–31; 14:24–25

Date used _____ Place _____

The monarch butterfly is a familiar sight in most of the United States. Few butterflies can compare with the beauty of its orange, yellow, and black wings. Each year people in many regions of the United States enjoy the unique pleasure of seeing thousands of monarch butterflies fill the sky in their annual migration south. They spend the winter in forests of fir trees in the volcanic highlands of south-central Mexico. Environmentalists have identified nine areas where the monarchs cluster in colonies, and Mexico has designated five of these sites as sanctuaries of protection.

But that isn't enough, say researchers. The sanctuaries cover only sixty-two square miles. Meanwhile poor farmers and commercial loggers are clearing fir forests, at times even in the restricted zones, putting increasing pressure on existing butterfly colonies. Lincoln Brower of the University of Florida said, "We're not going to have a monarch migration in twenty years if those reserves aren't expanded and protected."

Like these beautiful, fragile monarch butterflies coming to their winter home, God's Spirit usually fills our hearts in gentle ways. We must intentionally keep a sanctuary for him, for many things would encroach upon his home in us. Our sense of his manifest presence, our ability to hear his thoughts, our awareness of his direction—all can be lost if we do not safeguard a place for him.

Direction, God's Presence, God's Voice, Silence,
Solitude, Spiritual Disciplines, Spiritual Perception
1 Kings 19:9–13; Eph. 4:30; 5:18

Date used _____ Place _____

On September 22, 1997, the U.S. Army commissioned West Point's first black cadet—123 years after expelling him. James Webster Smith, a former slave, entered the U.S. Military Academy in 1870. For the next four years he was harassed for the color of his skin. White students refused to talk to him. He was forced to eat by himself, and others poured slop on him. Twice he was court-martialed. He had to repeat a year. Finally the academy expelled him after his junior year for failing an exam. Smith died of tuberculosis at age twenty-six. That seemingly was the sad final note for a life scarred by injustice.

But 123 years later the Army endeavored to some degree to right its wrong. Because he had no known descendants, the commissioning certificate and gold second lieutenant's bars of James Webster Smith were presented to South Carolina State University. In the end a courageous man finally received his due.

In this world people who deserve honor may temporarily receive dishonor. But it is only temporary. Eventually such people will be vindicated. Honor will come. Sometimes the honor that is deserved comes in this world, but that honor always comes in the kingdom of God. That honor, which comes from God, is what really matters.

Discrimination, Name, Persecution, Prejudice, Shame, Vindication
Matt. 5:10–12; John 12:26; Rom. 2:5–11;
1 Cor. 4:8–13; 2 Cor. 4:1–18; 6:3–10

Date used _____ Place _____

In *Imaginary Homelands* author Salman Rushdie writes of one of the family traditions of his home:

In our house, whenever anyone dropped a book, it was required to be not only picked up but also kissed, by way of apology for the act of clumsy disrespect. I was as careless and butterfingered as any child, and accordingly I kissed a large number of books.

Devout households in India still contain persons in the habit of kissing holy books. But we kissed everything. We kissed dictionaries and atlases. We kissed novels and Superman comics. If I'd ever dropped the telephone directory, I'd probably have kissed that too.

Is it any surprise that Salman Rushdie grew up to become an author? What we honor defines us.

Child Rearing, Honor, Respect, Reverence, Worship
Eph. 6:2

Date used _____ Place _____

Hope

In 1997 the journal of the American Heart Association reported on some remarkable research. According to the *Chicago Tribune,* Susan Everson of the Human Population Laboratory of the Public Health Institute in Berkeley, California, found that people who experienced high levels of despair had a 20 percent greater occurrence of atherosclerosis—the narrowing of their arteries—than did optimistic people. "This is the same magnitude of increased risk that one sees in comparing a pack-a-day smoker to a non-smoker," said Everson. In other words, despair can be as bad for you as smoking a pack a day!

That is just one more reason why God calls us to choose hope and faith. The Christian life contributes to good health, for God gives us a legitimate basis for hope.

Despair, Health
Rom. 15:13; 1 Cor. 13:13

Date used _____ Place _____

Humility

In *People Weekly* Richard Jerome and Elizabeth McNeil write:

Violin virtuoso Joshua Bell is that rare prodigy who has matured into a world-class musician and an acclaimed interpreter of Mozart, Beethoven and Tchaikovsky. The 29-year-old Bell has always been driven, even while growing up in Bloomington, Ind. Whether it was chess, computers, video games or the violin, Bell had a need to master his environment.

In some quarters, he's already arrived at his pinnacle. Years ago back home in Bloomington, a twelve-year-old boy approached him and announced, "You're Joshua Bell. You're famous."

"Well, ummm, not really," Bell replied.

"Yes, really," the kid insisted. "Your name is on every video game in the arcade as the highest scorer."

Greatness is measured in different ways by different people. The kingdom of heaven, too, has its own standard of greatness: namely, humility and servanthood.

Greatness, Servanthood, Success
Matt. 18:1–4; 20:26–28; Phil. 2:1–11; 3:4–11

Date used _____ Place _____

One of the most decisive moments in our lives is when we admit our need. That admission is what it took to turn Tracey Bailey around. Bailey writes in *Guideposts* that in 1993 he stood in the White House Rose Garden in the presence of the president of the United States to receive the National Teacher of the Year Award. He had come a long way. Some fifteen years earlier he had stood as a teenager in the presence of a county judge in an Indiana courtroom to be sentenced to jail. Bailey had gone on a drunken rampage with friends, vandalizing a high school, had been caught and found guilty. Nevertheless Bailey stood before the judge with his head held high, the words of his high school wrestling coach ringing in his ears: "Don't you ever hang your head. Don't admit defeat. The minute you do, it's over."

The judge looked at the proud teenager and stunned the courtroom with Bailey's sentence: five years in the Indiana youth center, a prison one step below the state penitentiary.

Tracey Bailey went to jail with his head still held high, but it took only a few months for reality to set in. One day as he sat in solitary confinement in a cell with nothing more than a metal cot, a sink, and a toilet, he realized what a mistake he had made. He began to weep. More important, he began to pray to God. "God, I need help," he said. "I am defeated without you."

That was the turning point for Tracey Bailey. He joined a prison Bible study and began taking college correspondence courses. After fourteen months in jail he was released on probation, and after further college studies he became a science teacher in Florida. With these words he summarizes the lesson he had learned in life: "I bowed my head and tasted victory."

Brokenness, Confession, Contriteness, Dependence, Need
Ps. 40:1–2; Isa. 66:2; Dan. 4; 1 Peter 5:5–6; 1 John 1:9

Date used _____ Place _____

In *Christian Reader* Jim Corley tells of a conversation he had with a friend named Alex who attended his church. Alex was struggling over his many failures to live the Christian life the way he knew he should. One day they met at the car dealership where Alex worked. Corley writes:

That day in his office Alex got straight to the point. "Jim, I feel like a hypocrite every time I go to church because I fail to live for Christ so often."

"Alex, what do you call this part of the dealership?" I asked, nodding to the area outside his cubicle.

"You mean the showroom?"

I smiled. "Yes. And what's behind the showroom, past the parts counter?"

"The service department," Alex said confidently.

"What if I told you I didn't want to bring my car to the service department because it was running rough?"

"That would be crazy! That's the whole point of service departments—to fix cars that aren't running right."

"You're absolutely right," I replied. "Now, let's get back to our initial conversation. Instead of thinking of church as a showroom where image is everything, start thinking of it as God's service department. Helping people get back in running order with God is what the church is all about."

Church, Discipleship, Failure, Guilt, Obedience, Sin
Matt. 9:9–13; 1 John 1:7–10

Date used _____ Place _____

According to the *Chicago Tribune*, a man named Joe from Rockford, Illinois, ran a live Internet sex site called Video Fantasy. Joe had a ten-year-old son. On his home computer Joe installed filtering software to limit the surfing that his son could do on the Internet.

Joe explained, "It's not that I keep him sheltered, but my wife and I pay close attention to what he reads, what he watches on TV and what he does on the computer because we have a responsibility to him to be the best parents we can."

Joe's sense of responsibility to his son is commendable. Joe's sense of responsibility to the children of other parents (and the parents themselves!) is deplorable.

Can there be a more stark illustration of hypocrisy?

Golden Rule, Pornography, Responsibility, Stumbling Blocks, Voyeurism
Matt. 7:12; 18:5–7; 23:28; 1 Tim. 4:2; 1 Peter 2:1

Date used _____ Place _____

When does sports as entertainment become sports as idolatry? Consider this banner seen at Lambeau Field in 1996, the season the Green Bay Packers won the Super Bowl in New Orleans and their quarterback Brett Favre was named the most valuable player:

Our Favre who art in Lambeau, hallowed be thy arm. The Bowl will come, it will be won, in New Orleans as it is in Lambeau. Give us this Sunday our weekly win. And give us many touchdown passes. But do not let others pass against us. Lead us not into frustration, but deliver us to Bourbon Street. For thine is the MVP, the best of the NFL, and the glory of the cheeseheads, now and forever. Go get 'em!

Apparently some fans recognize their team support for what it really is: worship.

Worship
Exod. 20:3, Matt. 6:24, Mark 12:30, James 4:4, 1 John 5:21

Date used _____ Place _____

Ignorance   118

According to Peter Kendall in the *Chicago Tribune,* Ruben Brown, age sixty-one, was known on the south and west sides of Chicago, as the friendly neighborhood cockroach exterminator with "the Mississippi stuff." The Mississippi stuff was a pesticide Brown had bought hundreds of gallons of in the South, and it really did the trick on roaches. Brown went from door to door with his hand sprayer, and his business grew as satisfied customers recommended the remarkably effective exterminator to others.

In the process, however, Brown is alleged to have single-handedly created an environmental catastrophe. The can-do pesticide—methyl parathion—is outlawed by the EPA for use in homes. Southern farmers use it on boll weevils in their cotton fields, and within days the pesticide chemically breaks down into harmless elements. Not so in the home. There the pesticide persists as a toxic chemical that can harm the human neurological system with effects similar to lead poisoning.

The EPA was called into Chicago for the cleanup. Drywall, carpeting, and furniture sprayed with the pesticide had to be torn out and hauled to a hazardous-materials dump. The U.S. Environmental Protection Agency estimated that the total cost of the cleanup would be some $20 million, ranking this as one of the worst environmental nightmares in Illinois history.

Brown was charged with two misdemeanors. He apparently didn't know much about the pesticide he sprayed so liberally. Brown's attorney said, "It's a tragedy. It is one of those situations where he did a lot of harm, but his intention in no way matches the damage he has done. He is a family man and handled it with his own hands. Do you think he knew how toxic it was?"

What you don't know can hurt you. That is true both of pesticides and of false teaching.

Doctrine, Error, False Teaching, Knowledge, Mistakes, Study, Teachers
Ezra 7:10; Matt. 4:4; Eph. 4:14; 1 Tim. 4:1–16; 6:3–5; 2 Tim. 2:15–17;
3:14–17; Heb. 5:14; James 3:1; Rev. 2:20

Date used _____ Place _____

In a *New York Times* book review of *John Wayne's America*, by Garry Wills, writer Michiko Kakutani illustrates what a powerful effect the movie image of John Wayne has had on American men. General Douglas MacArthur thought John Wayne was the model of the American soldier. Critic Eric Bentley thought he was the most important man in America. Politicians like Ronald Reagan imitated his manner. And phrases like "Saddle up!" and "Lock and load!" have become battle cries for some.

But Garry Wills's book points out that the real man behind the legend was not always what he appeared. "Wills notes that the big-screen warrior," says Kakutani, "who denounced those who refused to serve in Vietnam as 'soft,' got out of serving in World War II so he could focus on his career; that the star of so many horse epics actually hated horses; that the indomitable man of the West was born in Iowa with the very unmacho name of Marion Morrison. Indeed this volume's central narrative traces John Wayne's creation of a mythic persona: an invented self that projected an aura of authority, autonomy and slumberous power."

We expect film stars to create an image; that is part of the business. But a false image is never the business of real life.

Entertainment, Hypocrisy, Myth, Perception, Reality, Truth
John 1:47

Date used _____ Place _____

Imitating God

On September 6, 1995, Cal Ripken, Jr., broke the baseball record that many believed would never be broken: Lou Gehrig's iron-man feat of playing in 2,131 consecutive games. Ripken gives much of the credit for his accomplishments to the example and teaching of his father Cal Ripken, Sr., who played minor league baseball, and coached and managed for the Orioles.

During the 1996 season Ripken, Sr., was inducted into the Orioles Hall of Fame. After he gave his acceptance speech, the son came to the microphone, an emotional moment recalled in his book *The Only Way I Know:*

It was difficult. I wasn't certain I could say what I wanted about my father and what he means to me. So I told a little story about my two children, Rachel, six at the time, and Ryan, then three. They'd been bickering for weeks, and I explained how one day I heard Rachel taunt Ryan, "You're just trying to be like Daddy."

After a few moments of indecision, I asked Rachel, "What's wrong with trying to be like Dad?"

When I finished telling the story, I looked at my father and added, "That's what I've always tried to do."

What could be more right than to try to be like your heavenly Father? It brings true and lasting greatness.

Example, Fathers, Greatness, Holiness, Imitation
Matt. 5:48; 20:25–28; Luke 6:36; Eph. 5:1–2; 1 Peter 1:16

Date used _____ Place _____

In *The Wall Street Journal* Emory Thomas, Jr., writes:

Ernest "Bud" Miller, president and chief executive officer of Arvida, a real-estate company, closed regional offices, reorganized departments, and cut his work force of 2,600 in half. In the process he turned a money-losing company into a profitable one. But despite the trimming, Miller believed one layer of fat remained. So last March he resigned.

"I couldn't justify me to me," says Miller. "I couldn't look at the people I let go and say I applied a different standard to me. Every fiber of my person wanted to stay. But professionally this was the decision that had to be made."

The move eliminated one of the two senior jobs at the company. The chief operating officer of Arvida became the chief executive.

Miller, 53, gave up an "upper six-figure" salary package.

The greatest test of integrity is whether we will do what is right at our own expense.

Authority, Leadership, Sacrifice, Selflessness, Servanthood
Matt. 20:26–28; Phil. 2:2–8, 19–24

Date used _____ Place _____

In January of 1997 astronomers announced they had made another discovery through the orbiting Hubble space telescope. As scientists peered at a cluster of some 2,500 galaxies called Virgo, they saw for the first time heavenly bodies that had been theorized for some time. What they saw, writes John Noble Wilford, were lone stars without a galaxy to call home. These isolated stars drift more than 300,000 light years from the nearest galaxy—that's three times the diameter of the Milky Way Galaxy.

"Somewhere along the way," writes Wilford in the *New York Times*, "they wandered off or were tossed out of the galaxy of their birth, out into the cold, dark emptiness of intergalactic space. . . . Astronomers theorize that these isolated stars were displaced from their home galaxies as a result of galactic mergers or tidal forces from nearby galaxies. There they drifted free of the gravitational influence of any single galaxy."

Like these isolated, wandering stars, Christians can drift from the community of Christ. But God never created us for the cold of isolation. He created us to be together in deep devotion to one another. He made us for the warmth of fellowship. He designed us to live in community.

Church, Community, Fellowship, Togetherness
Acts 2:42–47; Rom. 12:10; Heb. 10:24–25

Date used _____ Place _____

In the *Christian Reader* Andy Woodland writes :

Working as Bible translators in Asia, we had come to two verses spoken by Jesus to his disciples: "I will pray the Father, and he will give you another Counselor . . ." (John 14:16 RSV) and "In that day you will ask in my name; and I do not say to you that I shall pray the Father for you" (John 16:26 RSV). Our immediate thought was to use the common vernacular for "pray" or "beg," but our cotranslator had a better idea.

"Use the phrase *do paarat*," he suggested. "It's a recommendation an influential person brings on behalf of someone else." Not until a trip to the hospital in our adopted country did I fully understand its meaning.

My wife, Ellie, and I had been asked to help a friend's daughter experiencing post-natal complications. Ellie found the girl, her mother, and mother-in-law waiting in the ward. I stayed outside with the father.

Immediately, he turned to me and said, "You must tell Ellie to speak to the doctor and *do paarat* on my daughter's behalf. We are just poor people from a minority group. They won't respect us or treat us well. But if you *do paarat*, they will give us proper treatment." Ellie agreed, not knowing if it would make a difference.

Thankfully, the doctors did listen and the girl recovered quickly. For us, it was a humbling illustration of how Jesus comes before the Father on our behalf.

Advocate, High Priest, Intercession, Prayer
John 14:16; 16:26; Heb. 4:14–5:10; 1 John 2:1–2

Date used _____ Place _____

In *Discipleship Journal* Paul Thigpen writes:

I remember coming home one afternoon to discover that the kitchen I had worked so hard to clean only a few hours before was now a terrible wreck. My young daughter had obviously been busy "cooking," and the ingredients were scattered, along with dirty bowls and utensils, across the counters and floor. I was not happy with the situation.

Then, as I looked a little more closely at the mess, I spied a tiny note on the table, clumsily written and smeared with chocolatey fingerprints. The message was short—"I'm makin sumthin 4 you, Dad"—and it was signed, "Your Angel."

In the midst of that disarray, and despite my irritation, joy suddenly sprang up in my heart, sweet and pure. My attention had been redirected from the problem to the little girl I loved. As I encountered her in that brief note, I delighted in her. With her simple goodness in focus, I could take pleasure in seeing her hand at work in a situation that seemed otherwise disastrous.

The same is true of my joy in the Lord. Many times life looks rather messy; I can't find much to be happy about in my circumstances. Nevertheless, if I look hard enough, I can usually see the Lord behind it all, or at least working through it all, "makin sumthin" for me.

Confusion, God's Love, Problems, Purpose, Trials
John 5:17; 16:33; Rom. 5:3–5; 8:28–39; Phil. 2:12–13; 4:4; James 1:2–4

Date used _____ Place _____

In *Your Health* Al Hinman writes :

A spotless kitchen may harbor as many bacteria as a less tidy one, says a surprising new finding from the University of Arizona, in Tucson. That's because the most germ-laden object in a kitchen is often the sponge. Researchers tested sponges and dishrags collected from five hundred kitchens across the U.S. and found that as many as one out of five contained salmonella bacteria. Almost two thirds had at least some other bacteria that, when ingested, could make people ill.

Some attempts to cleanse can cause more harm than good. So it is when a pharisaical attitude prevails. Condemnation, self-righteousness, and judgmentalism are the salmonella of the soul.

> Condemnation, Conscience, Faultfinding
> Pharisaism, Self-Righteousness
> Matt. 7:1–5; Rom. 14; Gal. 6:1

Date used _____ Place _____

How do you get a great parking space at a New York Yankees baseball game? One man thought he had a way. According to the Fresno, California *Bee,* this man pulled his car into the VIP parking lot and casually told the attendant that he was a friend of George Steinbrenner, owner of the Yankees. Unfortunately for the imposter, the person attending the parking lot that day was George Steinbrenner himself, doing some personal investigation of traffic problems at the stadium.

The surprised imposter looked at Steinbrenner and said, "Guess I've got the wrong lot." You can be sure that he did not park in the VIP lot that day or ever.

The owner knows his friends. The owner determines who gets in the VIP lot.

God also knows who his friends are and who the imposters are.

Imposters, Heaven, Love for God, Obedience
Matt. 7:21–23

Date used _____ Place _____

According to the Associated Press, in fall 1997 the journal *Cell* reported on an experiment that potentially has far-reaching potential for fighting disease. Dr. John Rose and his research team at Yale Medical School had successfully altered the genes of a virus that normally infects livestock and turned it into a virus that specifically and exclusively attacks AIDS-infected cells and destroys them. In other words, they created smart bombs out of a virus. They used infection against infection.

The experiments were successful in the test tube and had yet to be tried on animals or humans.

Just as viruses can be designed to kill viruses, one of the ways God judges evil is to withdraw his protection and allow evil to come against what is evil.

Demons, Evil, Punishment, Satan, Sowing and Reaping
1 Sam. 18:10; Ps. 109:6; Jer. 4; 1 Cor. 5:1–5; Gal. 6:7–8

Date used _____ Place _____

In the 1990s Chee Soon Juan was one of the few opposition politicians in the Parliament of Singapore. The ruling People's Action Party had an iron grip on the country, holding 77 of 81 seats, and had been in power since 1959. Through authoritarian means the People's Action Party had brought great prosperity to the country, but political opponents like Chee Soon Juan felt that the time had come to loosen up.

The People's Action Party did not take kindly to dissidents, though, and for many years the way it had gotten rid of them was financial. For one reason or another, party opponents would be sued, fined, and financially broken.

In 1993 Chee Soon Juan was forced to sell his home to pay a defamation suit brought against him by a member of the ruling party.

In 1996 the harassment continued. Chee Soon Juan made a report to Parliament, and to his regret it contained a statistical error. According to Seth Mydans in the *New York Times*, Chee Soon Juan reported that "government spending on health care had fallen from 40 percent of the nation's total costs in 1970 to 5 percent in 1990. The actual 1990 figure was 25 percent."

When party officials discovered the error, they pounced on it. Chee Soon Juan was accused of perjury, misconduct, and giving false information to Parliament. He blamed it on a typing error. Late in 1996 "the Parliamentary Privileges Committee issued a 196-page report on Mr. Chee's statistical error and found him guilty as charged." He was fined $18,000.

In Singapore that may be legal, but most people would agree it is unjust. And injustice grieves the heart of God.

Control, Error, Fairness, Forgiveness, Injustice, Mistakes, Oppression, Parenting, Punishment, Retribution, Vengeance
Prov. 29:14; Isa. 11:4; Mic. 6:8; Matt. 23:23

Date used _____ Place _____

In *Conspiracy of Kindness* Steve Sjogren writes:

On a typical hot, humid summer day in Cincinnati, Joe Delaney and his eight-year-old son were in the backyard playing catch. As the two lobbed the ball back and forth, Joe could tell something was on Jared's mind. At first they talked about Reds' baseball, friends, and summer vacation. Then the conversation took a more serious turn, and Joe felt like a backyard ballplayer who suddenly found himself in the major leagues.

"Dad, is there a God?"

Joe had the same helpless feeling he experienced on the high school baseball team when he lost sight of a fly ball in the blazing sun. He didn't know whether to move forward, backward, or just stay put. A string of trite answers raced through his mind. In the end Joe opted for honesty. "I don't know, Jared," he replied as the ball landed solidly in his glove.

Joe's agnosticism failed to stifle his son's curiosity. Jared dug a little deeper. "If there is a God, how would you know him?"

"I really have no idea, Jared. I only went to church a couple of times when I was a kid, so I don't know a lot about these kinds of things."

Jared seemed deep in thought for a few minutes as the game of catch continued. Suddenly, he headed for the house. "I'll be right back," he yelled over his shoulder. "I have to get something." Jared soon returned with a Mylar helium balloon fresh from the circus along with a pen and an index card.

"Jared, what in the world are you doing?" Joe asked.

"I'm going to send a message to God—airmail," the boy earnestly replied.

Before Joe could protest, his son had started writing. "Dear God," Jared wrote on the index card, "if you are real and if you are there, send people who know you to Dad and me."

Joe kept his mouth shut, not wanting to dampen his son's enthusiasm. *This is silly*, he thought as he helped Jared fasten the card to the balloon's string. *But God, I hope you're watch-*

ing, he added to his silent petition. After Jared let go of the balloon, father and son stood with their faces to the sky and watched it sail away.

Two days later I became part of the answer to this unusual inquiry. Joe and Jared pulled into the free car wash that our church was holding as part of our outreach into the community on this particular Saturday morning. "How much?" Joe asked as he neared the line of buckets, sponges, and hoses.

"It's free," I told him. "No strings attached."

"Really!" Joe exclaimed. He seemed intrigued with the idea of getting something for nothing. "But why are you doing this?"

"We just want to show you God's love in a practical way."

It was as if that simple statement opened a hidden door to Joe's heart. The look on his face was incredulous. "Wait a minute!" he practically shouted. "Are you guys Christians?"

"Yeah, we're Christians," I replied.

"Are you the kind of Christians who believe in God?"

I couldn't help but smile. "Yes, we're that kind of Christians."

After directing a big grin at Jared, Joe proceeded to tell me the story of releasing the helium balloon with its message only days earlier. "I guess you're the answer to one of the strangest prayers God's ever received," Joe said.

How often it is that our acts of kindness are an answer to someone's deepest prayer.

Evangelism, Outreach, Prayer, Providence
Matt. 5:14–16; Gal. 6:10

Date used _____ Place _____

In his book *I Was Wrong* former PTL president and television personality Jim Bakker, who was sent to prison for fraud, writes:

Not long after my release from prison, I joined Franklin Graham and his family at his parents' old log mountain home for dinner. Ruth Graham (Billy's wife) had prepared a full-course dinner. We talked and laughed and enjoyed a casual meal together like family.

During our conversation, Ruth asked me a question that required an address. I reached into my back pocket and pulled out an envelope. My wallet had been taken when I went to prison. I had not owned a wallet for over four-and-a-half years.

As I fumbled through the envelope, Ruth asked tenderly, "Don't you have a wallet, Jim?"

"This is my wallet," I replied.

Ruth left the room, returning with one of Billy's wallets. "Here is a brand-new wallet Billy has never used. I want you to have it," she said.

I still carry that wallet to this day. Over the years I have met thousands of wonderful Christian men and women, but never anyone more humble, gracious, and in a word, "real" than Ruth Graham and her family.

Kindness does not have to be extravagant to mean a great deal to people.

Acceptance, Community, Love, Giving, Grace, Mercy, Sharing, Sincerity
Gal. 5:22; Col. 3:12; 2 Peter 1:7

Date used _____ Place _____

In *Running on Empty*, author and speaker Jill Briscoe writes:
I had been traveling for two weeks straight, speaking at meetings. Somehow the tight schedule allowed only time for talking and not much for eating! Whenever it was mealtime, I found myself on one more airplane. On this particular day it was hot, it was summer, and I was tired and hungry. My flight had been delayed, and by the time I arrived at the next conference center, I discovered that my hosts had gone to bed. (In the morning I learned that because of the delayed flight, they presumed I would not be coming until the following day—hence, no welcoming committee.) I wandered around the large dining room, hoping to find something to eat, but all the doors into the kitchen had been locked. "Lord," I prayed, "I really don't care what I eat, but I need something—and while I'm talking to you about this, I've got a yearning for peaches! Oh, for a lovely, refreshing, juicy peach!" Then I smiled. That was just the sort of prayer I counseled others against offering! I sighed, picked up my bags, and went to my assigned cabin.

When I arrived at my room . . . a basket of peaches sat on the doorstep smiling up at me! I lifted them up and felt my loving Lord's smile. (It could have been oranges and apples, you know!) Never before or since have I received a whole basket of delicious, fresh peaches. . . . The Lord provided a sweet touch that reminded me of his great love.

If we will notice the little things, we will see there is no limit to God's kindness.

Love of God, Needs, Prayer, Providence, Provision, Wants
Pss. 23:1; 37:4; 107:4–9; Matt. 7:7–8; Titus 3:4

Date used _____ Place _____

Knowing God   132

In *The Cure for a Troubled Heart* author and pastor Ron Mehl writes:

I heard once about a dear, saintly old woman who was gradually losing her memory. Details began to blur. . . . Throughout her life, however, this woman had cherished and depended on the Word of God, committing to memory many verses from her worn King James Bible.

Her favorite verse had always been 2 Timothy 1:12: "For I know whom I have believed, and am persuaded that he is able to keep that which I have committed unto him against that day."

She was finally confined to bed in a nursing home, and her family knew she would never leave alive. As they visited with her, she would still quote verses of Scripture on occasion—especially 2 Timothy 1:12. But with the passing of time, even parts of this well-loved verse began to slip away.

"I know whom I have believed," she would say. "He is able to keep . . . what I have committed . . . to him."

Her voice grew weaker. And the verse became even shorter. "What I have committed . . . to him."

As she was dying, her voice became so faint family members had to bend over to listen to the few whispered words on her lips. And at the end, there was only one word of her life verse left.

"Him."

She whispered it again and again as she stood on the threshold of heaven. "Him . . . Him . . . Him."

It was all that was left. It was all that was needed.

Aging, Death, Security, Trust
John 10:27–29; 2 Tim. 1:12

Date used _____ Place _____

Date used _____ Place _____

Knowing God

133

Writer T. H. Watkins is in love with the unique region of the Southwest United States called the Four Corners. The Four Corners is the only place in the country where four states join at one point: Utah, Colorado, New Mexico, and Arizona. The region around that point is one of breathtaking beauty: graceful sand dunes, striking deserts, buttes that glow orange in the morning light, deep canyons, snow-covered mountains, fog-shrouded valleys, vertical rock, sandstone wedges jutting into the sky. It is a terrain so unusual in its character that those who explore there never weary of it.

Watkins writes in *National Geographic* that this area of 100,000 square miles is "endlessly various and fascinating in its forms. Much of this I have come to think of as my own country. . . .

"I have spent several years exploring this western landscape, driving its roads, flying over it, hiking into its canyons, camping along its rivers, soaking it up, taking it in, sometimes writing about it, most of the time just thinking about its warps and tangles of rock and sky. This is not an idle passion. It stems from a deeply held conviction that the Four Corners country has something essential to offer us."

Watkins's relationship with this landscape is much like the joy that is ours as we seek to know God. God invites us to spend this life and all eternity getting to know his inexhaustible character and nature.

Devotional Life, Spiritual Disciplines, Transcendence
Exod. 33:18–34:7; Jer. 9:23–24; Hos. 6:6;
John 17:3, 24–26; Phil. 3:10

Date used _____ Place _____

On the Fox River and Chain o' Lakes waterways of northern Illinois, officials annually face an expensive problem. Of the roughly six hundred buoys on these waterways, not one is expected to last the entire season. Each year the attrition rate for the lighted plastic buoys has been 125 percent.

What happens to them? Officials say the buoys are willfully smashed to pieces by vandals.

In so doing, boaters are only hurting themselves and others, of course. The buoys are there "to provide safety and direction for boaters," says writer Stephen Lee in the *Chicago Tribune.* "Some mark no-wake zones where powerboaters must go at slower speeds. They delineate shallow areas where boating could be dangerous, and show the way to mouths of channels."

Smashing buoys may bring laughs, but it is an expensive hobby. An agency ordinance levies a $1,000 fine on boaters convicted of maliciously vandalizing buoys.

Like vandals smashing buoys, many people take great delight in running over the commands of God. The Bible calls this the spirit of lawlessness. God's commands are given for our safekeeping, yet the sinful nature within us hates them nonetheless.

Commandments, Disobedience, Lawlessness,
Rebellion, Ten Commandments
Rom. 1–3; 1 Cor. 7:19; James 2:8–11; 1 John 3:4

Date used _____ Place _____

One of the shocking legal developments of the late 1990s was the settlement between the tobacco industry and the attorneys general of numerous states. After the $360 billion settlement, the *Wall Street Journal* published an article by Alix M. Freedman and Suein L. Hwang that gave credit for this change in the tobacco industry's fortunes to the largely independent actions of seven individuals.

According to the writers, Jeffrey Nesbitt was a spokesman for the Food and Drug Administration. As he watched his father, a heavy smoker, dying from cancer and his youngest brother becoming more devoted to cigarettes, he pressed his colleagues at the administration to take initiatives to regulate the tobacco industry. They were reluctant because they did not think they could succeed, but eventually they took up the fight.

Michael Lewis was a small-town lawyer in Mississippi. As he rode a hospital elevator following a visit to a smoker suffering from heart disease, he got an idea for a new way to sue the tobacco companies. In the past the tobacco industry had always won legal suits because they had been brought by individuals, and juries had decided that individuals were responsible for their own decisions. This Mississippi lawyer's idea was for states to sue the companies to recover state money used to pay Medicaid bills for the care of those suffering from smoking-related diseases.

Jeffrey Wigand was a researcher who had once worked for one of the big tobacco companies. The companies had long claimed that nicotine was not addictive. As a former insider, Wigand blew the whistle on the companies, showing that they did know of nicotine's effects and even designed cigarettes to enhance that addictive power.

Walt Bogdanich was an ABC television producer who championed a 1994 exposé that showed that tobacco companies carefully controlled the level of nicotine in their product.

Presidential advisor Dick Morris, who had watched his mother's health fall apart due to a three-pack-a-day habit, convinced President Clinton to put his weight behind the FDA's anti-youth-smoking initiative. Morris provided the polls that showed overwhelming support for such a move, proving that it was politically viable.

Bennett LeBow, a financier who controlled one of the tobacco companies, was the first to bolt from the ranks of Big Tobacco. He led his company to unilaterally settle with the attorneys general of four states. Then he officially admitted that nicotine is addictive and agreed to stamp warnings to that effect on cigarette packages.

Grady Carter was a smoker who had tried for more than twenty-five years to quit. He succeeded only after finding he suffered from lung cancer. Then he filed a personal suit against one of the tobacco companies and was the first to win such a case.

As these seven men show, individuals who take action can make a huge difference—even in causes thought impossible.

Activism, Change, Commitment, Initiative,
Ministry, Prayer, Revival, Zeal
Esther 4:14; Matt. 28:18–20; Acts 17:6

Date used _____ Place _____

On August 1, 1970, W. Lain Guthrie, a commercial airline pilot, decided he had had enough. He had dumped his last load of kerosene into the environment. Holcomb Noble writes in the *New York Times* that at that time the airline industry practice was to dump waste kerosene during takeoff or at high altitudes. Airline officials claimed that the kerosene evaporated and caused no harm to the environment, but Guthrie did not buy it. He claimed that in peak seasons as much as five hundred gallons of fuel was dumped every day over his home airport of Miami.

And so on his thirtieth anniversary as a pilot, he celebrated by following his conscience. He refused to take off until the waste fuel accumulated from the previous flight was pumped out of his jet. In subsequent flights he continued his demand, and two months later he was fired for insubordination. By now, however, he had become a cause célèbre, as other pilots rallied around him and also refused to dump fuel. Finally the airline backed down and rehired Guthrie at full pay. Soon the airline industry as a whole ceased the practice of aerial fuel dumping.

For wrongs to be righted, the question often is who will lead the way and be the first to pay the price of following his or her conscience. For some people it means deciding that they have told their last lie or cut their last corner. When we follow our conscience, it just may be that many other people will be encouraged to follow theirs. But even if others do not, the day we choose to do what we think is right is a cause for celebration.

Conscience, Conviction, Environment, Taking a Stand
Exod. 32:26

Date used _____ Place _____

Moderate exercise is good for you, right? Not necessarily. One study suggests that exercise may do more harm than good if you are being forced to work out against your will.

According to Jon Van and Ron Kotulak in the *Chicago Tribune*, University of Colorado researcher Monika Fleshner focused an experiment on the effects of forced and unforced exercise on the immune system, that part of the body that fights off colds and infectious diseases.

Fleshner studied two groups of lab animals. One group was allowed to run on exercise wheels whenever they liked. The result was an improved response of their immune systems. A similar improvement in the human immune system's response is seen after moderate exercise.

On the other hand, the other group of lab animals was forced to run; their immune systems responded negatively in several ways, including having reduced levels of antibodies. The negative effects likely resulted from the stress of being forced to exercise.

The negative effect of forced exercise is similar to the spiritual harm of legalism. When people are forced to follow a code instead of freely choosing to obey out of love, they stay immature rather than mature.

Freedom, Manipulation, Obedience, Righteousness, Submission, Will
Matt. 5:6; John 14:23–24; 2 Cor. 9:7;
Gal. 3:1–14; 4:1–11; 5:1–15; Phil. 2:12–13

Date used _____ Place _____

In *Moody*, pastor and author Dan Schaeffer writes:

In a popular Christmas movie called *Home Alone*, a family plans a European vacation for Christmas. The relatives all arrive for the big event, but the youngest son is feeling slighted. Easily ignored in all the last-minute details, he rebels and gets in trouble. He's sent to a room in the attic. While there, in a tantrum, he wishes his family and everyone else would go away, so he could be all alone.

In a bizarre plot twist, the family overlooks the little boy in the attic, leaves for the airport, and gets on the plane, all the while believing he is with them. When the boy wakes in the morning, he discovers no one there, and believes his wish has been granted. He is delighted.

For the next few days, he lives alone, while his mother and family try frantically to return to him. At first the boy is delirious with joy, as he has full run of the house. He eats all the junk food he wants, watches whatever movie he wants, sleeps wherever he wants, and doesn't have to answer to anyone.

Then burglars try to break into the house, and he finds himself involved in simply keeping his home safe. After the burglars have been taken care of, he realizes he is now lonely and alone. It wasn't what he thought it would be, this life without his parents. He becomes sorry he had treated them so badly, and desperately wants them back again.

Schaeffer writes that this story is similar to how people relate to God. Often we resent God's authority and want our freedom. When we exercise our freedom, we may have fun for a while, but we end up with a life of fear and loneliness. Without God we are home alone.

Alienation, Emptiness, Fear, Freedom, Hell,
Human Condition, Independence, Rebellion
Gen. 3

Date used _____ Place _____

There is a picture hanging crookedly on your living-room wall. It bothers you, so you walk to the picture and push up the side that is hanging low. You step back, squint your eyes, and decide now the picture is straight. You leave the room feeling good about getting things to look the way they should.

The next day you walk through the living room and are surprised to see the picture is once again hanging as crookedly as it did yesterday before you straightened it. You conclude you must have failed to get it really level the day before. Again you push up the side hanging low, step back, eyeball the picture, and decide this time you have it right.

The next day to your great frustration you find the picture hanging crookedly again. You are sure you had it right the day before. You push it straight and walk away wondering whether it will be crooked again tomorrow.

The next day it is crooked again. What's going on! Then it dawns on you. Perhaps the wire on the back of the picture is not centered on the wall hook. You take hold of the picture, slide it to the left a fraction of an inch, and then level it.

The next day when you return to the living room, you find your picture hanging straight and true the way you left it the day before.

A picture will stay level only if it is centered on the hook. Without that, any corrections are temporary. In the same way, until we center ourselves in Jesus Christ, no matter how hard we try to straighten out our lives they will eventually fall out of line.

> Balance, Conversion, Morality, Regeneration,
> Repentance, Self-Improvement, Will Power
> 2 Cor. 5:15; Phil. 1:21; 1 Peter 3:15

Date used _____ Place _____

On Sunday, December 22, 1996, Carnell Taylor was working on a paving crew repairing the Interstate 64 bridge over the Elizabeth River in Virginia. The road was icy, and a pickup truck slid out of control and hit Taylor, knocking him off the bridge. He fell seventy feet and hit the cold waters of the river below. His pelvis and some of the bones in his face were broken.

Joseph J. Brisson, the captain of a barge passing by at that moment, saw Taylor fall and quickly had to make a life-or-death decision. He knew Taylor would drown before he and his crew could launch their small boat and reach him. The numbingly cold water and strong currents of the river could kill him if he dived in to rescue Taylor. He had a family, and Christmas was three days away.

Brisson decided to risk his life for a man he had never met. He dived into the river, swam to Taylor, and grabbed hold of him. "Don't worry, buddy," he said, "I got you." Brisson held Taylor's face above the water and encouraged him to keep talking. Then he took hold of a piece of wood in the water and slid it under Taylor to help keep him afloat. The current was too strong for them to swim to safety, and eventually the cold caused Brisson to lose his grip on Taylor. So Brisson wrapped his legs around the injured man's waist and held on.

After nearly thirty minutes the crew from the barge was finally able to reach the two men and pull them from the water into the small boat. Taylor was hospitalized for broken bones. Brisson, the hero, was treated for mild hypothermia.

Brisson later told the Associated Press he knew what he had to do when he saw the man fall. "I have a family," he said. "I thought about that. But I thought about how life is very important. I'm a Christian man, and I couldn't let anything happen to him."

In this perilous rescue, Joseph Brisson shows us the heart of God. The God of love knows better than anyone the tremendous value of a human being and his or her eternal soul. For even one person Jesus was willing to leave the safety and joy of his family in heaven and give himself to save others.

Christmas, Courage, Evangelism, Incarnation, Love, Love of God, Redemption, Rescue, Risk, Sacrifice, Salvation, Sanctity of Life, Security of Believer, Selflessness
Luke 15; John 3:16; John 10:27–29

Date used _____ Place _____

Hall of Famer Walter Payton holds the NFL record for rushing yards, and in 1985 he climaxed his career by winning Super Bowl XX with the Chicago Bears. One of Payton's cherished possessions was his Super Bowl ring commemorating their triumph. According to writer Fred Mitchell in the *Chicago Tribune*, each ring was distinctive, marked with the player's name, uniform number, and position.

In the winter of 1996, Walter's invaluable ring disappeared. It happened when he delivered a motivational speech to a high school basketball team he had worked closely with for years. To give an object lesson on the importance of trust, he entrusted his ring to one of the players for the weekend. Reportedly, when friends of that player came to the boy's house to see the ring, it disappeared.

At first, because of his close relationship with the school, Payton did not report the theft to the authorities. Exercising remarkable patience, he hoped the boys would get the ring back for him. But after five months he could wait no longer. He had to have his keepsake ring back. So he reported the theft to the police and offered a reward for information leading to its recovery.

One of the most painful experiences in life is to lose what we highly value. That is precisely what happened to God. The people whom God made in his image became lost through sin. Lost people matter to God.

Evangelism, Love of God, Stealing, Stewardship, Trust
Matt. 28:18–20; Luke 15:1–32; 19:1–10; Rom. 2:4; 1 Tim. 2:4; 2 Peter 3:9

Date used _____ Place _____

In 1996 Disney came out with the movie *101 Dalmatians,* and it was a box-office success. Many viewers fell in love with the cute spotted puppies on the big screen and decided to get one for themselves. When they brought those adorable little puppies home, however, they found that living with a dalmatian is an entirely different experience from watching one on the movie screen. Soon, according to the Associated Press, all over the United States dog shelters saw a dramatic increase in the number of dalmatians being abandoned by their owners. A Florida organization called Dalmatian Rescue took in 130 dalmatians in the first nine months of 1997; usually they get that many dogs in two and a half years.

Dalmatians can be a challenge to own for several reasons. Dalmatians grow to be big dogs, weighing as much as seventy pounds. They are rambunctious and require a lot of exercise. They can be moody, becoming restless and even destructive if they don't get enough activity. They shed year-round, and 10 percent of dalmatians are born deaf.

Tracey Carson, a spokeswoman for the Wisconsin Humane Society, says, "Although Dalmatians are beautiful puppies, and can be wonderful dogs, you have to know what you're getting into."

Whether with pets or with people, infatuation with someone's appearance is a poor foundation for a relationship.

Appearance, Commitment, Expectations, Faithfulness,
Illusions, Infatuation, Marriage, Relationships, Romance
Rom. 12:10; 1 Cor. 13:7–8

Date used _____ Place _____

Rita Price writes in a 1995 issue of the *Columbus Dispatch:*

Katie Fisher, 17, pulled her unruly lamb into the arena of the Madison County Junior Livestock Sale last July. With luck the lamb would fetch some spending money—and she wouldn't collapse as she had during another livestock show the day before.

Fisher had been battling Burkitt's lymphoma, a fast-growing malignancy, since February. She had endured many hospitalizations and months of chemotherapy. "Sometimes, in the beginning, it hurt so bad all she could do was pace," said her 12-year-old sister Jessica.

Selling the lamb did raise pin money for Fisher.

"We sort of let folks know that Katie had a situation that wasn't too pleasant," said auctioneer Roger Wilson, who hoped his introduction would push the price-per-pound above the average of $2. It did—and then some.

The lamb sold for $11.50 per pound. Then the buyer gave it back. That started a chain reaction. Families bought it and gave it back; businesses bought it and gave it back.

"The first sale is the only one I remember. After that, I was crying too hard," said Katie's mother, Jayne Fisher. "Everyone kept saying, 'Re-sell! Re-sell!'"

"We sold that lamb 36 times," said Wilson. And the last buyer gave back the lamb for good. The effort raised more than $16,000, which went into a fund to help pay Katie's medical expenses.

It is blessed both to give and to receive.

Giving, Mercy, Sacrifice
Acts 20:35; Gal. 6:2; 1 John 3:16–18

Date used _____ Place _____

Researcher Beppino Giovanella knows what it means to give himself on behalf of others. In *Johns Hopkins Magazine* Melissa Hendricks writes:

Nobody put a gun to Beppino Giovanella's head and said, "Take this or else." It was the desire to find a safe but effective dosage that made the biologist swallow a gelatin capsule containing 100 milligrams of an experimental cancer drug. Like a modern-day Dr. Jekyll, Giovanella, director of laboratories for the Stehlin Foundation in Houston, chose himself as a guinea pig. Partly as a result of his self-experiment, the drug is now in clinical trials.

Science is rich with stories of self-experiments, but today an investigator like Giovanella, who has tested several drugs on himself without seeking formal approval of his institution, is a rare bird. As a result of his latest experiment, he temporarily lost his hair. But he did find that cancer drug doses effective in animals are too much for humans.

"As a biologist, you become acutely aware that drugs at times act very differently from one species to another," Giovanella says. "That is why I always test new drugs on myself first. It wouldn't be very nice to risk another person before I risk myself."

Love is considerate.

Golden Rule, Self-Sacrifice
1 Cor. 13:7; James 3:17–18

Date used _____ Place _____

How do we love someone who stumbles?

In a *Leadership* profile of pastor and author Stu Weber, Dave Goetz writes:

Growing up, Weber developed a temper, which blossomed in high school and college. "And then I went in the military," Weber said, "which doesn't do a lot to curb your temper and develop relational skills."

Early in his ministry, he stopped playing church-league basketball altogether; his temper kept flaring, embarrassing himself and the church. A decade passed. "I hadn't had a flash of temper for years," Weber said. "I thought, the Lord has been good. I'm actually growing."

Then his oldest son made the high school varsity basketball squad. "I began living my life again through my son." Weber terrorized the referees. On one occasion, seated in the second row, Weber wound up on the floor level, with no recollection of how he got there. He received nasty letters from church members, who, he says now, "were absolutely right on."

But then he got another note: "Stu, I know your heart. I know that's not you. I know that you want to live for Christ and his reputation. And I know that's not happened at these ballgames. If it would be helpful to you, I'd come to the games with you and sit beside you."

It was from one of his accountability partners.

"Steve saved my life," Weber said. "It was an invitation, a gracious extension of truth. He assumed the best and believed in me."

When we love others, we believe in and hope the best for them even when they fail.

Accountability, Anger, Belief, Community, Devotion, Discipleship, Failure, Forbearance, Loyalty, Men, Stumbling, Support, Temper
Rom. 12:10; 1 Cor. 13:7; Col. 3:8, 12–14

Date used _____ Place _____

Lying

Early in 1996 the body of the former ambassador to Switzerland, was buried in Arlington Cemetery, America's graveyard of war heroes. His granite tombstone read, "S1C [Seaman First Class] U.S. Merchant Marine."

But according to Don Van Natta Jr. and Elaine Sciolino in the *New York Times*, on December 11, 1997, cemetery workers hauled that tombstone away, and they exhumed the casket. The reason: the man had lied. For years he told others he had served on the Coast Guard ship *Horace Bushnell* during World War II. He said the Germans torpedoed the ship, and he had been thrown overboard, sustaining a head injury. In fact, records showed that at the time he said he was serving in the Merchant Marine he was actually attending Wilbur Wright College in Chicago. The Coast Guard had no record of his serving in the Merchant Marine, and of course he had never earned the rank of seaman first class.

Somehow his lie was not discovered when the State Department investigated his background, and he was approved as an ambassador. Somehow his body was permitted to be buried in Arlington Cemetery with a tombstone engraved with a lie. But to no surprise, the truth eventually came out.

The truth always will.

Character, Deception, Falsehood, Integrity, Truth
Matt. 10:26; Luke 12:1–3; Eph. 5:8–14

Date used _____ Place _____

Ruth Ryan, wife of Hall of Fame pitcher Nolan Ryan, had one moment she looked forward to in every one of her husband's games. In *Covering Home,* she writes:

It probably happened the first time on the high-school baseball diamond in Alvin, Texas, in the mid-1960s. Then it happened repeatedly for three decades after that. Inevitably, sometime during a game, Nolan would pop up out of the dugout and scan the stands behind home plate, looking for me. He would find my face and grin at me, maybe snapping his head up in a quick nod as if to say, There you are; I'm glad. I'd wave and flash him a smile. Then he'd duck under the roof and turn back to the game.

It was a simple moment, never noted in record books or career summaries. But of all the moments in all the games, it was the one most important to me.

Those who love us long for us to acknowledge them, to give them our attention. This is true not only in marriage and family, but in our relationship with God. Throughout our days, in both the big and small moments, God enjoys it when we "step out of the dugout" and smile in his direction.

Acknowledging God, Attention, Love, Prayer, Support, Thanksgiving
Prov. 3:5–6; Eph. 5:25

Date used _____ Place _____

Martyrs

In *Discipleship Journal* Navigator staff member Skip Gray writes:

When Joseph Ton was a pastor in Romania he was arrested by the secret police for publishing a sermon calling for the churches to refuse to submit to the communist government's demand for control over their ministries. When an official told him he must renounce his sermon, he replied, "No, sir! I won't do that!"

The official, surprised that anyone would respond so forcefully to the secret police, said, "Aren't you aware that I can use force against you?"

"Sir, let me explain that to you," Ton said. "You see, your supreme weapon is killing. My supreme weapon is dying. . . . You know that my sermons are spread all over the country on tapes. When you kill me, I only sprinkle them with my blood. They will speak 10 times louder after that, because everybody will say, 'That preacher meant it because he sealed it with his blood.' So go on, sir, kill me. When you kill me, I win the supreme victory." The secret police released him, knowing his martyrdom would be far more of a problem than his sermon.

Conviction, Courage, Death, Leadership, Persecution, Sacrifice, Witness
John 15:18–16:4; Acts 7:54–8:4; Phil. 1:20

Date used _____ Place _____

In the syndicated cartoon "Mister Boffo" Joe Martin pictures a middle-aged man lying on a psychologist's couch. The psychologist sits on a chair next to him, listens intently, and writes in a notebook. The man on the couch has a problem. "I drive a Mercedes," he says, "I have a beachhouse in Bermuda, a 12-room penthouse, a 90-foot yacht. My clothes are made by the finest tailors in London. I have a world-class wine cellar. And yet I'm still not happy."

The psychologist asks, "Do you have a Rolex?"

Abruptly the troubled man raises his head from the couch, points his finger in the air, and declares, "Why no, I don't !"

Such is the folly of those who pursue happiness in material possessions. They will always be one purchase away from a happy life.

Greed, Happiness, Possessions
Exod. 20:17; Luke 12:15

Date used _____ Place _____

Mercy 150

In *Reader's Digest* Jim Williams of Butte, Montana, writes:
I was driving too fast late one night when I saw the flashing
lights of a police car in my rearview mirror. As I pulled over and
rolled down the window of my station wagon, I tried to dream
up an excuse for my haste. But when the patrolman reached the
car, he said nothing. Instead, he merely shined his flashlight in
my face, then on my seven-months-pregnant wife, then on our
snoozing 18-month-old in his car seat, then on our three other
children, who were also asleep, and lastly on the two dogs in
the very back of the car. Returning the beam of light to my face,
he then uttered the only words of the encounter.

"Son," he said, "you can't afford a ticket. Slow it down." And
with that, he returned to his car and drove away.

*Sometimes mercy triumphs over law. So it is for sinners who
call out to Jesus.*

Grace, Law, Salvation
Luke 18:9–14; Rom. 11:32; James 2:12

Date used _____ Place _____

Ministry

In the early 1990s large numbers of upscale professionals and independent freelancers began moving from the cities to the country. When those accustomed to the conveniences of suburban and city living arrived in rural areas, many were in for a big surprise, writes Patrick O'Driscoll in *USA Today*. "Your neighbor's cattle may stink," he writes. "You may have to haul your own trash to the dump. The mail carrier might not deliver daily, or perhaps not at all. Power or phone lines may not reach your property. The fire department or ambulance may not come quickly enough in an emergency. And, yes, your remote mountain road may not get plowed—or paved, for that matter."

Life in rural America had hardships naive newcomers never expected. Some of these city slickers called to complain. One county commissioner named John Clarke of Larimer County, Colorado, got so many cranky calls that he finally decided to warn people who were planning to move to the country about the realities that awaited them. He wrote a thirteen-page booklet called "The Code of the West: The Realities of Rural Living." Some of the warnings went like this:

"Animals and their manure can cause objectionable odors. What else can we say?"

"If your road is gravel, it is highly unlikely that Larimer County will pave it in the foreseeable future. . . . Gravel roads generate dust. . . . Dust is still a fact of life for most rural residents."

"The topography of the land can tell you where the water will go in case of heavy precipitation. When property owners fill in ravines, they have found that the water that drained through that ravine now drains through their house."

Clarke's motive in writing the booklet wasn't to keep newcomers away. "We just want them to know what to expect," he says.

Just as moving from the city to the country may bring unexpected hardships, so does becoming an active worker in the church. We too need to know what to expect. Don't be surprised by people problems or organizational glitches that arise when you are involved in a volunteer work force. Even with these vexations, though, working for Christ is as beautiful as a gentle stream flowing through a mountain valley.

Change, Complaining, Expectations, Hardship,
Problems, Reality, Spiritual Warfare
Phil. 1:28–30; 2 Tim. 2:3

Date used _____ Place _____

# Ministry												152

In 1996 the U.S. auto industry celebrated its one hundredth anniversary. In observance, *Chicago Tribune* auto writer Jim Mateja selected what he called the "10 That Made a Difference." These were the ten vehicles that had made the most significant contributions in their time and whose reputations live on:

1. 1896 Duryea Motor Wagon. For the first time more than one vehicle was manufactured from the same design (thirteen the first year).
2. 1901 Curved Dash Olds. This was the first mass-produced vehicle (425 the first year).
3. 1908 Ford Model T. Known as the Tin Lizzie, this car put America on the road.
4. 1941 Willys Jeep. The jeep helped win World War II and proved to be the forerunner of the sport-utility vehicle.
5. 1949 Volkswagen Beetle. This was "The People's Car," and in 1973 it overtook the Ford Model T as the world's best-selling car.
6. 1953 Chevrolet Corvette.
7. 1964 Pontiac GTO.
8. 1964 Ford Mustang. The Mustang set a first-year record of 417,000 sales, and drew a cult following.
9. 1984 Chrysler minivan. It replaced the station wagon as a people carrier.
10. 1986 Ford Taurus. By 1992 it was the industry's top-selling car.

Ten cars that made a big difference in the auto world.

Like these cars, each of us is called to make a difference in our world. We are change agents. God calls us to be salt, light, ambassadors for Christ. He wants each of us to leave our workplace, family, neighborhood, church a better place than when we came.

Change Agents, Evangelism, Fruitfulness,
Leadership, Light, Outreach, Salt, Vision
Matt. 5:13–16; 28:18–20; John 15:8; Acts 1:8; 17:6; 1 Cor. 15:58

Date used _____ Place _____

At the 1997 Brickyard 400 auto race, NASCAR driver Lake Speed learned firsthand the amazing effect of prayer. His car had been having mechanical problems. Sitting on the track in preparation for a qualifying run, he waited in frustration because his car wouldn't start. Meanwhile he prayed. Finally his crew chief Jeff Buice took out a wrench and hand-cranked the engine Model-A style. The car started, and Lake Speed roared onto the track to post the second fastest qualifying time of the day.

Victor Lee writes in *Sports Spectrum:*

Later, when Speed returned to the pits to get ready for a final practice session, he found his crew tearing out the engine. Shocked, he asked what was going on.

"Lake, that engine was blown before you qualified," Buice said, noting that it had blown during NASCAR pre-race inspection. Lake looked more closely. Oil was everywhere.

Buice continued, "I wasn't going to tell you anything, because time had run out. But I was already trying to figure out how I was going to spend Saturday. Even if it started, I surely didn't expect it to make a lap, and surely not to run good enough to make the race."

Lake's assessment: "God did a major mechanical miracle. I always pray right before the race. Sitting on that track, when it didn't start, I prayed, 'Lord, I don't know what's going on here, but if there's any way, I'd like this thing to start.'"

Driver Lake Speed went on to finish twelfth in the race, his second best finish in 1997.

You may say this has a perfectly natural explanation; or you may call it a miracle; but without question according to the automobile experts on the scene this was a remarkable event that followed prayer. Funny, but remarkable events and coincidences often follow prayer.

Impossibilities, Prayer, The Supernatural
Gen. 18:14; Matt. 19:26

Date used _____ Place _____

Miracles 154

In the *Pentecostal Evangel* missionary Ian Hall tells the story of a Romanian woman named Cristina Ardeleanu, whom he met during a preaching crusade:

In March 1992 Cristina was in the hospital with an ectopic pregnancy. Before she learned she was pregnant, the fetus died and began to decompose in her body. Cristina was not expected to live.

My wife Sheila and I went to the hospital to pray for Cristina, and God healed her. Still, in their attempts to save her life, doctors removed most of her uterus and one ovary. They told her she would never bear a child.

Cristina's strength returned, and by May she was back in church. I was holding another series of meetings there, and she and her husband Stefan came forward for prayer.

"Will you pray that God will give us a child?" they asked. Knowing Cristina's diagnosis, they were hoping to adopt.

I began to pray, but suddenly I found myself prophesying: "In one year you will stand in this place holding a son born of your own body."

"Why did you say that?" Sheila asked later. "You know she can't bear children. You've really put yourself out on a limb."

I knew my predicament all too well. The words that came from my lips had astonished everyone, including me.

That year I returned to the area from time to time, but Stefan and Cristina said nothing of a baby. Although I was troubled at first, in time I stopped thinking about the prophecy.

In May 1993 I was conducting services again in the Cimpulung church. The pastor announced that a baby would be dedicated and informed me that I was to pray for the child. But as I surveyed the audience, I couldn't see anyone with a baby.

Then from the farthest corner of the church I saw Stefan and Cristina approaching, holding the son born to them 6 weeks earlier. As with Hannah of the Bible, the Ardeleanus had received their promise—and they named him Samuel.

Childbirth, Healing, Holy Spirit, Pregnancy,
Promise, Prophecy, Supernatural, Word of Knowledge
1 Sam. 1; Acts 2:17–18; 21:10–11; 1 Cor. 12; 14; James 5:14–16

Date used _____ Place _____

Miracles

Baseball fans will talk about the first game of the 1996 American League championship series between the New York Yankees and the Baltimore Orioles for years to come. The game was played in New York. Going into the bottom of the eighth inning Baltimore led 4–3. With one out and Armando Benitez on the mound, Yankee Derek Jeter hit a towering blast to right field. Orioles right fielder Tony Tarasco ran back to the wall and timed his jump perfectly to snatch the ball before it hit high off the right-field fence.

But before the ball landed safely in his glove, the unexpected happened. "To me it was a magic trick," said Tarasco later, "because the ball just disappeared out of midair."

Not quite. A twelve-year-old boy from New Jersey named Jeff Maier had skipped school that day to come to the game and was seated in the front row in right field. When that towering fly ball fell straight in front of him, he did what any Yankee fan would do: he reached out over the wall with his baseball glove and scooped the ball into the stands.

The "magic" continued. The umpire erroneously called it a home run, tying the score. The game went into extra innings, and in the bottom of the eleventh Yankee Bernie Williams hit the home run that won the game, giving the Yankees a 1–0 lead in the series. Afterward the Orioles called the fan interference an outrage. Yankee fans called it a miracle. The Yankees went on to win the series 4 games to 1.

Like the Yankees, sometimes we need outside intervention. We need God to reach out and break the rules of nature to help us. Miracles are possible for those who pray and believe.

Angels, Deliverance, Healing, Impossibilities, Prayer
Matt. 19:26; Mark 9:23; 10:27; Acts 12:1–11

Date used _____ Place _____

Author and professor Phillip Johnson has waged an all-out war on the theory of Darwinian evolution. In a *Christianity Today* article titled "The Making of a Revolution," Tim Stafford tells how Johnson took up the cause:

In the fall of 1987, Phillip Johnson, a middle-aged law professor at the University of California, Berkeley, began a sabbatical year in England. His distinguished academic career had specialized in criminal law and lately branched out into more philosophical fields of legal theory. Nevertheless, Johnson could not shake the feeling that his life amounted to a wasted talent, that he had used a first-class mind for only second-class occupations. He was "looking for something to do the rest of his life" and talked about it with his wife, Kathie, as they hiked around the green fields of England. "I pray for an insight," he told her. "I'd like to have an insight that is worthwhile, and not just be an academic who writes papers and spins words."

In London, Johnson's daily path from the bus stop to his office at University College took him by a scientific bookstore. "Like a lot of people," Johnson says, "I couldn't go by a bookstore without going in and fondling a few things." The very first time he walked by he saw and purchased the powerful, uncompromising argument for Darwinian evolution by Richard Dawkins, *The Blind Watchmaker.* Johnson devoured it and then another book, Michael Denton's *Evolution: A Theory in Crisis.* "I read these books, and I guess almost immediately I thought, This is it. This is where it all comes down to, the understanding of creation."

Johnson began a furious reading program, absorbing the literature on Darwinian evolution. Within a few weeks, he told his wife, "I think I understand this stuff. I know what the problem is. But fortunately, I'm too smart to take it up professionally. I'd be ridiculed. Nobody would believe me. They would say, 'You're not a scientist, you're a law professor.' It would be something, once you got started with it, you'd be involved in a lifelong, never-ending battle."

"That," says Phillip Johnson, remembering back with a smile, "was of course irresistible. I started to work the next day."

Every Christian needs a great mission worth giving one's life for.

Cause, Challenge, Defining Moments, Direction,
Leadership, Prayer, Purpose, Spiritual Gifts, Vision
Matt. 4:18–22; Rom. 12:1–2; Phil. 2:12–13; 3:7–14; 1 Peter 4:10

Date used _____ Place _____

According to the Associated Press, in the summer of 1996 a man named Joe from Janesville, Wisconsin, received a check from the Social Security Administration for $40,945. Though entitled to the money, Joe was not supposed to receive that check directly. Rather, the check was supposed to go to him through a responsible payee. That's because Joe has an IQ of about 70 and suffers manic depression. Although he had worked some menial jobs here and there, he was unemployed and mildly retarded. Joe also had a gambling problem.

As you might guess, that was his undoing. Whenever Joe felt down, he told his live-in girlfriend he was going on an errand, and he would end up being gone for days on a gambling binge at the casino in Baraboo. Joe often felt down, and so the money didn't last long. In a few weeks he had blown all of the $40,000.

That isn't the way Joe had planned to spend the money. He had planned to buy a house and provide for his three children. Instead, he blew a great opportunity to get ahead. In the end, he blamed the Social Security Administration.

The government won't be giving any more money directly to Joe. Those who can't manage money cannot expect to be given even more.

The same principle applies to us all. God entrusts what is valuable to those who prove their ability to manage it.

Faithfulness, Gambling, Management, Stewardship, Waste
Matt. 25:14–30; Luke 16:1–13; 1 Cor. 4:1–4; 1 Tim. 1:12

Date used _____ Place _____

The Bible says we are to be free of the love of money. Campus Crusade for Christ's founder Bill Bright and his wife Vonette are sterling examples of this attitude.

A 1997 *Christianity Today* article by Wendy Murray Zoba says that although Campus Crusade had worldwide revenues in 1996 of $300 million, Bill Bright, at age seventy-five, and his wife Vonette, still raise their own monthly support from individual donors just like any other Campus Crusade staff person. Together they earn $48,000 annually ($29,000 for Bill and $19,000 for Vonette). After Bill won the Templeton Award for Progress in Religion in 1996, he relinquished the prize money—in excess of $1 million—for the purpose of developing a ministry of prayer and fasting.

"He recently liquidated $50,000 of his retirement funds," writes Zoba, "to help start up a training center in Moscow. All royalties from his books go to Campus Crusade; he does not accept speaking fees and has no savings account (though Vonette has a small one). The luxury condo they live in was donated to CCC (they pay $1,000 a month rent). They do not own a car, and they have no property."

Giving
Matt. 6:19–21; 1 Tim. 3:3; Heb. 13:5

Date used _____ Place _____

In *Words We Live By,* Brian Burrell tells of an armed robber named Dennis Lee Curtis who was arrested in 1992 in Rapid City, South Dakota. Curtis apparently had scruples about his thievery. In his wallet the police found a sheet of paper on which was written the following code, sort of a robber's rules:

1. I will not kill anyone unless I have to.
2. I will take cash and food stamps—no checks.
3. I will rob only at night.
4. I will not wear a mask.
5. I will not rob mini-marts or 7-Eleven stores.
6. If I get chased by cops on foot, I will get away. If chased by a vehicle, I will not put the lives of innocent civilians on the line.
7. I will rob only seven months out of the year.
8. I will enjoy robbing from the rich to give to the poor.

This thief had a sense of morality, but it was flawed. When he stood before the court, he was not judged by the standards he had set for himself but by the higher law of the state.

Likewise when we stand before God, we will not be judged by the code of morality we have written for ourselves but by God's perfect law.

Codes, Ethics, Judgment, Justice, Law, Righteousness, Standards, Stealing, Ten Commandments, Truth
Isa. 64:6; Rom. 3:10–23

Date used _____ Place _____

In *Discipleship Journal* editor Susan Maycinik writes:

The line between obedience and performance can be a blurry one. Yet it is an important distinction to grasp, because obedience leads to life, and performance to death. . . .

Obedience is seeking God with your whole heart. Performance is having a quiet time because you'll feel guilty if you don't.

Obedience is finding ways to let the Word of God dwell in you richly. Performance is quickly scanning a passage so you can check it off your Bible reading plan.

Obedience is inviting guests to your home for dinner. Performance is feeling anxious about whether every detail of the meal will be perfect.

Obedience is following God's prompting to start a small group. Performance is reluctance to let anyone else lead the group because they might not do it as well as you would.

Obedience is doing your best. Performance is wanting to be the best.

Obedience is saying yes to whatever God asks of you. Performance is saying yes to whatever people ask of you.

Obedience is following the promptings of God's Spirit. Performance is following a list of man-made requirements.

Obedience springs from fear of God. Performance springs from fear of failure.

Jesus promised that his yoke is easy, and his burden light.

Grace, Perfectionism, Performance, Works
Matt. 28:20; John 14:23–24; Rom. 8:1–17; Eph. 2:8–10; 1 John 5:3

Date used _____ Place _____

Obedience

In *Discipleship Journal* author Elaine Creasman writes:

Pursuit of "good things" can hinder obedience. It has been said that "the good is the enemy of the best." I think of times my husband has asked me to do one thing for him during the day. When he gets home from work, I tell him all the good things I have done. But the question he always has for me is, "What about the thing I asked you to do?"

Many times I have answered, "I forgot," or "I didn't have time." Or I've dismissed his request as trivial.

God asks that same question of us: "What about the thing I asked you to do? . . ."

I'm sure Abraham could have thought of a lot of good things to do instead of taking Isaac to be sacrificed. But I see no excuses in Genesis 22. God commanded; Abraham obeyed.

Direction, Disobedience, Excuses, God's Leading,
God's Will, Good Deeds, Obedience, Rebellion
Gen. 22:1–18; 1 Sam. 15:22–23; Isa. 1:19;
Matt. 28:20; John 14:23–24; Heb. 5:8

Date used _____ Place _____

Obedience

According to the *Chicago Tribune,* in 1996 a professor at the University of Illinois found himself in an embarrassing situation. At that time Stuart Nagel was the most published professor at the university, with some sixty books to his credit. The subject of his writing was public policy, with an expertise in dispute-resolution theory. Nagel's car even bore a bumper sticker that said, "Mediate, Don't Litigate."

But in the spring of 1996 the professor who would eat and breathe conflict-resolution theory decided he had no choice but to take the University of Illinois to court. Nagel felt the university was trying to force him into early retirement, or worse, to terminate him without due process. His department head had put him under investigation, ostensibly over the quality of his classroom teaching. Nagel had sought a win-win resolution, but had failed to come to an agreement with the university. And so, with his interests at risk, the professor who abhors litigation went to court as a last resort.

We all know what he felt like. How difficult at times to keep from doing what we don't want to do. How hard at times to do what we want to do.

Conflict, Law, Peacemakers
Matt. 5:9, 23–26; Rom. 7:7–25; 12:18; 1 Cor. 6:1–8

Date used _____ Place _____

The appetite of Americans for Mexican food increased dramatically in the 1990s, to the point that in 1996 it was a $1.6 billion market. The market for salsa and refried beans and the like began to grow when small companies like El Paso Chile in Texas marketed an authentic-style Mexican food that even a native of Mexico City could love. Then several large American companies, such as Pillsbury, saw the potential in the market and began to buy out smaller companies and market Mexican-style food on a much larger scale. But what they labeled Mexican food was really a watered-down version of the original to suit American tastes.

"Heat must be carefully rationed at Old El Paso [the Pillsbury brand]," writes Glenn Collins in the *New York Times*. "'Forty percent of those on the East Coast want salsa as mild as it can be,' said Dr. Bernadette Piacek-Llanes, vice president of research and development for Pillsbury Specialty Brands. So Old El Paso, like Pace, has introduced mild, 'cool salsa' products."

Industry experts call these products gringo food, and it is clearly catching on. "About the only thing missing from the boom is Mexicans," writes Collins. "There are no Mexicans on Pillsbury's 10-member Old El Paso development team; its leader was born in India."

Bob Messenger, editor of the industry publication *Food Processing*, says that the "gringo-ization of Mexican food will continue. In 20 years, you won't even recognize what they'll be calling Mexican food."

In business there's nothing wrong with watering down a strong flavor, but the same impulse leads to disaster in our faith. Like the inauthentic gringo style of Mexican food, there is a gringo gospel that is simply not the real thing. The hot, offensive themes—such as the cross and the blood of Christ—are taken out, and a comfortable, people-pleasing substitute is found. The false gospel may be soothing to the taste, but it is powerless to save. The gospel will always be an offense to sinful humankind.

> Atonement, Blood, Commitment, Compromise, Cross,
> Doctrine, Evangelism, False Gospel, Gospel, Hell,
> Judgment, Original Sin, Pleasing People, Resurrection,
> Substitutionary Death, Tolerance, Universalism, Wrath
> John 6:41–66; Rom. 9–11; 1 Cor. 1:18–25; 15:1–57;
> Gal. 1:6–10; 5:1–11; 6:12–15; 2 Tim. 4:3–4

Date used _____ Place _____

Sometimes you can be tardy and get away with it; sometimes you can't.

According to the Associated Press, near midnight on the evening of June 30, 1997, United Airlines flight 728 from Chicago was bound for Harrisburg, Pennsylvania, and as happens it was behind schedule. Unfortunately the Harrisburg airport had informed the airlines that the lone airport runway would be closed from 11:30 P.M. to 6:30 A.M. for construction.

The pilot of flight 728 believed that he could land before the runway closed, but when he radioed the control tower he was refused permission to do so.

Well, it's a big country; you would think he could land say in Baltimore or Pittsburgh. But no, the plane was ordered to fly all the way back to Chicago so as not to disrupt other flight schedules. The airline put the 101 passengers up in hotels and gave them $25 travel certificates, and the next morning the 101 made the trip to Harrisburg one more time. Yes, they were angry.

A window of opportunity is just that. Never assume everything will be okay if you miss the cutoff time. Sometimes, as here, it just makes life harder; other times, we never get a second chance. So it is with the opportunity for salvation.

Assumptions, Authorities, Obedience, Rules,
Second Coming, Tardiness
Luke 4:19; Acts 17:30–31; 2 Cor. 6:1–2

Date used _____ Place _____

Original Sin 165

Movie director Ron Howard has been a repeat winner in the entertainment world. In his days as a child actor he played Opie on *The Andy Griffith Show,* and as a teen he starred in television's *Happy Days.* When he started directing movies, he had success with positive films like *Apollo 13, Parenthood, Splash, Cocoon, Backdraft,* and *Far and Away.*

But then in 1996 he went against the flow by choosing to direct a dark, troubling film called *Ransom,* starring Mel Gibson. The plot revolves around the efforts of the Mel Gibson character to rescue his kidnapped son.

According to Bernard Weinraub in the *New York Times,* Ron Howard chose this movie because he could identify with the Gibson character, a winning but flawed man.

"Ron seems to be a cheerful, easy-going guy," says Brian Grazer, Howard's friend and the movie's producer, "but inside is a very complex, very competitive person who has darkness and pain. He just doesn't show it to people. In his face he never shows it. And this movie was a creative way for him to express that. The complexity of the Mel Gibson character intersects with Ron personally. He's a winning character but flawed. Ron views himself that way. And what appealed to him about the movie is the idea of digging around psychologically into a person that he can relate to."

Ron Howard is honest enough to recognize that despite all his success there is a flaw within. Do you recognize that about yourself? The Bible calls that flaw sin, and every human being has it.

Adam, Confession, Redemption, Salvation, Sin, Success
Gen. 3; Rom. 3:9–20; 5:12–21; Eph. 2:1–10

Date used _____ Place _____

Outreach

Author and Nobel laureate Elie Wiesel was a survivor of the Buchenwald concentration camp during World War II. In *All Rivers Run to the Sea,* he recalls how he became a U.S. citizen:

I was working in New York City as a correspondent for a French newspaper when my travel permit expired. At the French consulate I was informed that the document could be validated only in France. I didn't have enough money to go back there, and I was anxiously wondering whether I would be deported from America. I went to the U.S. Immigration office, where an official smiled and said, "Why don't you become a U.S. Resident? Then later you can apply for citizenship." I stared at him. Could I actually become an American citizen?

It is hard to put into words how much I owe that kindly immigration official, especially when I recall my annual visits to the Prefecture de Police in Paris, with its long lines and humiliating interrogations. The refugee's time is measured in visas, his biography in stamps on his documents. There is nothing romantic about the life of the exile.

In later years, a high official asked whether I would like to have French nationality. Though I thanked him, I declined the offer. When I needed a passport, it was America that gave me one.

People go where they are welcome. In the church we must help seekers and sinners know we are glad they have come.

Acceptance, Evangelism, Kindness, Love, Mercy, Pharisaism, Welcome
Matt. 9:9–13; 11:19; Luke 15

Date used _____ Place _____

According to *U.S. News & World Report:*

When it comes to the needy, former president Jimmy Carter enjoys exploring new ways of helping them. But even he admits that when it comes to dealing with society's problems, the church has some catching up to do.

"Most church members—including me—rarely reach outside to people who are different from us or less fortunate. Quite often my Sunday school class will say, 'Why don't we take up a collection and give a nice Thanksgiving meal to a poor family?' The next question is: 'Who knows a poor family?' Nobody does. We have to call the welfare office to get the name and address."

The first step in reaching out in the name of Jesus is to be friendly enough to find out the name of your neighbor. That especially means your disadvantaged neighbor.

Compassion, Evangelism, Justice, Mercy, the Poor
Isa. 58:6–12; Luke 4:18; 7:22; 14:12–24

Date used _____ Place _____

In the book titled *Can a Busy Christian Develop Her Spiritual Life?* Jill Briscoe writes:

Years ago, as I waited in line at a local shop, I heard the gossip. My neighbor's husband had left her. The night before he had packed his things into a van and driven out of her life.

I knew my neighbor casually. When we did speak, which wasn't often, it was about the weather. Our subdivision was the type where people led their own lives and neighbors didn't really get to know one another.

When I returned home, I struggled with what to do. Should I visit my neighbor, or pretend I knew nothing about her situation and go on with my day? In my mind I could see her sitting at her kitchen table, alone. She was in her fifties and the kids were grown.

Finally, I got up the courage and walked over to her house. When she opened her door, I said, "I heard through the grapevine your husband left you last night. Can I do anything to help?"

Immediately, she burst into tears and said, "Come in. Come in." I spent the entire morning with her—listening, putting my arm around her, and having coffee. But it was the start of a relationship.

Sometimes when we think of a needy world, we think of faraway places and masses of people in desperate circumstances. In reality, our needy world might be right next door.

Evangelism, Love, Ministry, Missions, Neighbors
Matt. 28:18–20; Luke 10:25–37

Date used _____ Place _____

In *Leadership* pastor and author Gordon MacDonald writes:

For the first time in my life, in my early thirties, I was experiencing physical pain, a spate of migraine headaches that came close to unbearable. I worried they were caused by a brain tumor and feared I would live with pain the rest of my life.

This may sound unbelievable, but I could almost set my calendar and watch to the onset of the migraines: They came during the month of May of every even-numbered year. They generally hit about one o'clock in the morning every other night for about three weeks, and then they stopped. I had four sequences of these.

I finally went to a headache specialist. "Ninety percent of my patients remind me of you," he said. "They are young men, heads of organizations or wanting to be heads of organizations. They're not at peace with themselves; they've got some people in their lives with whom they have unresolved relationships."

He had never met me and didn't know what I did for a living, but he described me perfectly. I knew exactly the unresolved relationships to which the doctor was referring. . . .

Down through history, some of the greatest moments of kingdom production have come during physical pain. . . . The question then becomes, "What does God want to teach me while I'm in the theater of pain?" Pain humbles us, forcing us to recognize our reliance on others and God. It reduces us to our true size.

It was during this dark moment that Gail and I, ten years into our marriage, first learned to pray together. It was one way I worked through my unresolved relationships. Over the next nine months, Gail and I pursued God together in prayer, in more than just a perfunctory way, and it changed our lives. I discovered the importance of saying to her, "I need you to pray for me," and that was something I had not done before. Years later, when Gail and I faced the blackest of my dark moments, the discipline of prayer we had learned during my physical pain was in place.

We don't know all that God is doing by allowing pain in our lives, but one good thing is certain: pain leads us to prayer.

Conflict, Marriage, Prayer, Relationships, Suffering, Trials, Weakness
Rom. 5:3–4; 2 Cor. 12:7–10; James 1:2–4

Date used _____ Place _____

In 1995 the Northwestern Wildcats football team had one of the most remarkable seasons in college football history. Prior to 1995 the Wildcats were the most notorious losers in the Big Ten, and for that matter in college football. They had set an NCAA record by losing thirty-four consecutive games between 1979 and 1982. They had not had a winning season in twenty-four years.

Then in 1995, under head coach Gary Barnett, the Wildcats finished the season 10–2, won the Big Ten Conference title, and went to the Rose Bowl ranked eighth in the nation.

Coach Gary Barnett earned all the credit he received, winning seventeen national coach-of-the-year awards.

In the spring of 1996 as the team prepared for the next season, Coach Barnett knew he had to fight the natural tendency to keep looking back on 1995. So he called a team meeting in the auditorium of the football center. In the *Chicago Tribune Magazine* Andrew Bagnato writes:

As the players found seats in the gently banked rows of plush chairs, Barnett mounted the stage and announced that he was going to hand out the awards that many of the Wildcats had earned in 1995. . . .

As Barnett called the players forward and handed them placards proclaiming their accomplishments, the 70-plus players in the room cheered and chanted their teammates' names. . . .

The players roared as Barnett waved the placard representing his 17 national coach-of-the-year awards. Then, as the applause subsided, Barnett walked to the side of the stage, stopping in front of a trash can marked "1995." He took an admiring glance at his placard, then dumped it in the can.

As silence descended on the auditorium, Barnett stepped to the side of the stage. . . . Then, one by one, the stars of the team dropped their placards on top of Barnett's. Soon, the trash can was overflowing with the laurels of the previous season.

Barnett had shouted a message to his assembled charges without uttering a word: What you did in 1995 was terrific, lads. But look at the calendar: it's 1996.

The only way to continue to achieve great things in the present and the future is to leave the past behind us.

Complacency, Discipleship, Future, Growth, Success
Phil. 3:7–16; Rev. 2:1–7; 3:14–22

Date used _____ Place _____

One of the indelible images from the Vietnam War is the photograph of a nine-year-old girl named Phan Thi Kim Phuc. During a battle between North and South Vietnamese troops, an American commander ordered South Vietnamese aircraft to drop napalm bombs on her tiny village. Two of her brothers were killed, and she was burned badly. Wearing no clothes, she fled up the road toward the cameraman. Because of the pain her arms are held out sideways, and her mouth is open in a cry of agony.

According to Elaine Sciolino in the *New York Times*, Ms. Kim Phuc suffered third-degree burns over 50 percent of her body, but she lived. She endured fourteen months of painful rehabilitation and scores of skin grafts. "It was so painful to have her wounds washed and dressed that she lost consciousness whenever she was touched."

Since then she has married, emigrated to Canada, and become a Christian who hopes someday to attend Bible college. Her burned skin lost sweat and oil glands, and she is still in much pain. Scars stretch up her arms to her chest and back. But despite her past and present suffering, in 1996 she accepted an invitation from several Vietnam veterans groups to join in Veterans Day ceremonies held at the Vietnam Veterans Memorial, where she laid a wreath and spoke words of forgiveness.

"I have suffered a lot from both physical and emotional pain," she told the audience of several thousand people, who greeted her with two standing ovations. "Sometimes I could not breathe. But God saved my life and gave me faith and hope. Even if I could talk face to face with the pilot who dropped the bombs, I would tell him, 'We cannot change history, but we should try to do good things for the present and for the future to promote peace.'"

Those who suffer the most can be the greatest peacemakers.

Forgiveness, Mercy, Suffering
Matt. 5:9; 18:21–35; Acts 7:54–60

Date used _____ Place _____

Perfection   172

According to the Associated Press, in 1997 the U.S. Treasury Department planned to put into circulation a new-look fifty dollar bill with special features designed to thwart counterfeiters.

After printing an estimated thirty million copies of the new bills at a cost of $1.44 million, however, it was discovered that the bills had a flaw. There were small breaks in the fine concentric lines around the photo of Ulysses S. Grant.

That presented a dilemma to the Treasury Department. In the first year a new bill goes into circulation it is especially important that it have no flaws because persons unfamiliar with the bills may assume the defective bills are counterfeit.

Larry Felix, a spokesman for the Treasury's Bureau of Engraving and Printing, said, "Clearly if you're going to introduce notes for the first time, you're going to make sure the notes are as flawless as possible."

And so, the bills in question were put under seal at Federal Reserve district banks pending a decision whether to destroy them.

The more valuable something is, the more necessary that it be flawless. Human beings are infinitely more valuable than a fifty-dollar bill. Since we will live forever, since we are moral beings in a moral universe, since we are created in the image of a perfect and absolutely righteous God, God's standard for humanity can be nothing less than perfection.

Character, Flaws, Integrity, Judgment, Righteousness, Sin
Matt. 5:48; 12:36–37; Rom. 3:10–12, 23; 14:10–12

Date used _____ Place _____

Persecution 173

According to Michael Lewis in the *New York Times Maga-zine,* Senator John McCain of Arizona is much more than a politician. First and foremost he is a Vietnam War hero. As a Navy pilot, he was shot down by a North Vietnamese missile on October 26, 1967. Lewis writes:

For nine days, McCain received no treatment for the injuries he sustained when he parachuted into a North Vietnamese mob: two broken arms, a shattered knee, a shattered shoulder and bayonet wounds in his ankle and his groin. He survived in captivity for the next five and a half years under constant, exqui-site torture. . . . But McCain's capacity to suffer was the least of what the experience revealed about him. The truly aston-ishing part of the story . . . is that he did it . . . voluntarily.

McCain belongs to a distinguished military family; his father and grandfather were both admirals, and his father was com-manding the bombing of Hanoi at the time McCain's Navy fighter was shot down. The North Vietnamese planned for their famous P.O.W. to violate United States military policy, which dictated that prisoners return in the order they had arrived. His early release might demoralize American troops, they figured. Except that he wouldn't go along. For five and a half years, they tortured McCain. For five and a half years, he refused to go home.

He had no choice in the matter, he later explained. To accept early release would have dishonored not only himself but his family. You just didn't do that.

There are times when the only way to escape suffering is unworthy of who you are. Those who are persecuted for their faith in Christ may face that choice. The only path worthy of a Christian is at all costs to stand with Christ for all to see.

Courage, Endurance, Hardship, Honor, Perseverance, Suffering
Matt. 13:21; John 15:18–16:4; Acts 7:54–60; 2 Cor. 11:16–33; Phil.
1:28–30; 2 Tim. 2:3; 3:12; Heb. 10:33; Rev. 2:10

Date used _____ Place _____

In *The Calling* Brother Andrew writes:

We were planning to smuggle one million Bibles into China. Wanting to be sure that the believers in the country realized the immensity of the task and were willing to accept the risks, we sent Joseph, a Chinese team member, to meet with five key house-church leaders.

"Do you know how much space one million Bibles take up?" Joseph asked.

"We have already prepared storage places," they replied.

"Do you know what could happen to you," Joseph continued, "if you were caught with even a portion of these Bibles?"

"Joseph, all five of us have been in prison for the Lord," they replied. "All together, we've spent seventy-two years in jail for Jesus. We are willing to die if it means that a million brothers and sisters can have a copy of God's word."

With tears in his eyes, Joseph folded up his long list of questions and put it away.

Whether it is risking our life or risking our reputation, serving the gospel requires courage. God never said his work was safe.

> Courage, Dedication, Evangelism, Gospel, Ministry,
> Pleasing People, Reputation, Sacrifice, Scripture
> Rom. 1:16; Phil. 1:20; Heb. 12:1–4

Date used _____ Place _____

Even as a young amateur golfer Tiger Woods was known for mental toughness. In the *New York Times* Larry Dorman tells where some of that toughness came from:

His father and mentor, Earl Woods, traces it to an incident that occurred in 1992 when Tiger was 16 and playing in the Junior Orange Bowl Tournament at Miami. The young man was, as Earl recalls it, "a little full of himself" and when things started going badly for him, he began to pout. Then he went into the tank, and stopped trying.

Earl, a former Green Beret, chewed his son out. "I asked him who he thought he was," the elder Wood said. "I told him golf owed him nothing and that he had better not ever quit again." The way Earl remembers it, Tiger never said a word. And he has never quit again.

The best things in life don't come served on a platter to those who think they deserve it. They come to those who know they must persevere no matter who they are and no matter what happens.

Child Rearing, Expectations, Fathers,
Persistence, Quitting, Self-Pity
Ps. 27:14; 1 Cor. 15:58; Gal. 6:9–10; Heb. 10:36

Date used _____ Place _____

Leslie Hindman has served as president of the Midwest's premier auction firm. Each year she auctioned millions of dollars worth of decorative arts and home furnishings from the estates of the wealthy. This is a world of Van Gogh paintings and black lacquered desks that sell for tens of thousands of dollars. Nevertheless, her career has made material things one of the least of her priorities.

"I see people fighting about their stuff all the time," she says. "You realize life is not about possessions."

"A few experiences early in Hindman's career helped to cinch her disdain for material things," says writer Adrienne Fawcett in the *Chicago Tribune*. "Once, she was hired to hold an auction in the modest home of a suburban family whose mother recently had died. As Hindman held court, the siblings bid against each other for their mother's humble possessions, scarcely exchanging a word."

Another experience she will never get over was finding "a lifetime of diaries in the apartment of an elderly Oak Park woman who saved everything but had no children to whom to leave her things. Hindman tried to donate the diaries to historical societies, but none wanted them. . . . She saved them for a couple of years but finally threw them out. 'So,' she says emphatically, 'I save absolutely nothing.'"

After all is said and done, the true value of possessions is clearly seen.

Covetousness, Greed, Materialism, Things
Exod. 20:17; Matt. 19:16–30; Luke 12:15; James 5:1–6

Date used _____ Place _____

According to Eric Ferkenhoff in the *Chicago Tribune,* on Father's Day 1997 Ricardo Enamorado set out on a jet ski from Chicago's Wilson Avenue boat ramp and headed north along the shoreline of Lake Michigan. After traveling several miles north, at about 3 P.M. he turned around to head back south when the engine on the jet ski suddenly quit. Unable to restart it, he floated along nonchalantly, expecting help to come quickly on the busy waters off Chicago. Gradually, though, the wind and waves pushed Enamorado farther and farther from shore, and help did not come. By dusk he was frantic. Dressed only in cut-offs, tennis shoes, and a life preserver, he spent the night on the chilly waters of the lake.

The next day Coast Guard helicopters and a Chicago fire department chopper equipped with special radar began searching for the lost man. By the end of the day they still had not found him, and Enamorado, hungry and sunburned, spent another night on the dark waters of Lake Michigan.

Finally the next morning one of the search-and-rescue teams spotted a flash of light. Enamorado was signaling in the search team's direction with a mirror. The nearly two-day ordeal was over at last.

A loss of power can be more dangerous than we realize.

Goals, Holy Spirit, Motivation, Purpose, Zeal
Ezek. 37:1–14; Acts 1:4–8; Rom. 12:11;
Eph. 5:18; 6:10–18; 2 Tim. 1:7; 3:5

Date used _____ Place _____

Prayer   **178**

In 1996 the Chicago Bulls basketball team won their fourth
world championship behind their leader Michael Jordan. Jordan's contract ended after the season, however, and fans in
Chicago were uneasy about whether the Bulls could re-sign Jordan for the upcoming year. Would owner Jerry Reinsdorf be
willing to pay the huge salary that everyone knew Jordan would
request for a new contract?

On July 12, 1996, the Chicago media discovered the answer.
The Bulls announced they had agreed to pay some $30 million.

Bob Verdi reported later in the *Chicago Tribune* that months
prior to the negotiations, when snow was on the ground, Reinsdorf had joked with Jordan and his agent that when the season
ended, if the negotiations took more than five minutes, they would
be wasting their time. At a dinner with Jordan less than two weeks
before negotiations began, Reinsdorf repeated his intention to wrap
things up quickly. And when the time came to talk numbers,
Reinsdorf paid Jordan's asking price without a qualm.

"I could have tried to talk Michael down from what he
asked," said Reinsdorf. "But why? . . . Michael is unique. I can
afford what he's getting, he deserves what he's getting, and if
it's not the best business transaction I ever made, so what? This
wasn't a business deal in the truest sense, anyway. Call them
psychic dollars. When we couldn't give Michael what he
deserved because of the salary cap, I told him there would be a
day. Well, the day has come."

Like Michael Jordan asking for a big salary, we often come to
God with large requests, and we wonder how he will feel about
it. Jesus taught us that God's response to our prayers is guided
in large measure by how he feels about us. God's sons and daughters are more special to him than Michael Jordan is to the owner
of the Chicago Bulls. For God, prayer isn't some spiritual negotiation; prayer is love. God is giving "heart dollars."

Faith, Favor from God, Love of God
Ps. 37:4; Matt. 7:7–11; Mark 1:40–42; Rom. 8:31–32; Eph. 3:20

Date used _____ Place _____

In "Total Eclipse" Annie Dillard writes:

The Ring Nebula, in the constellation Lyra, looks, through binoculars, like a smoke ring. It is a star in the process of exploding. Light from its explosion first reached the earth in 1054; it was a supernova then, and so bright it shone in the daytime. Now it is not so bright, but it is still exploding. It expands at the rate of seventy million miles a day. It is interesting to look through binoculars at something expanding seventy million miles a day. It does not budge. Its apparent size does not increase. Photographs of the Ring Nebula taken fifteen years ago seem identical to photographs of it taken yesterday.

Huge happenings are not always visible to the naked eye—especially in the spiritual realm. How often it is that this nebula resembles the process of prayer. Sometimes we pray and pray and seemingly see no change in the situation. But that's only true from our perspective. If we could see from heaven's standpoint, we would know all that God is doing and intending to do in our lives. We would see God working in hearts in ways we cannot know. We would see God orchestrating circumstances that we know nothing about. We would see a galaxy of details being set in place for the moment when God brings the answer to fulfillment.

Appearances, Change, Patience, Perseverance, Perspective
Dan. 10:12–14; Luke 12:5–13; 18:1–8

Date used _____ Place _____

In May 1996, ValuJet Flight 592 crashed into the Florida Everglades, killing 110 passengers. To determine the cause of the crash, the National Transportation Safety Board needed the plane's black box. That would not be easy to find. The crash had scattered plane debris across a large area of swamp. Dozens of searchers descended on the scene to sift through muck and water as much as eight feet deep in an attempt to find the black box.

Navy experts tried using special technology that detected submerged metal, without success.

Holding a rope that kept them spaced three feet apart, other searchers systematically poked through every square foot of the crash area. After fourteen days, they had found nothing.

For workers the physical conditions were nigh unbearable. The Florida sun beat upon them, and temperatures hovered in the 90s. Diesel fuel and caustic hydraulic fluid from the wrecked plane floated in the water, forcing searchers to wear several layers of protective rubber and latex despite the heat and humidity. Fourteen days of that had left many searchers dehydrated, but they had to find the black box.

Sergeant Felix Jimenez, of the Metro-Dade police, was one of the searchers. For fourteen days he had prayed for the bereaved families and for the safety of his fellow workers, but on the fifteenth day as he took a break, suddenly he realized he had failed to pray for one important thing: that God would help them find the black box. So he asked God for direction, resumed the search, and when he stuck his pole into the water, he hit something metallic. He pulled the object out of the muck. It was the black box.

Jimenez writes in *Guideposts*, "At the end of the day . . . I thought of the many days we had spent searching for the recorder, how we must have tromped over it many times, and I wondered why its retrieval had taken so long. Amid the low rustle of saw grass and the call of a great white heron, I seemed to hear the response: 'Why did it take you so long to ask?'"

Dependence
James 4:2

Date used _____ Place _____

Prayer

James David Ford, chaplain of the United States House of Representatives since 1979, told the following story about prayer to *Leadership* journal:

In the spring of 1976 I sailed the Atlantic Ocean with a couple of friends. In a thirty-one-foot vessel, we sailed from Plymouth, England, to New York—5,992 miles. During the trip, we hit a real hurricane—some of the waves were thirty-five feet high—and frankly, I was scared. My father had said, "Don't go. You have five children. Wait till they're grown."

The hurricane went into its third day, and I thought of my father's words about the children. I thought, *Why am I out here? Was this thing that I thought was courage and adventure really just foolhardy?*

The skies were black, and clouds were scudding by. I wanted to pray for God to stop the storm, but I felt guilty 'cause I'd voluntarily gotten into this. I didn't have to go across the ocean. . . .

Finally I came up with a marvelous prayer, seven words: "O God, I have had enough. Amen."

Within half an hour of that simple prayer, the sky in the west lifted like a screen in a theater, and there was blue sky.

Was my prayer tied to the opening of the sky? I don't worry about it.

One thing is certain: simple, sincere prayers are sufficient.

Deliverance, Desperation, Fear, Help, Rescue, Sincerity, Storms, Trials
Ps. 107:23–32; Matt. 6:7–8; Mark 4:35–41; James 4:2; 5:13–18

Date used _____ Place _____

In *How I Pray*, Billy Graham writes:

I heard about a young president of a company who instructed his secretary not to disturb him because he had an important appointment. The chairman of the board came in and said, "I want to see Mr. Jones." The secretary answered, "I'm terribly sorry, he cannot be disturbed; he has an important appointment."

The chairman became very angry. He banged open the door and saw the president of his corporation on his knees in prayer. The chairman softly closed the door and asked the secretary, "Is this usual?" And she said, "Yes, he does that every morning." To which the chairman of the board responded, "No wonder I come to him for advice."

To those who pray, God promises wisdom and help.

Spiritual Disciplines, Wisdom
James 1:5

Date used _____ Place _____

Bill Cowher took over as coach of the Pittsburgh Steelers in 1992. He quickly showed himself to be a man with a future. The Steelers made the playoffs each of his first several seasons as coach and went to Super Bowl XXX in 1996. One thing that made Cowher an effective coach was that he focused on his priorities. In *Sports Illustrated* Tim Crothers writes:

After almost every game, every practice, Pittsburgh Steelers head coach Bill Cowher drives straight home to his wife, Kaye, and their three daughters. He doesn't do ads for cars or frozen yogurt. He exists inside his two passions, family and football, exclusive of everything else.

Cowher is so focused that one afternoon he was seated next to a woman at a civic luncheon and politely asked, "What is it you do?"

The woman responded, "I'm the mayor of Pittsburgh."

Granted, it's a good idea to know who your mayor is, but Cowher shows us one essential truth: A person cannot focus on everything. A person with priorities must let some things go by the wayside. The more we focus on the Lord, the less we focus on the unimportant things of this world.

Devotion, Focus, Passion, World
Matt. 10:37–39; 2 Cor. 11:2–3; Phil. 3:7–16; Col. 3:1–3; Heb. 12:1–3

Date used _____ Place _____

In *The Door* Mike Yaconelli writes:

Author Susan Howatch made a fortune writing blockbuster novels like *Penmarric*. She had houses in several countries, drove a Porsche, and, after divorcing, had a number of "transient liaisons." But at age 30, she says, "God seized me by the scruff of the neck and shook me until my teeth rattled."

Now a Christian, she reflects: "I was promiscuous, but finally one morning I woke up and said, 'What am I trying to prove and to whom?' I knew exactly what—that even though my marriage broke up, I could still attract men. The fact that I could control men boosted my fractured ego."

Her conclusion: "Promiscuity is a sign that you're not aligned right with God or yourself."

Divorce, Ego, Self-Image, Sex
1 Thess. 4:3–7; 1 Peter 4:2–4

Date used _____ Place _____

In 1979 Verna Bowman of Telford, Pennsylvania, gave birth to her fourth child, Geoff, and quickly learned from doctors the frightening news: the baby had defective kidneys. Writing in *Guideposts,* she tells that doctors ordered the child rushed to a children's hospital in Philadelphia, where he would receive kidney dialysis.

Still hospitalized herself, Verna prayed and prayed for her son, and as she did she soon felt God's nearness. Unbidden, the words of a Scripture text began to repeat in her heart: "This sickness is not unto death, but for the glory of God" (John 11:4). She wrote the words down.

Later her husband called to report on the baby's condition: "It's too soon to tell if he's going to make it," he said.

"He's going to make it," Verna replied, and she read him the verse that God had breathed into her heart. "I believe those words," she said.

"So do I, Verna," replied her husband. "So do I."

After three months of dialysis, Geoff's kidneys, though still defective, began to function on their own. Throughout his childhood Geoff took medication and tired easily. During that time Verna collected in her journal other Scriptures which encouraged her faith that her son would be all right.

When Geoff was thirteen, the doctors reported he would need a kidney transplant. Though unsettling at first, this news turned out to be the answer to her prayers. Verna herself provided the kidney, and the operation was a complete success. Geoff would be able to live a normal life.

Later Verna's daughter suggested they do something special with the Scriptures that had meant much to them during Geoff's long sickness. Verna often made quilts and her daughter was skilled at cross-stitch, so they decided to make a quilt that displayed twelve of the cherished promises from the Bible. Each Scripture was stitched onto white linen and bordered in a pattern of hunter green and burgundy. Three months later the quilt was completed and hung on the wall of their guest room. When others admired the quilt, it eventually was hung in their church as well as other churches in the area.

God's promises had made a great difference for Verna Bowman. When she chose to have these promises stitched onto a quilt, she made a fitting choice. As comforting as a quilt on a cold wintry night, so God's promises ward off soul-chilling fear. They warm the soul.

Faith, Fear, Revelation, Scriptures, Word of God
Ps. 145:13; 2 Peter 1:4

Date used _____ Place _____

Provision 186

In *Pentecostal Evangel* pastor Dale Alan Robbins writes of an occasion early in his ministry when he and his wife were barely making ends meet:

When I arrived home, my wife Jerri saw the worry on my face. I had $3 in my wallet and there was one can of soup in the cupboard. After our meager supper, I quietly leafed through my Bible in the dim light. Tears streamed from my eyes. I wondered whether we were really called by God. I felt like giving up. Then I thought, *What alternative do I have? Who else but God do I have to turn to?*

I read the verse: "The effectual fervent prayer of a righteous man availeth much" (James 5:16). . . . Encouraged, yet still burdened, Jerri and I knelt at opposite ends of the little trailer to seek God. Into the night we prayed, until sleep finally overtook us.

I was awakened by a pounding at the door. From the window I could see the brilliant orange sunrise behind the city skyline. A fresh, white blanket of snow now covered the ground. Again, the knocking came.

"Who is it?" I asked.

A mystery voice replied, "I've got something for you."

Cautiously, I opened the door. There stood a short man with a grin on his face and two brown grocery bags in his arms. He quickly shoved the bags in the doorway, then turned, and walked away.

Jerri joined me. Stunned, we began to look through the bags. There were bread, meat, canned goods, and several cans of my favorite soup. They were the same items and brands we normally purchased. There was also a can of shaving cream. Who knew I had just used my last ounce of shaving cream? On the bottom of one sack was an envelope with cash. (Later I discovered it was the precise amount needed to fill our gas tank to get us to our next destination.)

On that wintry Saturday morning in Syracuse, my wife and I wept in our trailer and thanked God for hearing and answering our prayer. No one on the planet knew about our need; only our Lord God Almighty. And he dispatched a little grinning man to minister to us.

Earnestness, Money, Needs, Prayer, Seeking God, Supply
Gen. 22:14; Matt. 6:25–34; Phil. 4:19; Heb. 11:6; James 5:16–18

Date used _____ Place _____

Provision   187

In *Fresh Wind, Fresh Fire*, Jim Cymbala, author and pastor of the Brooklyn Tabernacle, tells the story of the first financial obstacle he faced upon coming to the tiny church:

When the first mortgage payment rolled around at the end of the month, the checking account showed something like $160 in hand. We were going to default right off the bat. How soon would it take to lose the building and be tossed out into the street? That Monday, my day off, I remember praying, "Lord, you have to help me. I don't know much—but I do know that we have to pay this mortgage."

I went to the church on Tuesday. Well, maybe someone will send some money out of the blue, I told myself, like what happened so often with George Mueller and his orphanage back in England—he just prayed, and a letter or a visitor would arrive to meet his need.

The mail came that day—and there was nothing but bills and fliers.

Now I was trapped. I went upstairs, sat at my little desk, put my head down, and began to cry. "God," I sobbed, "what can I do? We can't even pay the mortgage." That night was the midweek service, and I knew there wouldn't be more than three or four people attending. The offering would probably be less than ten dollars. How was I going to get through this?

I called out to the Lord for a full hour or so. Eventually, I dried my tears—and a new thought came. Wait a minute! Besides the mail slot in the front door, the church also has a post office box. I'll go across the street and see what's there. Surely God will answer my prayer!

With renewed confidence I walked across the street, crossed the post office lobby, and twirled the knob on the little box. I peered inside . . .

Nothing.

As I stepped back into the sunshine, trucks roared down Atlantic Avenue. If one had flattened me just then, I wouldn't have felt any lower. Was God abandoning us? Was I doing something that displeased him? I trudged wearily back across the street to the little building.

As I unlocked the door, I was met with another surprise. There on the foyer floor was something that hadn't been there just three minutes earlier: a simple white envelope. No address, no stamp—nothing. Just a white envelope.

With trembling hands I opened it to find . . . two $50 bills.

I began shouting all by myself in the empty church. "God, you came through! You came through!" We had $160 in the bank, and with this $100 we could make the mortgage payment. My soul let out a deep "Hallelujah!" What a lesson for a disheartened young pastor!

To this day I don't know where that money came from. I only know it was a sign to me that God was near—and faithful.

Money, Needs, Prayer, Providence, Supply
Matt. 6:25–34; 2 Cor. 12:8–10; Phil. 4:19; Heb. 13:5–6

Date used _____ Place _____

Purity

In the spring of 1995, revival broke out on many college campuses across America. One characteristic of this visitation from God was students dealing with sinful habits that they had previously let linger in their lives. Bonne Steffen interviewed several of the students for the *Christian Reader;* one student named Brian at Asbury College said:

I was a leader on campus. We had invited Wheaton students to come and share. At first, I was praying for other people, but then I began to think about my own struggles. I stood in line for three hours with one of my best friends all the time thinking, *How can I get up here and admit I'm less than perfect?* But I also realized that being on a Christian campus isn't protection from the world. I have really struggled with lust. I found I wasn't alone. It was an issue for a lot of others. Personally, I wanted the chain to be broken; I wanted that stuff out of my life. If it meant no magazines, no television, I was willing to eliminate them. A number of us signed a paper stating our desire for purity, which we put in a box and placed on the altar. I'm still accountable to other people. My deepest desire is to be pure in my heart and thoughts.

As this student shows, the desire for purity is the beginning of purity. Purity comes when we pursue it actively and forcefully.

Accountability, Confession, Lust, Repentance, Revival
Matt. 5:8, 27–30; 2 Cor. 7:1; James 5:16

Date used _____ Place _____

When we are in conflict with those near to us, God calls us to seek reconciliation as a first priority. Among the reasons is personal safety.

According to the Associated Press, in 1994, hospital emergency rooms in the United States treated 1.4 million victims of violence or suspected violence. Is this all about crime on the streets?

No. The Justice Department analyzed the data and reported in 1997 that roughly half of these victims were hurt by someone they knew. Seventeen percent of the victims, 243,000 people, were injured by a spouse, former spouse, or a current or former boyfriend or girlfriend. Eight percent of the victims were injured by a relative such as a parent or child. Twenty-three percent were hurt by friends or acquaintances. (These figures, which come from hospital emergency rooms, differ from those reported by the FBI's annual Uniform Crime Report, which reflects only offenses reported to police.)

God knows that hostile feelings between family and friends are literally dangerous. There is no telling how broken relationships will end.

Anger, Divorce, Family, Forgiveness, Peace,
Relationships, Ten Commandments, Violence
Exod. 20:12–17; Mal. 2:13–16; Matt. 5:21–26, 38–48;
18:15–35; Luke 6:27–37; James 3:8–18

Date used _____ Place _____

In an interview with Will Norton, Jr., best-selling novelist John Grisham recalls:

One of my best friends in college died when he was 25, just a few years after we had finished Mississippi State University. I was in law school, and he called me one day and wanted to get together. So we had lunch, and he told me he had terminal cancer.

I couldn't believe it. I asked him, "What do you do when you realize that you are about to die?"

He said, "It's real simple. You get things right with God, and you spend as much time with those you love as you can. Then you settle up with everybody else." Then he said, "You know, really, you ought to live every day like you have only a few more days to live."

That left an impression on me.

Few things impart more wisdom than to face up to the fact that we will all die sooner or later.

Conversion, Death, Family, Priorities, Repentance, Wisdom
Ps. 90:12; Eccles. 12:13–14; Heb. 9:27

Date used _____ Place _____

In the early nineties the plight of Keiko the orca whale, star of the movie *Free Willy*, stirred the concern of millions of people. Keiko's saga began when the media discovered that, like the whale in the movie, Keiko actually lived in an unhealthy environment.

Life magazine reported: "His tank at Mexico City's Reino Aventura theme park, full of chlorinated and artificially salted water, was barely large enough . . . for the 21-foot animal to turn around in. His muscles had turned flabby, and constant swimming in one direction had curled his dorsal fin. His water was far too warm—80 degrees—for his Nordic blood. An inadequate filtration system had him swimming in his own wastes, and he was breathing the world's smoggiest air. These hardships, along with an improper diet, had weakened his immune system. He was 1,300 pounds underweight, and warty eruptions, caused by the papillomavirus, marred his skin. In his frustration he had taken to gnawing at the edge of the pool—a habit that wore his teeth down to stubs."

Various activists crusaded to try to improve the whale's lot. After several years Dave Phillips at the Earth Island Institute formed the Free Willy Foundation, and millions of dollars began to pour in. The foundation built a new tank for Keiko at the Oregon Coast Aquarium in Newport, Oregon.

Life reported that Keiko's new home was "four times bigger than the one in Mexico. Filled with healthful 40-degree seawater from nearby Yaquina Bay, the new pool featured reversible currents to work against, waterjets to play among, even submerged rocks for navigation practice."

On January 7, 1996, Keiko was flown to his new home. Within a year Keiko had gained 1,000 pounds. The lesions on his skin were healing. And his fallen dorsal fin was on the rise.

The Free Willy-Keiko Foundation redeemed one very grateful whale. In the same way, God redeems us. Through Christ he rescued us from a hurtful situation that we had no power to escape and brought us into a healthful one.

Abundant Life, Deliverance, Healing,
Kingdom of God, Restoration, Salvation
John 10:10; Col. 1:13–14

Date used _____ Place _____

On December 20, 1995, an American Airlines jet crashed into a mountainside in Colombia, killing 159 passengers. Months later, airline officials determined that the cause of the crash was an error by the flight captain and a mix-up in computer coordinates.

According to Reuters, as flight 965 approached Cali airport from the north, the control tower radioed to the flight captain that he was to fly a straight path over the "Rozo" navigational radio beacon near the airport. The captain punched the letter "R" into the on-board computer, which he assumed would cause the autopilot to fly the plane toward the beacon. Unfortunately there was another radio beacon with a code name that began with the letter "R," the "Romeo" beacon, 132 miles to the left and behind the plane at the Bogota airport. The autopilot sent the plane to the wrong beacon—with disastrous results.

Accuracy and details are essential not only in navigation but also in religion. Punching in the letter "R" for any old religion will not do. The only way to have a relationship with God is through faith in Jesus Christ and the essential doctrines of orthodoxy.

Doctrine, Exclusiveness of the Gospel,
Orthodoxy, Truth, Universalism
John 14:6; Acts 4:12; Rom. 10:1–4; Gal. 1:6–9; 1 John 5:12

Date used _____ Place _____

What causes ulcers? Stress, coffee, spicy food? Wrong, wrong, wrong, according to Daniel Haney of the Associated Press. For years that is what doctors presumed caused ulcers, but in the early 1980s two doctors—Barry Marshall and Robin Warren— discovered a bacterium in the lining of the digestive system that they suspected might be the real cause. The bacterium is called *Helicobacter pylori.*

The proof of Marshall and Warren's idea was slow in coming, but by the early 1990s—after some two thousand articles had appeared in medical journals on the subject of the bacterium—gastroenterologists agreed with them.

"It turns out that about half of all U.S. adults are infected with *H. pylori*," writes Haney. "Most don't get ulcers. But when ulcers do occur, the bug is probably responsible for 80 percent or more. The only major exception is ulcers triggered by aspirin and some other pain killers."

Nevertheless, most people suffering stomach discomfort don't go first to a gastroenterologist; they go to their family practitioner or general internist. And news about the real cause of ulcers has been slow to reach them. Instead of prescribing an antibiotic that would cure the problem, many persist in prescribing acid-blocking drugs that may heal ulcers temporarily, but in time they often come back.

In a similar way, many people get only temporary relief for spiritual and emotional problems. If a person has a sin problem, no amount of self-help or technique will completely take away the pain or cure the disease. The antibiotic is repentance.

Pain, Self-Help, Sin, Technique, Therapy
Luke 5:27–32

Date used _____ Place _____

In *Guideposts* Joann C. Jones writes:

During my second year of nursing school our professor gave us a pop quiz. I breezed through the questions until I read the last one: "What is the first name of the woman who cleans the school?"

Surely this was some kind of joke. I had seen the cleaning woman several times, but how would I know her name? I handed in my paper, leaving the last question blank.

Before the class ended, one student asked if the last question would count toward our grade. "Absolutely," the professor said. "In your careers you will meet many people. All are significant. They deserve your attention and care, even if all you do is smile and say hello."

I've never forgotten that lesson. I also learned her name was Dorothy.

We have not begun to show the love of Christ to others until we have treated them with respect.

Dignity, Humility, Love, Significance, Worth
Rom. 12:16; Phil. 2:3; 1 Peter 2:17

Date used _____ Place _____

In 1987 Donna Rice was involved in a scandal with presidential hopeful Gary Hart. She accompanied Hart, who was a married man, on a pleasure cruise to the Bahamas on a yacht called *Monkey Business.*

At the time, Donna Rice was a backslidden Christian, says Ramona Cramer Tucker in *Today's Christian Woman.* As a freshman in high school, Rice had received Christ at a Cliff Barrows crusade. Throughout high school her life revolved around choir, youth group, mission trips, and inviting friends to church.

When she went away to college, though, she gradually compromised to the point where she was far from God. Then, the Gary Hart scandal put her and her picture on the front page of newspapers and magazines across the country.

Her life fell apart. She resigned her job, and she was hounded by the press. She was offered millions to tell her story. As she wrestled with what to do, her mother and grandmother said something to Rice that would seem obvious: "Before you make any decisions, get your life straight with God."

But it wasn't obvious to Rice. She says, "I was stunned because I hadn't yet realized I could put the entire mess in his hands."

Then Rice's mother gave her a cassette tape from a former youth-group friend. "Donna, I imagine you're in a lot of pain right now," the friend said. "I just want you to know that God loves you and I love you."

Rice recalls, "When she began to share songs we used to sing together, I collapsed on the floor in my apartment and sobbed. I knew I—and no one else—was responsible for my choices. I cried out, (God, it took falling on my rear in front of the whole world to get my attention. Help me to live my life your way!) God answered my plea by flooding me with his presence and forgiveness and by surrounding me with Christian fellowship."

Those who have slipped away from God can be restored. Never underestimate the role your words can play in leading someone to God.

Admonishment, Backsliding, Counsel, Evangelism, Exhortation, Intervention, Love, Repentance, Reproof
2 Cor. 5:10–11; Gal. 6:1–2; Heb. 3:12–13; James 5:19–20

Date used _____ Place _____

Restoration 196

In the United States, businesses use millions of wood pallets each year to haul products. After a pallet has borne heavy, sometimes crushing weights and taken abuse from truck travel and forklifts, eventually it can no longer be used. Now cracked and smashed, or loose and floppy, pallets are something businesses must pay other companies up to five dollars per pallet to dispose of. Disposal companies burn the pallets, chew them into wood chips, or dump them in landfills.

One nonprofit company in New York had a better idea, writes Andrew Revkin in the *New York Times.* Big City Forest in South Bronx takes other companies' junk and turns it into treasure. The raw material of pallets is valuable hardwoods like rosewood, cherry, oak, mahogany, and maple. Big City Forest workers dismantle the pallets, salvage the usable wood, and recycle it into furniture and flooring. Recycled wood chips are worth only $30 a ton. But when used as flooring the value of the recycled wood is $1,200 a ton, and as furniture $6,000 a ton.

If that is what can be done with lifeless wood, how much more can people be restored to lives of value. Like Big City Forest, God is in the business of restoration. He takes people that seem worthless, people broken by the weight of sin, and transforms them into works of beauty and usefulness.

Discipleship, New Creation, Regeneration, Renewal, Worth
Ps. 23:3; Isa. 61:3; 2 Cor. 5:17

Date used _____ Place _____

In *100 Meditations on Hope* Wayne A. Lamb writes:

In the midst of a storm, a little bird was clinging to the limb of a tree, seemingly calm and unafraid. As the wind tore at the limbs of the tree, the bird continued to look the storm in the face, as if to say, "Shake me off; I still have wings."

Because of Christ's resurrection, each Christian can look the experience of death in the face and confidently say, "Shake me off; I still have wings. I'll live anyway."

Death, Easter, Hope
Matt. 28:1–10; 1 Cor. 15; 2 Cor. 5:1–10; Phil. 1:21–23

Date used _____ Place _____

As Christmas 1996 approached, the Kingston Technology corporation of Orange County, California, informed its 523 employees they would soon receive an extra special Christmas bonus.

Having started in the owner's garage in 1987, Kingston Technology, like many high-tech companies, had experienced explosive growth, to the point where it now was the world's largest supplier of add-on memory boards for personal computers. And each year since the company had begun with just a handful of employees, the owners had followed a generous policy of giving 10 percent of the annual profits to the workers.

Well, in 1996 another company bought Kingston Technology for $1.5 billion. The arrangement called for Kingston's owners to retain control of their company, and they decided to carry on generosity as usual: they gave 10 percent of a billion or so dollars to their employees as a Christmas bonus! With the bonus computed on the basis of seniority and performance, that meant the average employee would receive $75,000, and the highest bonuses could reach $300,000.

This story had only one downside. When it hit the national news, Kingston Technology was besieged by a flurry of applications for employment, but alas they were not hiring.

The decision makers at Kingston Technology believe in giving lavish rewards to their workers. So does God. At the final judgment, the Christmas bonuses of this company will look like peanuts compared to the heavenly rewards God will shower upon those who have served him in this life. What's more, anyone who is willing is hired.

Heaven, Judgment Day, Treasures in Heaven
Matt. 6:19–21; 10:40–42; 25:14–30; Eph. 6:8; Rev. 22:12

Date used _____ Place _____

Good posture contributes to good health. That is what several studies and physicians suggest, says writer Brenda Kearns.

"Poor posture can cause headaches," says back specialist Laura Fleck, M.D. "The problem is your head," says Kearns. "It weighs 20 pounds, and when it's hanging forward, it strains the muscles that hold the neck vertebrae together."

Dr. Fleck also says that "many patients with low back pain have it because of poor posture." A spine out of proper alignment adversely affects the spinal disks and overworks back muscles.

Posture may have something to do with carpal tunnel syndrome. One study found that "women who practice good posture for most of their work day are four times less likely to get CTS."

Chiropractors have long claimed that poor posture affects a person's blood pressure and heart rate by adversely affecting the nerves that run from the spine to the rest of the body.

One of the visual words the Bible uses to describe a person of character is uprightness. Just as good physical posture contributes to health, so good spiritual posture—a righteous lifestyle—brings health to our spirit, soul, and body.

Character, Honesty, Integrity, Uprightness
Ps. 32:10; Isa. 48:22

Date used _____ Place _____

Author Ken R. Canfield, president of the National Center for Fathering, writes in *New Man:*

Some 20 years ago, I was a "Big Brother" to a boy named Brian whose parents were divorced. Brian was caught in that time of his life when he was figuring out his identity as a young man and a son. My wife, Dee, and I were newlyweds with no children—yet. We came to know Brian's family, and his mother asked if I could spend some time with him.

Brian and I spent many Saturdays together, and I'll never forget the way he watched me and listened closely to everything I said. We never did anything extravagant—usually just hung out together. Then one experience helped me realize that it's on God's heart to provide a male role model for the fatherless.

One day I sat down and wrote Brian a short one-paragraph letter. It wasn't anything profound or heartwarming but said something like: "Dear Brian, I'm looking forward to getting together again with you this Saturday. I've enjoyed our time together, and I just want you to know that you're a great guy to be around. Your Big Brother, Ken."

Nothing life-changing from my perspective. But the next time I visited Brian, I noticed my letter was proudly displayed on his wall and surrounded by posters of sports heroes. When I saw that, I realized the impact I could have in Brian's life.

Attention, Caring, Child Rearing, Encouragement, Example, Family, Fathers, Influence, Love, Men, Togetherness
1 Thess. 5:11; Heb. 3:13

Date used _____ Place _____

In *Sports Spectrum* Harold Reynolds, ESPN baseball analyst and one-time all-star second baseman for the Seattle Mariners, writes:

When I was growing up in Corvallis, Oregon, there was an NBA player named Gus Williams. Gus tied his shoes in back instead of in front like normal. I thought that was so cool. So I started tying my shoes in the back. I wanted to be like Gus. He wore number 10; I wore number 10. He wore one wrist band; I wore one wrist band.

One day I was lying in bed and my stomach was killing me. I noticed that it wasn't my sports hero, Gus Williams, who came to my room to take care of me.

It was my mother.

That's when I began to understand the difference between heroes and role models. I stopped looking at athletic accomplishments to determine who I wanted to pattern my life after. Instead, I tried to emulate people with strong character who were doing things of lasting value.

Whom we look up to largely determines who we become. Choose your heroes well.

Character, Heroes, Mothers
1 Cor. 11:1; Phil. 3:17; 4:9

Date used _____ Place _____

Rumors 202

Imagine trying to put out a wind-blown forest fire with a squirt gun. That's what Gerber Products, the baby-food company, felt they were doing in 1997. Someone somewhere started a false rumor about the company that spread like wildfire.

According to John Schmeltzer in the *Chicago Tribune*, the rumor said Gerber had been involved in a class-action lawsuit and would give a $500 gift certificate to families with children to settle the suit. Supposedly all the parents had to do to get the money was send a claim form and copies of their children's birth certificates and social security numbers to a post-office box in Minneapolis by October 1, 1997.

Once the rumor caught fire, it began to spread along channels that gave it an appearance of legitimacy: notices were posted in hospitals and sent home with children by schoolteachers. One corporation even put the false notice in the envelope with their employees' paychecks.

Gerber Products tried to stomp out the bogus story, putting a notice on several internet web sites, tracking down sources of the rumor, and informing the media. Nevertheless, they received over 18,000 phone calls to their toll-free telephone number in the three-week period before October 1 from people requesting the bogus claim form.

According to Schmeltzer, the cost to Gerber Products of fighting this rumor was in the millions of dollars.

Passing along a rumor may seem harmless, but someone pays an undeserved price if we are not careful about the truth. Never take lightly the power of the tongue to do others harm.

Gossip, Speech, Tongue, Truth, Words
Rom. 1:29; 1 Tim. 5:13; James 3:1–12

Date used _____ Place _____

Extended rest is an essential regimen for the physical recovery of those who run in a marathon. Many athletes, however, try to return to hard training too quickly, says writer Bob Condor in the *Chicago Tribune.*

Joe Henderson, a columnist for *Runner's World,* says, "Runners make the incorrect assumption that once the soreness in muscles is gone, then they are recovered. But thousands of microscopic tears in the muscles can take four to six weeks for complete healing."

Henderson recommends that marathon runners take a day off from regular training for every mile run in a competitive race.

Gregory Florez, president of First Fitness Inc., says, "There is also a risk of long-term damage to your joints if you don't force yourself to get enough rest."

Condor says, "Research reveals a biochemical phase of recovery. It takes time to balance fluids and hormones in the body after the extraordinary requirements of running 26.2 miles. . . .

"One study revealed faster recovery for muscle tissue by marathoners who did not exercise for a full 10 days after the race. But taking time from the running trail can be difficult for some people."

Runners aren't the only ones who don't want to get all the rest they need. With many things to do and goals to reach, taking a weekly day of rest for spiritual renewal can seem impossible. Nevertheless God instituted the Sabbath principle not just for the sake of our bodies but also for our soul and spirit.

Endurance, Healing, Renewal, Rest, Work
Exod. 16:22–30; 20:8–11; Matt. 11:28–29; Mark 6:31

Date used _____ Place _____

The name Norma McCorvey probably doesn't mean anything to you. But the pseudonym that Norma McCorvey used in the landmark Supreme Court case in which she was the plaintiff you will probably recognize—Jane Roe, of *Roe versus Wade*, the infamous decision in 1973 that legalized abortion on demand.

According to Kathleen Donnelly, in 1969 Norma McCorvey was working as a barker for a traveling carnival when she discovered she was pregnant. She asked a doctor to give her an abortion and was surprised to find it was against the law. She sought help elsewhere and was recruited as the plaintiff in *Roe versus Wade* by two attorneys seeking to overturn the law against abortion. Ironically, because the case took some four years to be finally decided, McCorvey never was able to abort the child and instead gave her baby up for adoption.

She remained anonymous for a decade or so, and then Norma McCorvey went public. Donnelly writes:

> Shaking, sick to her stomach and fortified by vodka and Valium—she told a Dallas television reporter she was Jane Roe of Roe v. Wade. . . . Next, she admitted she had lied about that pregnancy in the hope it would help her get an abortion: It was a casual affair that made her pregnant, not rape as she told her Roe lawyers. And, little by little, through occasional interviews, sporadic speaking engagements and a 1989 television movie, she revealed that before she gave birth to the Roe baby and gave her to adoptive parents, she had given birth to two other children. . . . Slowly, she began speaking of her long-term lesbian relationship. . . . [Her memoir *I Am Roe*] leaves little out: not her childhood of petty crime and reform school, or the affairs with lovers of both sexes, or the long nights spent drinking in Dallas dives, or the days of low-level drug-dealing that preceded Roe.

According to writer Jeff Hooten in *Citizen*, McCorvey soon went to work answering phones for a Dallas abortion clinic.

Next door to the clinic the pro-life group Operation Rescue leased an office. After a time, Norma began to have a change of heart. One day she began referring callers to Operation Rescue. Hooten writes:

> Her turning point came when a 7-year-old girl named Emily—the daughter of an Operation Rescue volunteer who greeted McCorvey each day with a hug—invited McCorvey to church. On July 22, [1995], McCorvey attended a Saturday night church service in Dallas. "Norma just kept praying, 'I want to undo all the evil I've done in this world,'" said Ronda Mackey, Emily's mother. "She was crying, and you knew it was so sincere."
>
> In August of 1995 she announced she had become a Christian and was baptized in a swimming pool in front of ABC "World News Tonight" television cameras. For a short time she said she still supported abortions in the first trimester, but before long that conviction fell by the wayside. Says McCorvey, "I still feel very badly. I guess I always will . . . but I know I've been forgiven."

Norma McCorvey proves once again that our Lord Jesus came to seek and to save those who are lost.

Abortion, Conversion, Forgiveness, Mercy of God,
Patience of God, Repentance, Sinners
Matt. 9:9–13; Mark 2:13–17; Luke 15:1–32; 1 Tim. 1:12–16; 2 Peter 3:9

Date used _____ Place _____

In thirty years of marriage James Dobson of Focus on the Family says he never considered committing adultery. But in *Focus on the Family* magazine he recalls one time when Satan tried his best to lure him into that trap:

Shirley and I had been married just a few years when we had a minor fuss. It was no big deal, but we both were pretty agitated at the time. I got in the car and drove around for about an hour to cool off. On the way home, an attractive girl drove up beside me in her car and smiled, obviously flirting. Then she turned onto a side street. I knew she was inviting me to follow her. I didn't take the bait. I just went home and made up with Shirley. But I thought how vicious the devil had been to take advantage of the momentary conflict between us. That's why Scripture refers to him as "a roaring lion looking for someone to devour."

No one, not even the most prominent of Christian leaders, is immune from Satan's temptations. We need to be on our guard.

Adultery, Marriage, Sex, Temptation
Gen. 39:6–12; Exod. 20:14; 1 Cor. 10:12–13; 2 Tim. 2:22; 1 Peter 5:8

Date used _____ Place _____

In 1997 the Central American city of Managua, Nicaragua, adopted a program that most cities take for granted: The city named its streets and numbered its buildings.

Larry Rohter writes in the *New York Times* that for twenty-five years Managua, with a population of 1.5 million, had been without that basic necessity following a devastating 1972 earthquake, which relocated most residents. During that time people learned to make do, wandering down the wrong streets, asking strangers where to go, and making one wrong turn after another until they hopefully found their destination.

Illogical is a good word to describe the system, if you can call it that. "Formal addresses have come to be defined neither by numbers nor street names," writes Rohter, "but in relation to the nearest landmark, as in: 'From El Carmen Church, a block toward the National Stadium' or 'Across from Los Ranchos Restaurant.'

"That, in turn, has made it necessary to name the points of the compass in giving directions or addressing a letter, an issue that has been resolved in an equally baffling fashion. 'Toward the lake' has come to mean north, 'toward the mountain' means south, 'up' means east and 'down' means west.

"Furthermore, though some of the original guideposts still exist, many others have vanished, leaving all but pre-quake residents confused. A leading economic research institute, for instance, offers visitors the following address: 'From where the gate of El Retiro Hospital used to be, two blocks toward the lake, one block down.'"

Finding your way in Managua sounds a lot like trying to live without the clear guidance of God's Word. You're dependent on directions from others who may not know the right way. You live by trial and error. You wander and feel lost. How much better to have a map!

> Absolutes, Culture Wars, Ethics, Lostness, Morality,
> Postmodernism, Ten Commandments, Truth, Values
> Prov. 14:12; 2 Tim. 3:16–17

Date used _____ Place _____

Secrets

On February 9, 1996, a railroad train running from Waldwick, New Jersey, to Hoboken ran through a red signal and smashed into the side of another train at a crossing. The crash killed the engineers of both trains and one passenger, and injured 158 other passengers.

One year later the National Transportation Safety Board announced the results of its investigation into the cause of the accident. The engineer of the train that ran the red signal was going blind. According to Matthew Wald in the *New York Times*, for nine years the engineer had progressively been going blind because of diabetes. He and his doctor both knew it. But he had kept his medical condition secret, no doubt for fear of losing his work, and the doctor, who reportedly knew that his patient was a railroad engineer, had not reported the man's condition to the railroad.

New Jersey requires that its engineers have a physical exam each year by the company's own occupational medicine specialist, but each year the engineer had "always answered no to the annual questions about whether he had diabetes, was taking any prescription medication or was under another doctor's care. He had had eye surgery twice, but apparently paid for it out of pocket rather than filing insurance claims," says Wald.

Unfortunately, the truth came out in a deadly way.

Some things we must not keep secret.

Community, Confession, Darkness, Denial, Healing, Honesty, Openness, Repentance, Transparency, Truth, Walking in the Light
2 Sam. 11–12; Eph. 5:13–14; James 5:16; 1 John 1:6–9

Date used _____ Place _____

Glen Keane has done significant work as a Disney animator. He drew Ariel for *The Little Mermaid*, as well as the Beast and Aladdin in other Disney movies. He served as supervising animator for Disney's *Pocahontas*. One issue of *Premiere* magazine listed him as the one-hundredth most powerful person in Hollywood.

Keane came to work for Disney in 1974. "During that time, Keane was also increasingly open to questions of faith," writes Kevin Dale Miller in *Christian Reader*.

Raised a Catholic, he felt condemned by his sins and began looking for relief from his guilt.

Seeing his colleague Ron Husband reading a Bible one day during the lunch hour, Keane asked him what the Bible said about getting to heaven. Ron, who was also searching for answers, was studying John 3:16. He pointed it out to Keane and also gave him a Gideon's New Testament, which he had taken from a hotel room.

With the New Testament in hand, Keane walked down the street for lunch. On the way back, he read John 3:16 over and over. Slowly the truth and the implications of the verse sank in, and suddenly Keane found himself saying out loud, "I believe it! I believe it!"

"It was like suddenly I reached down and there was something there that wasn't before," Keane remembers. "There was a faith I could actually apply and believe with. From that moment on, I knew I was secure. I didn't need to fear judgment or hell or anything anymore."

Assurance, Belief, Conversion, Faith, Fear, Hell, Judgment
John 1:12; 3:16; Rom. 10:9–10

Date used _____ Place _____

According to Alex Heard in the *New York Times Magazine,* for those who just can't get enough of themselves, a doll company in Denver, Colorado, has the perfect item: the My Twin Doll. For between $130 and $170 you can have a doll custom-made to be a mirror image of your adolescent self, right down to the hairstyle and wardrobe selections. Just send the company a photo, and soon you can go to sleep cuddling a doll-sized version of the one and only you.

Arrogance, Egotism, Pride, Self-Love
2 Tim. 3:2

Date used _____ Place _____

Sandra had an unusual problem, and it would be the ruin of her family. She lived in Cincinnati, Ohio, with her husband, Alexander, and three children ages two, three, and five. When her husband could no longer bear with her problem, he moved out of the home. Two weeks later he called the police to report that his wife was neglecting the children. The police drove to Sandra's apartment and found deplorable conditions. The children's playroom was littered with broken glass and debris, and there were children's handprints in human feces.

Sandra's problem, said her husband, was a compulsion for surfing the Internet. She spent up to twelve hours a day at the computer.

Police Sergeant Paul Neudigate said, "She would lock the children in their room so as not to be bothered. The place was in complete shambles, but the computer area was clean—completely immaculate."

Police took custody of the children and charged Sandra with three counts of child endangerment.

In a world filled with interesting and pleasurable things, self-control is a survival skill.

> Addictions, Balance, Interests, Moderation, Pleasure, Priorities
> Prov. 25:16; Gal. 5:22–23; 2 Tim. 1:7

Date used _____ Place _____

In May 1996, 5-foot–7-inch, 118-pound Miss Venezuela won the Miss Universe contest. According to the *Chicago Tribune,* after her victory reporters asked her what she wanted to do first. "I'm going to do something," she said, "I haven't been able to do for three weeks—eat, eat, eat and sleep."

Apparently she kept her word. She quickly gained weight, to the point where pageant officials were complaining. One pageant official explained, "She has various swimsuit contracts, and they're not happy that she has gone a bit chubby."

She kept on gaining, though. According to *People Weekly,* by January 1997 a new personal trainer weighed her in at 155 pounds, and at one point she weighed 160 pounds. But with the help of her trainer within a few months she was back down to an ideal weight of 130 pounds.

Without ongoing self-discipline how quickly we can squander our accomplishments. Self-control must be a lifestyle, not an occasional event.

Discipleship, Discipline, Indulgence, Sinful Nature
Judg. 16; 2 Sam. 11; Gal. 5:13, 23; Col. 3:23

Date used _____ Place _____

In 1997 Timothy McVeigh was convicted of bombing the Federal Building in Oklahoma City, killing 168 people. During the trial one of McVeigh's old army friends testified in court and made a revealing observation about human nature.

According to Jo Thomas in the *New York Times*, the friend said, "I'd known Tim for quite a while. If you don't consider what happened in Oklahoma, Tim is a good person."

Most of us have a similar outlook on ourselves as we consider the prospect of standing before the Judge of all the earth someday. No, we likely have not been found guilty of murder, but we can downplay our sins and judge ourselves by what we have done right. We think, If this or that isn't taken into account, I'm a good person.

The problem for us is that these failings of ours are gravely serious in the sight of a holy God, whose standard is perfect righteousness. He does not overlook any sin. Without a Savior, every person faces eternal judgment.

Guilt, Judgment
Gen. 3; Rom. 3:10, 23

Date used _____ Place _____

The thirty-seven-year-old New York man was a small-time crook, the kind who would mug little old ladies for the cash in their purses. But on Sunday, July 21, 1996, this crook messed with the wrong little old lady. According to the *Chicago Tribune*, the mugger bumped into a ninety-four-year-old woman in Greenwich Village and snatched her wallet. The NYPD later picked him up, and as they drove him to the station, police lieutenant Robert McKenna told the suspect, "You just robbed the mother of the biggest mob chieftain in New York."

The ninety-four-year-old woman was Yolanda Gigante, and her son is Vincent Gigante, described by authorities as head of the Genovese mob, the nation's most powerful Mafia family.

The police lieutenant later said, "When the perp heard that, he just slumped down into the back seat of the radio car. He had a sort of stunned, resigned look on his face, sort of saying, 'How could I be so stupid?'"

Whenever we sin, we get ourselves into more trouble than we bargained for.

Consequences, Death, Satan, Sin, Sowing and Reaping, Temptation
John 8:34–44; 10:10; Rom. 6:23; 1 John 5:19

Date used _____ Place _____

On the afternoon of August 2, 1997, James Aliff, a thirty-nine-year-old unemployed construction worker, woke up and found himself in a tough spot: He was lying face down between the rails of a railroad bed.

According to the *Chicago Tribune* news service, "Police believe Aliff might have been drinking and passed out on the track. Aliff said he slipped on a rock while walking his dog and was knocked out."

Whatever the cause, when Aliff woke up, he quickly realized he was not alone. Passing over him was a 109-car freight train.

"I got a headache, let me tell you," he later said from his Oak Hill, Florida, hospital bed. "About every three or four seconds an axle would come along and crack me upside the head. It's a good thing I wasn't on my back, or that train would have torn my face off."

If you are asleep in a dangerous place, you never know what can come upon you. Stay alert, and stay out of danger.

Alertness, Danger, Drunkenness, Problems, Troubles, Vigilance
Col. 4:2; 1 Thess. 5:1–8; 1 Tim. 4:16; 1 Peter 5:8

Date used _____ Place _____

Ed Hinton writes in *Sports Illustrated* that champion race car driver Dale Earnhardt was known for being so calm before races that occasionally he would take a catnap just before the start. While other drivers would have a pulse rate of 100 to 120 before a race, his would be less than 60.

But on August 31, 1997, at the Southern 500 race in Darlington, South Carolina, Earnhardt unintentionally took catnapping to a dangerous new level. At the start of the race, Earnhardt fell asleep at the wheel—he went into a semiconscious state but kept on driving. When he reached the first turn, he hit the wall but kept on going. At the second turn he again hit the wall, harder this time. He continued slowly around the track for two laps, looking for his pit but unable to find it. Finally he pulled off the track. Later he would say he remembered nothing of this.

Sixteen doctors examined Earnhardt to find out what had happened. They found nothing definite but suggested three possible explanations. A small blood vessel may have spasmed and restricted blood to the brain. Or he may have had a temporary short-circuit of the brain because of a previous accident. The third option was vasodepressor syndrome, in which the pulse rate falls rather than rises under stress.

The doctors didn't think the problem would recur, and they cleared Earnhardt to continue racing.

Frightening but true, it is possible, for a while, to drive over one hundred miles an hour and yet be asleep. In the same way, we can be busily racing through life—our eyes seemingly open, our hands on the wheel, our foot to the floor—yet spiritually asleep. Sooner or later, though, the trouble begins.

Busyness, Complacency, Stress, Watchfulness
Mark 13:32–37; Luke 12:35–40; Eph. 5:14; Col. 4:2; 1 Thess. 5:4–7

Date used _____ Place _____

According to Matthew Wald in the *New York Times*, on Friday, January 17, 1997, David Riach and his mother Dorothy, both pilots, were flying a single-engine Piper Dakota over the northeastern United States. Their destination was Saranac Lake, New York. Twenty-five minutes after takeoff, however, Mr. Riach did not respond to a radio message from a flight controller in New York. The plane was apparently on automatic pilot. After the third attempt by the flight controllers, the pilot's mother radioed to the tower that he was not responding. A few minutes later, she radioed that her son was vomiting.

Then she, too, began to experience physical problems. She radioed that she was getting tired. A minute later she said she was very, very tired. Another minute later she said she felt nauseated. A few minutes later, in the final communication she had with controllers, she said she just wanted to get the airplane down.

For an hour and a half the airplane continued to fly on autopilot. Finally it ran out of gas and crashed in Alton, New Hampshire, with no survivors.

Authorities investigated and several days later reported that the cause of the accident was a triangular hole in the plane's muffler, which allowed carbon monoxide to be sucked into the plane's heating system. The chief investigator said that at the time of the crash the victims were unconscious but alive.

Sleep can be dangerous in the wrong place. One such place is in your spiritual life.

Alertness, Self-Control, Wakefulness, Watchfulness
Mark 13:32–37; Luke 12:35–40; Eph. 5:14; 1 Thess. 5:4–7

Date used _____ Place _____

According to *New Man* magazine, writer, theologian, and one-time Harvard professor Henri Nouwen once broke away from his busy schedule to live for six months in a monastery. Here is why:

I realized that I was caught in a web of strange paradoxes. While complaining about too many demands, I felt uneasy when none were made. While speaking about the burden of letter writing, an empty mailbox made me sad. While speaking nostalgically about an empty desk, I feared the day in which that would come true.

In short, while desiring to be alone, I was frightened of being left alone. The more I became aware of these paradoxes, the more I started to see how much I had fallen in love with my own compulsions and illusions, and how much I needed to step back and wonder, "Is there a quiet stream underneath the fluctuating affirmations and rejections of my little world?"

That quiet stream of contentment, of course, is found only in the Lord. And periods of solitude with him can be crucial to finding it.

Busyness, Compulsion, Contentment, Loneliness, Peace, Rest, Sabbath, Security, Spiritual Disciplines, Work
Ps. 62:1–2; Matt. 11:28–30; Mark 1:35–37; 6:31; Phil. 4:7

Date used _____ Place _____

A certain very practical man, whom we'll call Bob, took absolutely nothing for granted.

Bob kept a large toolbox and first-aid kit in the trunk of his Volvo, just in case.

He had a Swiss Army knife and cell phone in his briefcase, just in case.

Bob had insurance on everything. Why, he had insurance on his insurance, just in case.

He carried an umbrella with him to work even when the weatherman said there was more chance that the Cubs would win the World Series than that it would rain, just in case.

He filled his safe-deposit box with solid-gold Krugerands, just in case.

He had enough pension-fund money and IRAs to live well and travel often, even if he lived to 125, just in case.

But in all his preparation there was one thing Bob gave scarce thought to: What would happen to his soul after he died? What could be more impractical? he thought. He did not read the Bible seriously for himself. He avoided church. "Most likely," he would joke with his friends, "we die like a dog, and then it's over."

Wouldn't you know it, when Bob was forty-nine, his car was broadsided in an intersection by a drunk driver, and Bob died instantly. To Bob's surprise, though, his soul did not extinguish like a candle.

God said to him, "How could you be so foolish! You prepared for everything but what matters most: where your soul will spend eternity. And now forever and ever you will have nothing—nothing but unremitting sorrow."

After several thousand years in hell, Bob admitted to himself, What a fool I was to focus all my attention on that brief life on earth and ignore the life that will never end.

So will it be for all who do not prepare to meet God.

Afterlife, Death, Hell, Judgment
Amos 4:12; Luke 12:13–21

Date used _____ Place _____

Sowing and Reaping 219

Comedian and actor Chris Farley, of *Saturday Night Live* fame, was found dead in his downtown Chicago apartment on December 18, 1997. The Cook County medical examiner's office later reported that he died of an opiate and cocaine over-dose. According to Mark Caro and Allan Johnson in the *Chicago Tribune*, Farley's problems with drugs were no secret, and his death at age thirty-three, though a shock, was no surprise to his friends. He had been in and out of various programs to clean up his life many times.

In Farley's obituary in the *New York Times*, James Barron quoted from a recent interview of Farley in *Playboy:* "I used to think that you could get to a level of success where the laws of the universe didn't apply," said Farley. "But they do. It's still life on life's terms, not on movie-star terms. I still have to work at relationships. I still have to work on my weight and some of my other demons. Once I thought that if I just had enough in the bank, if I had enough fame, that it would be all right. But I'm a human being like everyone else. I'm not exempt."

Sadly, his words proved to be prophetic.

Addiction, Consequences, Drugs, Laws, Money,
Self-Control, Spiritual Laws, Success
Gal. 6:7–8

Date used _____ Place _____

In the mid-1990s a system of exercise that had long been a staple of the dance community became popular in health clubs. It is called the Pilates method.

The system was developed by Joseph Pilates during World War II as a way to strengthen the bodies of immobilized patients. By using springs attached to beds, Pilates experimented with ways to strengthen muscles especially in the patients' midsection.

In the *Chicago Tribune* Bob Condor writes, "The Pilates system focuses on first building your 'power center'—the abdomen, buttocks and lower back—to make all body movements easier. 'If you don't have a strong torso, you will not be in full control of your arms and legs,' says Sean Gallagher, a physical therapist and athletic trainer who owns the Pilates Studio in New York. 'Everything we do starts with our center of gravity.'"

That certainly makes sense. It makes sense not only with our body, but in every area of our lives, including finances, relationships, work, and emotions. Our power center is our spiritual life. Those who are spiritually strong in the Lord find strength flowing into all areas of their lives. For that reason, nothing can benefit our lives more than the exercise of spiritual disciplines.

Devotional Life, Power, Spirit, Strength
Prov. 4:23

Date used _____ Place _____

In 1997 the Russian space station Mir became a byword for serial glitches. On June 25, 1997, it collided with a cargo ship, and the space station then suffered one problem after another, from computer failures to oxygen shortages.

The glitch on July 3, 1997, was with the eleven gyroscopes that kept the space station oriented toward the sun. According to the Associated Press, NASA reported that five gyroscopes in one of the ship's modules shut down apparently after communication problems with the control computer on Mir. The crew then shut off the remaining gyroscopes.

The purpose of the eleven gyroscopes was to keep the space station in the best position for its solar panels to soak up energy from the sun. To lose the gyroscopes, therefore, meant the loss of precious power.

Spiritual disciplines serve a purpose in our lives similar to these gyroscopes. We naturally tend to veer away from God and toward darkness. Spiritual disciplines keep us oriented toward the light, toward our power source.

Devotional Life, Light, Power, Prayer
Ps. 119:105; Matt. 4:4; 2 Cor. 3:18; 1 Peter 2:2–3

Date used _____ Place _____

In *Discipleship Journal* author Mark Galli writes about the motivation for spiritual disciplines:

I love to play basketball. Just being on a court, dribbling, shooting, making moves, rebounding—to me it's a type of dance, an art.

One afternoon during my college years, I was shooting hoops at my girlfriend's house. I was working on my Earl-the-Pearl (Monroe) move—dribble to the top of the key, fake right, spin left, accelerate to the basket for a lay-up. I practiced it fifteen or twenty times.

A few weeks later, I overheard my girlfriend's father say to a friend: "Mark sure is a disciplined young man. You should see him practice basketball. He just never lets up."

Me, disciplined? I wondered. Basketball workouts weren't discipline for me. I loved playing. I enjoyed perfecting those moves. Although I panted and sweated and wore myself out, I never had to "discipline" myself to practice. . . . I just loved the sport. Basketball was its own reward.

We should practice the spiritual disciplines for the intrinsic satisfaction they can give us. Jesus has taught us something that should be obvious but often is not: Knowing God is its own reward. The disciplines are merely the dribbling, the moves, the jump shots of the spiritual life.

You can no more enjoy God without the spiritual disciplines than you can enjoy basketball without dribbling or shooting. But the disciplines are not duties, laws, demands, or requirements. They are merely the conditions in which the joy of God is experienced.

Devotional Life, Joy, Prayer
Matt. 4:4; 1 Peter 2:2

Date used _____ Place _____

Of the thousands of professional baseball players who have stepped up to the plate over the game's history, until the morning of September 2, 1997, only seventy-three had had the distinct thrill of hitting a home run the first time at bat in their major league career. On this date Montreal Expos outfielder Brad Fullmer became the seventy-fourth, with a pinch-hit two-run shot off Boston Red Sox pitcher Brett Saberhagen. Does such an auspicious beginning suggest great things to come for Brad Fullmer? Fullmer thinks so: "It has to be a good sign," he said.

Gary Gaetti would add weight to that argument. In 1981 as a Minnesota Twin he hit a homer his first time up and went on to hit 330 more by September 1997.

But after Gaetti and a handful of other fast starters, the numbers aren't very impressive. "Of the 73 players who preceded Fullmer," say Richard O'Brien and Hank Hersch in *Sports Illustrated*, "13 never hit another homer. Only two of the group's members have been enshrined in the Hall of Fame: Earl Averill and Hoyt Wilhelm, a pitcher."

When we take our first steps in serving the Lord, it's nice to start with a bang, but whether we do or don't says little about what we're really made of. That is proven over time.

Beginnings, Character, Ministry, Perseverance, Success
Mark 4:16–17; Eph. 4:11–12, 16; Phil. 1:6; Heb. 10:32–39

Date used _____ Place _____

One morning in 1992, as scientist Sid Nagel of the University of Chicago stood at his kitchen counter getting breakfast, something caught his attention. What he saw was a dried coffee drop on his counter. Nothing unusual about that, but what caught his eye was the way the spot had dried. Rather than having a uniform color, the coffee spot had a dark concentration of minute coffee granules at the outer edges and a much lighter color toward the middle.

To Nagel that didn't make sense. It contradicted the physics principle that says materials suspended in liquid spread randomly and as uniformly as possible.

That night Nagel discussed his observation with another professor. After suggesting some theories, he too came to the conclusion that the dried coffee spot didn't make sense. The following Friday Nagel brought the problem to a weekly bag-lunch gathering of scientists, and the mystery of the coffee spot quickly became the buzz among the university's math, computer science, chemistry, and physics faculty. For months, though, no one could solve the puzzle.

Finally a group of scientists came up with this solution: "The liquid," writes William Mullen in the *Chicago Tribune*, "puddles out until it is stopped or 'pinned' by roughness on the surface it travels across. Evaporation along those edges becomes a capillary 'pull' that draws tiny coffee grains dispersed evenly in the liquid out to the edge. By the time evaporation is complete, virtually all the coffee particles are at the edge, thus creating the telltale dark rim."

The discovery could have practical application for paint manufacturers, electronic and computer engineers, and molecular biologists.

The ability to see the profound in the commonplace—to see a principle of physics in a coffee spot—is what makes for breakthroughs in understanding. A similar way of seeing helps us know God better. Either we can go through daily life oblivious to the activity of God around us, or we can pay attention to what God is trying to tell us in our circumstances. Those who are looking see the glory of God all around them. Those who pay attention find God's direction in even the mundane events of daily life.

Curiosity, Direction, God's Will, Hearing God,
Insight, Learning, Observation, Questions, Wonder
1 Kings 19:9–13; Isa. 58; Jer. 14:1–7, 22; Amos 4;
Jonah 4:5–11; Haggai 1:5–11; 1 Cor. 11:30–32

Date used _____ Place _____

In *World Vision* magazine John Robb writes:

Seven years ago, a giant tree stood on the banks of the Awash River, in an arid valley about two hours' drive southeast of Addis Ababa, Ethiopia. It had stood there for generations, seemingly eternal.

For years, the people who lived in the surrounding district had suffered through famines. . . . In their suffering, the people looked to the tree for help. Believing a spirit gave it divine powers, they worshipped the towering giant. Adults would kiss the great trunk when they passed by, and they spoke of the tree in hushed, reverential tones. Children said, "This tree saved us."

In 1989, World Vision began a development project there, including an irrigation system. . . . But even as they labored to build the system, the great tree stood like a forbidding sentinel of the old order, presiding over the community, enslaving the people through fear. For spirits need to be propitiated with animal sacrifices and strict observance of taboos.

When World Vision workers saw how the villagers worshipped the tree, they knew it was an idolatrous barrier to the entrance of Christ's kingdom and transformation of the community.

One morning as the staff prayed together, one of Jesus' promises struck them: "If you have faith, you can say to this tree, 'Be taken up and removed' . . . and it will obey you." In faith, they began to pray that God would bring down the menacing goliath.

Soon the whole community knew the Christians were praying about the tree. Six months later, the tree began to dry up, its leafy foliage disappeared, and finally it collapsed like a stricken giant into the river.

The people of the community were astonished, proclaiming, "Your God has done this! Your God has dried up the tree!" In the days and weeks afterwards, approximately 100 members of the community received Jesus Christ because they saw his power displayed in answer to the Christians' prayers.

Authority, Evangelism, Faith, Idolatry,
Impossibilities, Missions, Power, Prayer
1 Kings 18:17–40; Matt. 16:18–19; 19:26; 21:18–22;
Mark 9:23; 10:27; 11:12–26; Luke 10:17–18; 17:6; 18:27; Eph. 3:20

Date used _____ Place _____

259

The waters off Natal province in South Africa are shark-infested, writes Hugh Dellios in the *Chicago Tribune*. To maintain the tourist trade in the area, the Natal Shark Board has tried many different solutions. They have attempted using various odors as shark repellents, without success. They tried piping in sounds, such as that of the shark's archenemy the killer whale, without success. In earlier days they encircled bathing beaches with steel cages, or called in the navy to drop depth charges. Finally in the 1950s they stretched long nets around the circumference of the beach. That kept the sharks out but also accidentally caught and killed a large number of other marine life.

Now it appears the Natal Shark Board has a better solution. They have developed and patented what they call the Protective Ocean Device (POD). The POD puts out electrical impulses that irritate the shark's nose, which is sensitive to muscle movements in nearby fish and ultrasensitive to electrical currents. The new device, says writer Hugh Dellios, "will surround its owner with a low-level electric pulse that annoys the shark and persuades it that it isn't bearing down on a seal or other favorite taste-treat."

And so it is now possible with technology to drive away sharks.

Far more dangerous than a shark is our enemy Satan. But God has given us sure ways to repel his attacks: the Lord's name and Word, our righteousness and faith.

Name of Jesus, Prayer, Satan
Matt. 4:1–11; John 17:11–12; Eph. 6:10–18; James 4:7

Date used _____ Place _____

George Johnson writes in the *New York Times* that in October 1997 scientists at the University of California and the Space Telescope Science Institute released a "photograph" taken by the Hubble space telescope of a massive, unseeable star. Dubbed the Pistol Star, it stands near the center of our Milky Way Galaxy, burns as bright as 10 million suns, and is as large as the entire space inside of the Earth's orbit. Nevertheless neither the human eye nor telescopes can see it because it is shrouded by an impenetrable cloud of cosmic dust.

This raises the question: Where did the scientists get the photograph?

In reality, the picture is a computer-generated image based on measurements of infrared rays, which are not visible to the human eye but are detectable with scientific instruments. Computers convert these waves into colors, and, voilà, we see a picture of the biggest star in the galaxy.

Imagine, a colossal star blazing 10 million times brighter than the sun, but we can't see it without special equipment. Just as huge realities like this star are not perceptible without special equipment, so there are spiritual realities that a person cannot perceive without spiritual equipment. The fact that scientific instruments cannot detect the dimension of spirit does not mean that the spiritual world is not there, just that the instruments are limited.

Invisible Things, Naturalism, Perception,
Science, Sight, Spiritual Perception, Vision
Matt. 16:13–20; Mark 8:17–30; 1 Cor. 2:6–16; Eph. 1:17–18

Date used _____ Place _____

The Stradivari Society of Chicago performs an important role in the music world. The society entrusts expensive violins into the hands of world-class violin players who could never afford them on their own.

Top-flight violins made by seventeenth- and eighteenth-century masters like Antonio Stradivari produce an incomparably beautiful sound and now sell for millions of dollars each. Their value continues to climb, making such violins highly attractive to investors. But "great violins are not like great works of art," writes music critic John von Rhein. "They were never meant to be hung on a wall or locked up under glass. Any instrument will lose its tone if it isn't played regularly; conversely, an instrument gains in value the more it is used."

And so it is that those who own the world's greatest violins are looking for first-rate violin players to use them. The Stradivari Society brings them together, making sure that the instruments are preserved and cared for. One further requirement made by investors in such violins: the musician will give the patron at least two command performances a year.

Like the Stradivari Society, God also entrusts exquisite "violins" into the care of others. He gives us spiritual gifts of great value, which remain his property. He wants them used. He delights to hear beautiful music from our lives. And he wants us to play for him.

Faithfulness, Ministry, Spiritual Gifts
Matt. 25:14–30; Luke 12:48; Rom. 12:5–8; Eph. 4:8–16; 1 Peter 4:10–11

Date used _____ Place _____

According to the Associated Press, on the evening of February 6, 1996, three friends drove the rural roads east of Tampa, Florida, with the intent of playing pranks. Tragically, their game was anything but funny. They pulled some twenty street signs out of the ground, including the stop sign at one fateful intersection.

The next day three eighteen-year-old buddies, who had just finished bowling, breezed through that intersection without stopping. Their car sailed into the path of an eight-ton truck, and they were all killed.

One year later the three perpetrators of the deadly prank were convicted of manslaughter. In June of 1997 they stood in orange jail jumpsuits and handcuffs before a judge in a Tampa courtroom, weeping and wiping their eyes, and were sentenced to fifteen years in prison.

It is a dangerous thing with tragic consequences for anyone to take down a signpost on the highway. It is no less dangerous for anyone to vandalize the signposts that God puts on the highway of life. When we honor God's commandments, we point the way to the signposts of life. If we dishonor God's commandments, we can unwittingly lead others to destruction.

Consequences, Example, False Teachers, Golden Rule,
Immorality, Law, Lawlessness, Morality, Responsibility,
Rules, Ten Commandments
Matt. 5:19; Luke 17:1–2; Rom. 14:13–15:4;
1 Cor. 8:9–13; 10:32; James 3:1; Jude 4; Rev. 2:20–21

Date used _____ Place _____

In an article about former *Today* show host Bryant Gumbel, Cheryl Lavin writes in the *Chicago Tribune Magazine:*

Gumbel loves golf. Loves golf. Belongs to four clubs. Plays 200 times a year, sometimes 54 holes a weekend. Owns 2,000 golf clubs. "It's the one thing that you do that is only about you. It's the thing I enjoy the most," he says.

Gumbel and Al Roker were discussing a poll in *Golf* magazine that asked, "Which would you rather give up, golf or sex?"

Without hesitating, Gumbel said sex. Roker was surprised. Gumbel said, "Maybe you've never had a great round of golf."

"Which would you rather give up?" is not always a hypothetical question. Sometimes God asks us to give up something enjoyable for something that is far, far more enjoyable. The more we see the true joys of the things of God, the easier any sacrifice becomes.

Accomplishment, Dedication, Devotion, Love,
Obsession, Passion, Sacrifice, Sex
Matt. 5:29–30; 13:44–46; 16:24–26; 26:6–13; Phil. 3:7–11; 1 John 2:15–17

Date used _____ Place _____

In a *Chicago Tribune* profile about the creator of the syndicated comic strip "Dilbert," Jane Meredith Adams writes:

In an office just slightly bigger than a cubicle, Scott Adams transforms tales of idiotic bosses and meaningless empowerment teams into Dilbert, the chinless comic-strip hero to millions of cubicle-confined workers.

Since Adams published his Internet address (scottadams@ aol.com), he has been deluged with questions from readers who wonder how he knows the exact level of ineptitude with which their company operates. It's because he has been there. Adams endured 17 years of cubicle employment—most recently as an applications engineer with Pacific Bell, a job he left last year after six years of "Dilbert" syndication.

"I don't think I'll ever forget what it feels like to sit in a cubicle," says the cartoonist, "and realize you've been there for eight hours . . . and everything you did today will become unimportant in the next reorganization."

Scott Adams expresses a feeling we're all familiar with. We want what we do to last. Our work (and even our life) doesn't seem important if it is only temporary. The sure hope we have in God is that all we do for him has eternal significance.

Eternal Things, Futility, Future, Kingdom of God, Ministry, Obedience, Significance, Will of God, Work, World Eccles. 1:2–11; 12:13–14; Matt. 7:24–27; 1 Cor. 3:10–15; 15:58; 2 Cor. 4:18; 1 John 2:17

Date used _____ Place _____

Temptation

During the Christmas season of 1996, a bizarre story came over the news about a hair-eating doll. The main feature of the doll in question, according to the Associated Press, was a mechanical mouth that chewed on plastic carrots and french fries. Unfortunately the doll couldn't tell the difference between plastic vegetables and children's hair. During the first five months the doll was on the market, the Consumer Product Safety Commission received thirty-five complaints from parents whose children had their hair caught in the mouth of the doll. One woman in Campbell, Ohio, had to cut off a shank of her daughter's hair after it became snarled in gears in the doll's throat.

Some things that appear quite harmless can entangle and hurt us. Most of us know what it's like to get involved innocently in a relationship or a pastime only to eventually find that we were caught up in something hurtful from which we could not break away. Temptation can come in an attractive package.

Addictions, Distractions, Entertainment, Habits, Money, Pastimes, Pleasure, Priorities, Snares, Time Management
Gen. 3:6; Matt. 4:3; 1 Cor. 15:33–34;
2 Cor. 11:14–15; 1 Tim. 6:9–10; Heb. 12:1

Date used _____ Place _____

Playing for the Seattle Mariners in 1996, left-hander Terry Mulholland had one of the best pickoff moves in baseball. Over a period of five years, from opening day in 1992 until June 19, 1997, a total of only six runners were successful at stealing a base off Mulholland. Mulholland's pitching motion was so deceptive that a runner on first would think the pitch was going home, and he would start to lean toward second. At that instant, Mulholland would turn and throw to first, often catching runners in no-man's land for an embarrassing out.

Kansas City's speedy Bip Roberts knew that embarrassing feeling. Despite his base-stealing skill he too got picked off by Mulholland. Roberts said, "Sometimes, it seems as if he gives up a hit just so he can pick you off."

That statement perfectly describes the tempter. Sometimes people have the mistaken idea that Satan wants to give people pleasure. Satan no more wants to give us pleasure than a baseball pitcher wants to give up hits. Satan hates us and wants to inflict as much suffering into our lives as he possibly can. Satan offers the pleasure of sin only to inflict suffering later and to make that suffering permanent.

Pleasure, Satan, Sin, Sowing and Reaping
Matt. 4:1–11; John 10:10; Gal. 6:7–8; Heb. 11:25

Date used _____ Place _____

Many are familiar with the promise of Romans 8:28 that "in all things God works for the good of those who love him." But have you ever wondered how anything good can come out of temptation? Why does God allow Satan to attack our faith, to shower us with doubts? One clue comes from the world of football.

Running back Rashaan Salaam won the Heisman trophy in 1995 for his outstanding rushing career in college. But in his rookie year with the Chicago Bears, the pros uncovered a weakness in Salaam's game: He was prone to fumble. Although he led the Bears in rushing during his rookie season, he coughed up the ball nine times.

The coaches devised a practice drill to try to correct the problem. They tied a long strap around a football. As Rashaan ran with that ball clutched against his chest, another Bear ran behind him yanking on the other end of the strap. Rashaan had to squeeze the ball with all his might to keep from losing it.

In many ways, that's what temptation does to us. The more the enemy of our souls tries to yank away our faith, the tighter we squeeze it to our heart. God allows temptation so that we will cling more fiercely to him.

Doubt, Faith, Perseverance, Testing
1 Cor. 10:13

Date used _____ Place _____

In *Sports Spectrum* Ken Walker tells how after a Monday night football game in 1990 several players did something for the first time that would later become a common sight. When the game ended between the San Francisco 49ers and the New York Giants, eight players from both sides gathered in a huddle in the center of the field at the 40-yard line nearer to the scoreboard. There they bowed their knees for all to see and prayed together in the name of Jesus Christ.

The brief prayer meetings caught on and gained their highest visibility several years later with Reggie White and his 1997 Super Bowl champion Green Bay Packers. One Packer, Eugene Robinson, explains the purpose of the players coming together to bow their knees: "We don't pray about who wins the game or any of that stuff. That's not what it's there for. We pray basically as an acknowledgment of who God is and that men will see that He exists."

The players have taken heat for their public stand. An article in *Sports Illustrated* advised the players to pray in private, and the NFL made noises for a while as though they would shut the practice down. But the players stood firm, some saying they were willing to be fined for the practice, and the prayer huddles went on.

One moment of truth for a believer is when he or she decides to publicly identify with Jesus Christ. Whether it be praying over a meal at a restaurant, carrying a Bible, wearing a pin, mentioning the Lord in conversation—it solidifies our commitment to Christ.

Acknowledging God, Boldness, Evangelism, Light,
Prayer, Salt, Taking a Stand, Witness
Matt. 5:13–16; Mark 8:38; Acts 4:29; 2 Cor. 3:12

Date used _____ Place _____

In *Charles Kuralt's America* the author recalls a town meeting he once attended in Strafford, Vermont:

What happens at a town meeting is pure democracy. Every citizen may have his or her say on every question. For a half-hour that day, for example, they debated the question of whether to go on paying $582.50 a year for outside health services deemed unsatisfactory by a farmer named Brown.

The moderator, rail-fence-maker James Condict, said, "I'm going to ask for a standing vote. All those in favor . . ." and there it came, the Yankee expression that is the soul of the town meeting, "stand up and be counted."

By a standing vote, Strafford agreed with farmer Brown.

To stand up and be counted is both pure democracy and pure commitment. Jesus calls his true followers to stand up and be counted as Christians.

Baptism, Boldness, Convictions, Courage, Witness
Mark 8:38; Phil. 1:20

Date used _____ Place _____

In the 1996 summer Olympics, sprinter Michael Johnson set records in the 200- and 400-meter races. To do so he had trained for some ten years to cut a mere second or two from his time. In *Slaying the Dragon* he writes:

Success is found in much smaller portions than most people realize. A hundredth of a second here or sometimes a tenth there can determine the fastest man in the world. At times we live our lives on a paper-thin edge that barely separates greatness from mediocrity and success from failure.

Life is often compared to a marathon, but I think it is more like being a sprinter: long stretches of hard work punctuated by brief moments in which we are given the opportunity to perform at our best.

The Christian life also resembles the life of a sprinter: long stretches of obedience and spiritual disciplines punctuated by great tests in which God gives us the opportunity to choose his eternal best.

Choices, Devotional Life, Discipleship, Discipline, Growth,
Holiness, Obedience, Perfection, Preparation,
Sanctification, Spiritual Disciplines
Gen. 22; Pss. 66:10–12; 81:7; Matt. 5:48; 28:20; 2 Cor. 7:1; 13:9;
Phil. 3:7–15; Heb. 12:1–4; James 1:2–4; 1:12

Date used _____ Place _____

An outbreak of cholera is nothing to take lightly, and in September 1996 Manila, the capital city of the Philippines, was in the grip of just such a plague. Three hundred people were suffering from acute symptoms of the disease, wrote Uli Schmetzer in the *Chicago Tribune*, and seven had already died.

The source of the problem was not a mystery. In the rainy season of August and September the streets and sewage canals of Manila become flooded and clogged. Flies and cockroaches proliferate, feed on the trash that floats on the surface, and become carriers of the cholera germs.

To combat the epidemic, Alfredo Lim, the mayor of Manila, had a novel idea. He put a bounty on flies and cockroaches: 1 peso (4 cents) for every ten flies brought dead or alive to health officials; 1.5 pesos (6 cents) for every ten cockroaches. Health officials targeted some of the poorest areas of the city, and on the first day of the program officials from the Department of Public Health went into the Paco district. Residents brought some two thousand insects in plastic bags and were paid on the spot.

"If we kill the flies at once," said Egmidio Espiritu, the chief of the health department, "we can stop the spread of these diseases."

Creepy little things can lead to big problems. Likewise, naughty little thoughts can someday result in serious, harmful sins. Work on cleaning up your thought life, and watch how your lifestyle changes.

Habits, Imagination, Rewards, Sin, Small Things, Words
Ps. 19:14; Matt. 6:24–34; Mark 7:20–23; Phil. 4:8; James 1:13–15

Date used _____ Place _____

When the Green Bay Packers football team won the Super Bowl in 1997, many people thought back to the previous era of Packer greatness under legendary Green Bay coach Vince Lombardi. One of the players on those earlier world championship teams, offensive lineman Jerry Kramer, recalled this story:

One day during the first year I played for him, he rode me unmercifully, pointing out how slow I was, how weak I was, how stupid I was. He convinced me. By the time I dragged myself into the locker room, I suspected I was the worst guard in league history. I sat in front of my locker, head down, contemplating quitting, when Lombardi came up behind me, mussed up my hair and said, "Son, one of these days you're gonna be the greatest guard in the league." Suddenly I was 10 feet tall, ready to do anything for him.

The tongue has awesome power to whittle other people down to nothing or to turn them into giants capable of great things.

Affirmation, Child Rearing, Confidence, Criticism,
Discipleship, Encouragement, Leadership, Words
Prov. 12:18; 1 Thess. 5:11; Heb. 3:13

Date used _____ Place _____

In the *New York Times Magazine* Robert Bryce writes:

Autumn is prime time for the use of eyeblack in sports: baseball players in daytime playoff games and football players put dark stuff under their eyes, supposedly to reduce glare bouncing off their cheeks. One popular smear, called No Glare, contains crushed charcoal, paraffin, beeswax and petrolatum. Does it do anything? Dr. Oliver Schein, an ophthalmologist at Johns Hopkins School of Medicine, says, "Probably not." Even so, it's a tradition. The Pro Football Hall of Fame has a photo of the Washington Redskins fullback Andy Farkas using it way back in 1942. Bobby Valentine, when he managed the Texas Rangers, once wore eyeblack in the dugout. Boog Powell, the former Baltimore Orioles star, used it during his 17 years in the majors. "I don't remember it ever doing any good," he says. "But you looked cool."

We do well on occasion to examine our traditions to see whether we really know their purpose—and whether they accomplish that purpose.

Appearance, Ceremony, Effectiveness, Purpose, Religion, Ritual
Matt. 15:1–9; Mark 7:1–13; Col. 2:8

Date used _____ Place _____

Tradition 241

Until 1996 the Cleveland Browns football team had some of the most loyal fans in all of sports. For them Sunday was the main event of the week. Early on Sunday morning they came to Cleveland Stadium to enjoy tailgate parties and talk about their beloved Browns, and then in the afternoon they filed to the stadium to cheer and holler.

But all that changed in 1996. Owner Art Modell moved the team to Baltimore and changed its name to the Ravens, crushing the hearts of Cleveland fans.

Surprisingly, that didn't stop these fans from doing what they had done for years. On opening day, September 1, 1996, some fans showed up at Cleveland Stadium just as they had done for the last forty-six years and held tailgate parties. They wore Browns jerseys, waved Browns flags, and chanted, "Let's go, Brownies." Then shortly before 1 P.M. they refilled their cups and marched to the stadium gates. But the stadium was quiet and empty.

Traditions die hard, especially religious ones. An empty tradition is an end in itself, a habit without meaning. It is cheering fans without a team or a game, for God is gone.

Atheism, Habits, Religion, Ritual, Rules, Secularism
Ezek. 10; Mark 7:1–13; Col. 2:16–23

Date used _____ Place _____

In a *Reader's Digest* article titled "You Can Make a Million," Randy Fitzgerald tells the story of how one immigrant couple amassed a fortune:

Humberto and Georgina came to America from Cuba as penniless refugees in 1960. Humberto learned English in a Long Island, N.Y., high school; Georgina spent her early years in Los Angeles. They met when Georgina was a student at the University of Miami, and married in 1972. Both eventually landed jobs as reporters for a Fort Lauderdale, Fla., newspaper, a profession that rarely leads to great wealth. But a math teacher had taught Humberto the importance of compound interest, and early in the couple's marriage, they decided to save every possible dollar for investment.

Their formula was simple though challenging. They bought only compact cars and paid their credit-card bills in full every month. They shopped at discount stores, clipped "cents off" coupons and took sack lunches to work. Some years the couple saved up to 66 percent of their income. In 1987 they began investing $1250 a month in five diversified-stock mutual funds. And that strategy over eight years produced the bonanza that gave them millionaire status. Last year they made more money from their investments than from their two salaries.

Storing up treasures like this sounds wonderful, doesn't it? But if this sounds good, imagine how great a treasure stored up in heaven will be. Jesus said the value of heavenly treasures far surpasses any treasure on earth. We should make the same effort and have the same focus as this couple did when we give our money to God.

Giving, Goals, Money, Rewards, Saving, Self-Control
Matt. 6:19–24

Date used _____ Place _____

One of the healthiest things that can happen to a ponderosa forest is to have a forest fire every five to twenty years. Without a regular fire two things happen that can ultimately lead to destruction that lasts for hundreds of years.

First, "a healthy ponderosa forest is made of widely spaced, fire-resistant trees," writes Michael Parfit in *National Geographic.* "With overprotection young trees and competing species make a flammable understory so shaded that ponderosa seedlings can't grow." Thus new ponderosas stop springing up.

Second, dead wood, needles, and cones pile up in a thicker and thicker layer of combustible kindling on the forest floor. When a fire eventually does come to an overprotected forest—as it eventually must—the fire burns hotter and deeper. Instead of a healthy fire that burns quick and low over the floor of the forest, blackening the trunks of healthy trees but nothing more, the fire explodes in the crown of the trees. It also destroys the roots. The result is total destruction of every tree.

Such a fire ruins the forest ecosystem. The soil no longer absorbs rain, and it erodes.

As odd as it may seem, ponderosa forests need fire in order to be healthy and viable.

Christians also benefit from fiery trials, even though they are painful. They can burn away the temporal, worthless things that so easily pile up in our lives.

Affliction, Fire, Hardship, Pain, Troubles
Ps. 119:71; Rom. 5:2–5; Heb. 12:28–29; James 1:2–4

Date used _____ Place _____

Star NFL wide receiver Robert Brooks of the 1997 Super Bowl champion Green Bay Packers suffered a terrible season-ending knee injury after six games in 1996. Drew Baker writes in *Sports Spectrum* that Brooks (who started the Packer tradition of jumping into the stands after a touchdown) is a Christian, and as he sat in the locker room that day after the injury, he thought about what purpose God could have in this discouraging blow:

"God was telling me He needed to use me," says Brooks, "to show people that through Christ you can overcome anything— based on the way I was going to handle my injury. It was going to touch a lot of people's hearts and change a lot of people's lives in their everyday struggles. It wasn't a personal thing. I knew I was going to be okay. If I didn't play in the Super Bowl, that's fine, because it is more important that God is going to use me."

Before surgery, team chaplain Steve Newman visited Brooks's home and shared 2 Corinthians 1:3–4. This passage confirmed Brooks's postinjury conclusions: "It was the exact reason God was telling me He was using me. It took me to another spiritual level with God. If I hadn't known God was using me, I wouldn't have handled it as well."

Packer teammate and free safety Eugene Robinson, NFL leader in interceptions among active players, has observed the change in Brooks. He describes him as "real fired up. The Lord got hold of Robert."

To everyone's surprise, Robert Brooks recovered completely from his injury and played outstandingly the following season.

God's Will, Priorities, Purpose, Suffering, Trials, Trust
Rom. 8:28; 2 Cor. 1:3–7; Phil. 1:12–26; 2:12–13

Date used _____ Place _____

The purple dinosaur named Barney is loved by millions of children. According to Reuters, on July 15, 1997, Barney had an accident. During filming of the *Barney & Friends* show, a cooling fan inside the sixty-pound dinosaur suit short-circuited and started to smoke. The actor playing Barney quickly got out of the suit but suffered smoke inhalation. He was taken to the hospital and soon released.

The story of the accident was carried on the news, and it upset many children. Scores of parents called the television station to say their children were afraid that Barney had been burned, or worse, that he was a fake.

A spokeswoman for the producers of the program said, "It can be really devastating to a three-year-old. They love Barney and they think that something terrible has happened to him, or that he's not real."

Fantasies like Barney can bring a person good feelings. But a fantasy is a fantasy, and sooner or later the truth comes out.

There are all sorts of fantasies. Those hostile to the God of the Bible must hold on to a great number of fantasies to justify their thinking and behavior. Sooner or later those fantasies are seen for what they really are.

Authenticity, Belief, Deception, Disillusionment, Doctrine, Error, Evolution, Fantasy, Illusion, Lies, Morality, Reality
Isa. 44:9–20; 1 Cor. 6:9; Eph. 4:22; 2 Tim. 3:13; Titus 3:3

Date used _____ Place _____

In *Discipleship Journal* author Mack Stiles tells the story of how he led a young man from Sweden named Andreas to Christ. One part of their conversation is especially instructive:

Andreas said, "I've been told if I decide to follow Jesus, He will meet my needs and my life will get very good."

This seemed to Andreas to be a point in Christianity's favor. But I faced a temptation—to make it sound better than it is.

"No, Andreas, no!" I said.

Andreas blinked his surprise.

"Actually, Andreas, you may accept Jesus and find that life goes very badly for you."

"What do you mean?" he asked.

"Well, you may find that your friends reject you, you could lose your job, your family might oppose your decision—there are a lot of bad things that may happen to you if you decide to follow Jesus. Andreas, when Jesus calls you, He calls you to go the way of the cross."

Andreas stared at me and asked the obvious: "Then why would I want to follow Jesus?"

Sadly, this is the question that stumps many Christians. For some reason we feel that unless we're meeting people's needs they won't follow Christ. Yet this is not the gospel.

I cocked my head and answered, "Andreas, because Jesus is true."

Those on the side of truth come to Jesus.

Cross, Evangelism, Gospel, Jesus, Persecution, Witnessing
Matt. 16:24–27; John 8:31–47; 14:6; 15:18–16:4; 18:37; Acts 14:22; Phil. 1:29; 1 Thess. 3:3; 2 Tim. 3:12; 1 Peter 2:21; Rev. 1:9

Date used _____ Place _____

When the new technology of high-definition television came on the scene, it had an immediate effect on how things were done in the studio. Low-tech television had such poor picture resolution that the visual details of a studio did not show up on the screen. Actors and newscasters wore thick pancake makeup to hide wrinkles, moles, and blemishes, but the makeup was invisible to the relatively crude camera. Fake books rested on shelves, and cardboard backdrops with painted wood grain stood as walls. Still, with low-tech television, the viewer was none the wiser. Says Jim Fenhagen, a set designer who works for the major networks, "With the old TV, you can get away with murder."

But high-definition television, using high-resolution digital technology, changed all that. The studio camera picks up everything from scratches on the desk to blemishes on the skin. That has forced a change in how things are done.

Like television personalities facing an unforgiving high-definition camera, when we come to God, we come to the one who sees us as we really are. We must be completely truthful with him.

Authenticity, Confession, Conviction, Faults, Guilt, Honesty,
Hypocrisy, Scripture, Sin, Transparency, Vulnerability
John 16:8; Acts 5:1–11; 2 Tim. 3:16; Heb. 4:12–13

Date used _____ Place _____

In *Leadership*, Ben Patterson, dean of the chapel at Hope College and a former pastor, writes:

In the spring of 1980 I was suffering great pain from what was diagnosed as two herniated discs in my lower back. The prescription was total bed rest. But since my bed was too soft, the treatment ended up being total floor rest. I was frustrated and humiliated. I couldn't preach, I couldn't lead meetings, I couldn't call on new prospects for the church. I couldn't do anything but pray.

Not that I immediately grasped that last fact. It took two weeks for me to get so bored that I finally asked my wife for the church directory so I could at least do something, even if it was only pray for the people of my congregation. Note: it wasn't piety but boredom and frustration that drove me to pray. But pray I did, every day for every person in my church, two or three hours a day. After a while, the time became sweet.

Toward the end of my convalescence, anticipating my return to work, I prayed, "Lord, this has been good, this praying. It's too bad I don't have time to do this when I'm working."

And God spoke to me, very clearly. He said, "Stupid (that's right, that was his very word. He said it in a kind tone of voice, though). You have the same twenty-four hours each day when you're weak as when you're strong. The only difference is that when you're strong you think you're in charge. When you're weak you know you aren't."

Prayer is an admission of weakness and the single most important expression of true dependence on God.

Dependence, Ministry, Prayer
2 Cor. 12:8–10

Date used _____ Place _____

Weakness   249

In the 1996 Masters golf tournament, Greg Norman, the White Shark, had one of the most devastating experiences an athlete of any sort can suffer. After three rounds he had a virtually insurmountable six-stroke lead. Eighteen more holes of even average golf would assure him of his Masters victory and possession of the coveted green jacket. But the bottom fell out for Greg Norman. On the fourth and final day of the tournament he shot a 78, and Nick Faldo shot 67 to come from six shots back and win by five strokes.

In the *New York Times* Larry Dorman writes:

After the debacle, the golf star says he experienced "the most touching few days" of his life. People from all over the world contacted him with words of encouragement. The mail ran four times the volume of what Norman received when he won the British Open in 1993.

"It's changed my total outlook on life and on people," Norman says of last April's defeat. "There's no need for me to be cynical anymore. My wife said to me, 'You know, maybe this is better than winning the green jacket. Maybe now you understand the importance of it all.' I never thought I could reach out and touch people like that. And the extraordinary thing is that I did it by losing."

When we are weak, some of the most beautiful things in life can happen to us.

Cynicism, Encouragement, Failure, Losing, Strength
Matt. 5:1–5; 2 Cor. 12:7–10

Date used _____ Place _____

283

In the *Christian Reader*, Ramon Williams writes that on April 28, 1996, a gunman walked into a crowded cafe in Port Arthur, Australia, and started shooting. Tony Kistan, a Salvation Army soldier from Sydney, and his wife Sarah were in the restaurant when the bullets began to fly. Courageously Tony stepped in front of his wife to shield her from the gunfire, and he was one of the first to fall. Thirty-four victims eventually died in the incident, including Tony Kistan. As he lay dying in his wife's arms, he spoke his last words, "I'm going to be with the Lord."

Those final words of faith were quoted by the Australian media and carried to the world. "At a press conference," writes Williams, "Tony's son Nesan, 24, explained why his father held this assurance and described his father's dedication to the gospel. Hardened journalists and photographers were seen wiping tears from their eyes. In life, Tony had been a man who witnessed for his Lord to strangers and friends alike, and now in death, he had witnessed to others through his simple last statement."

Being a witness for Christ in this evil world brings eternal purpose to even the most tragic and painful events.

Courage, Death, Faith, Heaven, Hope, Love, Paradise,
Protection, Purpose, Testimony
1 Cor. 13:7; 2 Cor. 5:1–9; Phil. 1:20–24

Date used _____ Place _____

In April 1996 Sotheby's auctioned the estate property of former first lady Jacqueline Kennedy Onassis. The prices that bidders were willing to pay exceeded by far what anyone at the auction house had expected. A rocking chair sold for two hundred times what Sotheby's estimated. A faux pearl necklace, once tugged on by the toddler John F. Kennedy, Jr., in a now famous photo, had an estimated value of $500–$700 but sold for $211,500. A textbook of French verb conjugations brought $42,000. A humidor sold for half a million dollars.

Helyn Goldenberg of Sotheby's tried to explain the phenomenon: "This auction is merely a vehicle to get a piece of the magic, a piece the dream. This is about a woman who was once the most admired woman in the world."

The greatness of the person increases the value of the property. In a similar way, God in his great glory brings indescribable value to his people.

Children of God, Creation, Dignity, Identity, Respect, Self-Respect
Rom. 8:28–30; Eph. 1:3–14; 1 John 3:1–2

Date used _____ Place _____

Alan G. Artner writes in the *Chicago Tribune* that in 1995 the Art Institute of Chicago owned a treasure that they knew nothing about. In the institute's permanent collection was a chalk drawing of an upraised hand in a position of blessing (or as we might view it today, in a position of waving hello). The drawing appeared to have suffered serious damage: highlights in lead white chalk had oxidized and turned black. The drawing came into the institute's permanent collection in 1943, when the widow of a University of Chicago paleontologist donated two thousand drawings. At that time scholars noticed nothing unusual about the drawing, and the appearance of damage deterred further interest. It went into storage with thousands of other drawings and copies by lesser artists.

But then in 1987 the Art Institute decided to reexamine and catalogue every work in its permanent collection. Again, institute scholars first assumed the drawing of the hand was a copy done by an assistant of the Renaissance master Raphael. When they showed it to Raphael scholar Konrad Oberhuber, however, they were in for the surprise of a lifetime. He believed the drawing came from Raphael himself.

So institute scholars flew the drawing to England to show to more experts and to compare it with other Raphael originals. The verdict: the chalk drawing was a bona fide work of the master Raphael, one of the greatest figures in art history.

The prized work needed restoration, however. The oxidized paint was chemically converted into a light grey. When the cardboard mount was removed, the institute found further evidence of authenticity: a watermark in the paper similar to ones used in Florence around the time of Raphael's death in 1520.

The chalk drawing became an invaluable part of the Art Institute's collection, the only original Raphael they owned and one of only twelve Raphael originals in North America.

The value of a picture depends on who created it. The same is true of a person. When we realize that we are fashioned by

God—and not only fashioned by God but fashioned in his image—our worth skyrockets. As God's handiwork, our value exceeds all measure.

Creator, Dignity, Evolution, Self-Respect
Gen. 1:26–27; Ps. 139:14–16; Eph. 2:10; 1 John 3:1–3

Date used _____ Place _____

Cal Ripken, Jr., is the Iron Man of baseball. On September 6, 1995, he broke the record held by Lou Gehrig of 2,130 consecutive games played. Of course, there were days when that consecutive streak was in danger. In a June 1993 game Ripken was involved in a bench-clearing brawl. In *Time* Steve Wulf writes:

Ripken twisted his knee, and when he woke up the next morning, he couldn't put his weight on it. He told his wife, Kelly, he might not be able to play that night.

According to Kelly, "Just before he left for the ball park, I said, 'Maybe you could just play one inning and then come out.' He snapped, 'No! Either I play the whole game or I don't play at all.' I told him, 'Just checking, dear.'"

Ripken did play the full nine innings that night. In fact, he has played in 99.2 percent of every Orioles game since the streak began.

In any high pursuit, we face the temptation to lower our standards, to do just enough to get by. Cal Ripken, Jr., had committed himself to walk worthy of the title Iron Man.

Commitment, Compromise, Determination,
Overcoming, Perseverance, Standards, Walking Worthy
Eph. 4:1; Col. 1:27

Date used _____ Place _____

In a *Time* article prompted by the movie *Dante's Peak,* Jeffrey Kluger describes the physics behind the eruption of a volcano:

Volcanologically active areas generally lie atop clashing tectonic plates, where fractures five or six miles below ground create chambers into which magma rises and pools. . . . Magma held in the chamber eventually makes its way toward the surface through channels in the overlying rock. As the ascending ooze climbs higher, the pressure on it is dramatically reduced, allowing gases trapped within to bubble out like carbonation in an opened bottle of soda. As this happens, the magma takes on a foamier consistency, increasing its speed and mobility. When this scalding froth rises high enough to make contact with subterranean water, the water flashes into steam, turning the whole hellish mix into a natural pressure cooker. Finally, the explosively pressurized magma blasts out of the earth in an eruption that can send rocks, ash and gases flying out at near supersonic speeds. . . .

The first debris disgorged by a volcano is often a great gray mass of ash. The opaque cloud, made of pulverized rock and glass, falls like concrete snow on land and buildings miles away and may blot out the sun for days.

After the ash, some volcanoes produce what is known as a pyroclastic flow, a ground-hugging cloud of superheated gas and rock that forces a cushion of air down the mountainside at up to 100 m.p.h., incinerating anything in its path. Other mountains spew that signature substance of the volcano: lava.

For decades Mount St. Helens in Washington was a disaster waiting to happen, with a great chamber of molten magma cooking beneath it. In 1980 Mount St. Helens exploded, killing sixty people. Kluger writes that Mount Rainier has a similar profile, with a huge chamber of magma boiling beneath it— and with little towns like Orting, Washington, in its shadow. According to government geologists, the question is not whether Mount Rainier will blow, only when—and will people be ready.

The same is true of God's wrath. We live in a window of mercy, but do not let the relative calm deceive you. Wrath is going to come suddenly upon the earth. Will you be ready?

Anger, Day of the Lord, Judgment, Prophecy, Second Coming, Tribulation
Rom. 1:18; 2:4–6; 2 Thess. 1:5–10; Rev. 14–16; 19:11–21

Date used _____ Place _____

Notes

(Referenced by illustration number)

1. Doug Cumming, *Atlanta Journal-Constitution.* As seen in *Reader's Digest,* September 1997, 141–142.

2. "Boy, 12, Commits Suicide before Beginning School," *Chicago Tribune,* 27 August 1996, sec. 1, p. 7.

3. Associated Press, "Cervical Cancer Risk Rises with Infidelity," *Chicago Tribune,* 7 August 1996, sec. 1, p. 6.

4. Evan Thomas, "Inside the Mind of a Spy," *Newsweek,* June 1997, 34–35.

5. Shirley W. Belleranti, Scope , 1984; as seen in "Home Scuffed Home," *Christian Reader,* Sept/Oct 1995, 42.

6. Associated Press, "13 Years Later, Henderson Apologizes to Dallas Fans," *New York Times,* 6 January 1997, C10.

7. T. Ray Rachels, "Blemishes," *Pentecostal Evangel,* 21 April 1996, 14.

8. Mary B. W. Tabor, "Determined Student Proves SAT Wrong," *New York Times,* 7 February 1997, A1.

9. Gene E. Bradley with Wesley G. Pippert, "Miracle in the Desert," *New Man,* July/August 1997, 49, 51.

10. Canadian Press Photo, "An Act of Faith," *Chicago Tribune,* 17 December 1997, sec. 1, p. 11.

11. Richard Conniff, "Racing with the Wind," *National Geographic,* September 1997, 52–67.

12. Erma Landis, "Lite Fare," *Christian Reader,* March/April 1997, 11.

14. Lynette Holloway, "Noxious Mold Chases Families From Homes," *New York Times,* 9 November 1997, 17.

15. "Researcher: Monday Funk All in the Mind," *Chicago Tribune,* 2 July 1997, sec. 1, p. 8.

16. V. Dion Haynes and Jim Mateja, "According to Security Experts, Few Celebrities Hire Trained Drivers," *Chicago Tribune,* 5 September 1997, sec. 1, p. 19.

17. Moira Hodgson, "Lethal Wild Mushrooms Deceive the Unwary," *New York Times,* 22 January 1997, B6.

18. Bill McCartney, *From Ashes to Glory,* (Nashville: Thomas Nelson, 1995).

19. Philip Yancey, "A Bad Week in Hell," *Christianity Today*, 27 October 1997, 112.

20. Kevin A. Miller, "You Can Say No (Without Feeling Guilty)," *Discipleship Journal*, Mar/Apr 1996, 49.

21. Julie V. Iovine, "Style over Substance," *Chicago Tribune*, 29 March 1997, sec. 4, p. 1.

22. Kevin Dale Miller, "Ordinary Heroes," *Christian Reader*, Mar/April 1996, 81; Rick Bragg, "She Opened World to Others; Her World Has Opened, Too," *New York Times*, 12 November 1996, A1, A10; *Guideposts*, Sep. 1996, 2–5.

23. Haman Cross Jr., "Daddy, I'm Pregnant," *New Man*, May 1997, 63; as adapted from *Urban Family*.

24. "Breathing Lessons," *People Weekly*, 15 January 1996, 26.

25. Devlin Donaldson, *Contemporary Christian Magazine*; as seen in *Christian Reader*, July/Aug 1996, 43.

26. Barnaby J. Feder, "Quaker Chief, Tied to Losses From Snapple, To Step Down," *New York Times*, 24 April 1997, C1.

27. Reuters, "Runway record," *Chicago Tribune*, 16 October 1997, sec. 1, p. 15.

28. Philip Yancey, "A Pilgrim's Progress," *Books & Culture*, Sept/Oct 1995, 10.

29. Jim Bradford, "Of Countries and Kingdoms," *Pentecostal Evangel*, 11 January 1998, 12–13.

30. Associated Press, "Here's the Dirt—Check Your Hands," *Chicago Tribune*, 17 September 1996, sec. 1, p. 11. Gordon Walek, *Daily Herald* (Chicago Suburban), 18 September 1996, sec. 3, p. 9.

31. B. Drummond Ayres Jr., "At 72, Bush Leaps Into Open Sky, Again," *New York Times*, 26 March 1997, A10.

32. John Ortberg, "What's Really Behind Our Fatigue?" *Leadership*, Spring 1997, 110.

33. New York Times News Service, "Friends Aren't a Cure for Common Cold, but They Help, Study Finds," *Chicago Tribune*, 25 June 1997, sec. 1, p. 9; *The Journal of the American Medical Association*, 25 June 1997.

34. Bill Jauss, "Catcher and Sox Both Seriously Hurt," *Chicago Tribune*, 20 July 1996, sec. 3, p. 10; Steve Rosenbloom, "Hit & Run," *Chicago Tribune*, 29 September 1996, sec. 3, p. 1.

35. Jo Thomas, "Satisfaction in Job Well Done Is Only Reward for E-Mail Software Inventor," *New York Times*, 21 January 1997, A6.

36. Dan Quayle, *Standing Firm* (Grand Rapids: Zondervan).

37. Carolyn P. Hagan, *Child*; as seen in *Reader's Digest*, November 1996, 113.

38. William Palmer, "Roots of Rage," *Chicago Tribune Magazine*, 28 September 1997, 20–21.

39. John Feinstein, *Inside Sports.*

40. Jean Fleming, "Growing in the Good Times," *Discipleship Journal*, Sept/Oct 1996, 26.

41. Robert Coles, *The Moral Intelligence of Children*, (Random House, 1997).

42. Tribune News Services, "Health News," *Chicago Tribune*, 12 September 1996, sec. 1, p. 14; *New England Journal of Medicine*, 12 September 1996.

43. Ken Walker, "Ordinary Heroes," *Christian Reader,* Sept/Oct 1995, 62.

44. Neil McAleer, *The Mind-Boggling Universe* (Garden City, New York: Doubleday & Company, 1987).

45. Ron Kotulak and Jon Van, "Jupiter Might Be Key to Our Survival," *Chicago Tribune,* 28 September 1995, sec. 5, p. 4.

46. Tim Keller, "Preaching Hell in a Tolerant Age," *Leadership,* Fall 1997, 44.

47. "Skydiver Killed Saving a Novice," *Chicago Tribune,* 25 June 1997, sec. 1, p. 7; Reuters, "Skydiving Instructor Dies in Breaking Novice's Fall," *New York Times,* 25 June 1997, A16.

48. Andrea Midgett, *Christianity Today,* 3 April 1995, 43.

49. Jeff Zeleny and Susan Kuczka, "Those Who Said No Shudder with Relief," *Chicago Tribune,* 30 March 1997, sec. 1, pp. 1, 15.

50. Associated Press, "Man Dies While Running in Honor of Late Daughter," *Chicago Tribune,* 14 October 1997, sec. 1, p. 9.

51. John Wimber. *Living with Uncertainty.* (Anaheim, California: Vineyard Ministries International); as seen in *Christianity Today,* 7 October 1996, 50–51.

52. Robert R. Jackson, "Portia Spider: Mistress of Deception," *National Geographic,* November 1996, 104–114.

53. Jeffrey Bils & Stacey Singer, "Gorilla Saves Tot in Brookfield Zoo Ape Pit," *Chicago Tribune,* 17 August 1996, sec. 1, p. 1.

54. Associated Press, "Ship's Crew Is Faulted in New Orleans Crash," *New York Times,* 19 December 1997, A18; Associated Press, "Hundreds Flee As Ship Rams Mall in New Orleans," *Chicago Tribune,* 15 December 1996, sec. 1, p. 3.

55. Andy Griffith, "Journey to Health," *Guideposts,* November 1996, 9.

56. Associated Press, "Overbearing Neighbor? Bank on It," *Chicago Tribune,* 26 June 1997, sec. 1, p. 12.

57. "Objecting to 'Acts of God,' Governor Balks at Bill," *New York Times,* 21 March 1997, A10.

58. Tony Evans, *Returning to Your First Love* (Chicago: Moody Press, 1995), 128–129.

59. Jeff Gammage, "'Sponging' Investigated at Racetracks," *Chicago Tribune,* sports, p. 16.

60. Richard Conniff, "Racing with the Wind," *National Geographic,* September 1997, 52–67.

61. "Demand for Killer Heroin Rises, Police Say," *Chicago Tribune,* 16 July 1996, sec. 1, p. 9; "The Night the Music Ended," People, 29 July 1996, 92–93.

62. Michael Kelly, *The New Yorker.*

63. Alex Tresniowski, "Oprah Buff," *People Weekly,* 9 September 1996, 80–81; Lisbeth Levine, "It's Not Who You Know . . . It's Who You Train," *Chicago Tribune,* 12 September 1996, sec. 5, pp. 1, 11. Newsmakers, "Oprah Hires an Ally in Battle of the Bulge," *Chicago Tribune,* 2 September 1996, sec. 1, p. 2.

64. Chris Edwardson, "Chris Edwardson, M.D., Discusses Evangelism in the Workplace," *Pentecostal Evangel,* 26 October 1997, 7.

65. Ira Berkow, "Born to Coach Basketball," *New York Times,* 21 April 1997, C14.

66. *Today's Christian Woman;* as seen in *Christian Reader,* May/June 1996, 75–76.

67. Roy Maynard, "Strong Arms," *World,* 13 December 1997, 13–14.

68. Associated Press, "Driver Ed Teacher Quits After Road Rage Lesson," *Chicago Tribune,* 16 October 1997, sec. 1, p. 11.

69. Don Shula & Ken Blanchard, *Everyone's a Coach* (New York: Harper Business, 1995; Grand Rapids: Zondervan Publishing House, 1995) 56–57.

70. Marshall Shelley, "My New View of God," *Leadership,* Fall 1996, 90.

71. Leon Jaroff, "Still Ticking," *Time,* 4 November 1996, 80.

72. J. Allan Petersen, *Better Families;* as seen in *Leadership,* Summer 1996, 69.

73. Peter Gorner, "On the Record," *Chicago Tribune,* 20 July 1997, sec. 2, p. 3.

74. Gary J. Oliver, "The Cult of Success," *New Man,* September 1997, 74.

75. Associated Press, "Oops! Kidnap Note Aside, Couple Are OK," *Chicago Tribune,* 25 June 1997, sec. 1, p. 10.

76. John M. Broder, "Warning: A Batman Cape Won't Help You Fly," *New York Times,* 5 March 1997, A1.

77. Richard Stevenson, "A Buried Message Loudly Heard," *New York Times,* 7 December 1996, 19, 21; Floyd Norris, "Greenspan Asks a Question and Global Markets Wobble," *New York Times,* 7 December 1996, 1, 20.

78. Paul Hoversten, "Lucid Quick to Get Feet Back on Ground," *USA Today,* 25 October 1996, 4A.

79. Tim Franklin, "Tyler, U.S.: Agony of da-feet," *Chicago Tribune,* 27 July 1996, sec. 3, p. 1.

80. Patti Davis, *Angels Don't Die* (HarperCollins); as seen in *Christian Reader,* Nov/Dec 1995, 60.

81. David Wallis, "A Question for: Jimmy Carter," *New York Times Magazine,* 26 October 1997, 19.

82. Jill Briscoe, *Running on Empty* (Wheaton: Harold Shaw, 1995), 101.

83. Christopher Thomas, "Old Foes Cross a Bridge to Forgiveness," *The Times of London,* 16 August 1995, sec. 1, p. 1.

84. Julie V. Iovine, "A New Cash Crop: The Farm as Theme Park," *New York Times,* 2 November 1997, 1.

85. "'Tis The Season—To Be Wasteful," *National Wildlife,* Dec/Jan 1997, 12.

86. Judith Miller, "He Gave Away $600 Million, and No One Knew," *New York Times,* 23 January 1997, A1.

87. David W. Dunlap, "Zoo Gift Is Revoked Because Name on Plaque Is Too Small," *New York Times,* 15 May 1997, A19.

88. Ron Barefield, "Bethesda Outreach Ministries: Making Missions Their Business," *Pentecostal Evangel,* 4 February 1996, 8–10.

89. Melissa Isaacson, "Getting assistant a ring would be Jordan's pleasure," *Chicago Tribune,* 1 June 1997, sec. 3, p. 8.

90. Stuart N. Robinson, "Letters," *Sports Illustrated,* 15 September 1997, 10.

91. Wendy Murray Zoba, "Bill Bright's Wonderful Plan for the World," *Christianity Today,* 14 July 1997, 24.

92. Associated Press, "Fireworks Set Off Fire at Valley Forge Park," *New York Times,* 18 March 1997, A10.

93. Max Lucado, *In the Grip of Grace,* (Dallas: Word, 1996).

94. Stuart Briscoe, "Why Christ Had to Die," *Preaching Today,* #163, 4.
95. Luis Palau, "God's Ocean of Grace," *Pursuit,* vol. 4, no. 11.
96. Carey Goldberg, "Real-Space Meetings Fill In the Cyberspace Gaps," *New York Times,* 25 February 1997, A8; "Bill Gates: Richest American Ever," *Fortune,* 4 August 1997, 38–39.
97. Gary Thomas, "The Freedom of Surrender," *Discipleship Journal,* Sep/Oct 1996, 52.
98. "The Best and Worst of Everything," *Parade,* 28 December 1997, 6–7.
99. Mitchell May, "Assumed-Identity Crisis," *Chicago Tribune,* 17 August 1997, sec. 2, p. 5.
100. Associated Press, *Chicago Tribune,* 1 September 1996, sec. 1, p. 6.
101. Scorecard, "The Razor's Edge," *Sports Illustrated,* 4 November 1996, 22.
102. George O. Wood, "Psalm 103: Deep Healing," *Pentecostal Evangel,* 26 October 1997, 6.
103. John Wimber, *Living with Uncertainty,* (Anaheim, California: Vineyard Ministries International); as seen in *Christianity Today,* 7 October 1996, 50–51.
104. Paul Hoversten, "Jupiter's Winds: 10,000-Mile-Deep 'Giant Flywheel,'" *USA Today,* 22 May 1996, 3A.
105. Leith Anderson, "Next Life in the House of the Lord," *Preaching Today* (Christianity Today, Inc.), tape #157.
106. Joni Eareckson Tada, *Preaching Today* (Christianity Today, Inc.), tape #157.
107. Quotables, *Chicago Tribune,* 23 September 1996, sec. 1, p. 17; "Stranded U.S. Astronaut at Last May Be Retrieved," *Chicago Tribune,* 16 September 1996, sec. 1, p. 7.
108. Paul Grabill and Eric Harrah, "One of the Nation's Largest Abortion Providers Discusses His Decision to Follow Jesus," *Pentecostal Evangel,* 18 January 1998, 8.
109. John L. Eliot, "Earth Almanac," *National Geographic,* August 1996, 136.
110. "Black Cadet Commissioned 123 Years Later," *Chicago Tribune,* 23 September 1997, sec. 1, p. 6.
111. Salman Rushdie, *Imaginary Homelands,* (Viking Penguin).
112. "Male Despair Tied to Atherosclerosis," *Chicago Tribune,* 26 August 1997, sec. 1, p. 8.
113. Richard Jerome and Elizabeth McNeil, "Stringed Victory," *People Weekly,* 28 April 1997, 111–114.
114. Tracey Bailey, "Lesson of a Lifetime," *Guideposts,* April 1997, 14–17.
115. Jim Corley, "Getting Past the Showroom," *Christian Reader,* Jan/Feb 1998, 52.
116. "Quotable," *Chicago Tribune,* 11 July 1997, sec. 1, p. 21.
117. *Sports Illustrated Presents* (special commemorative edition), February 1997, 72.
118. Peter Kendall, "Exterminator's lethal brew leaves expensive residue," *Chicago Tribune,* 3 July 1997, sec. 1, p. 1.
119. Michiko Kakutani, "The Making of a Myth Who Rode Into the Sunset," *New York Times,* 25 February 1997, B6.
120. Cal Ripken, Jr. and Mike Bryan, *The Only Way I Know* (New York: Viking, 1997).

121. Emory Thomas, Jr., *Wall Street Journal*, 21 March 1995, 1; as seen in *Reader's Digest*, January 1996, 89.

122. John Noble Wilford, "Hubble Detects Stars That Belong to No Galaxy," *New York Times*, 15 January 1997, A9.

123. Andy Woodland, "He Loves Doing 'Paarat' for You," *Christian Reader*, May/June 1997, 44.

124. Paul Thigpen, "Where's the Joy," *Discipleship Journal*, May/June 1996, 21.

125. Al Hinman, *Your Health*; as seen in *Ladies' Home Journal*, May 1996, 45.

126. "The Best and Worst of Everything," *Parade*, 28 December 1997, 7.

127. Associated Press, "Lab-Made Virus Destroys Cells Infected by HIV," *Chicago Tribune*, 5 September 1997, sec. 1, p. 3.

128. Seth Mydans, "Singapore, Where Ruin Is the Reward for Error," *New York Times*, 12 December 1996, A11.

129. Steve Sjogren, *Conspiracy of Kindness* (Ann Arbor, Michigan: Servant Publications, 1993), 15–17.

130. Jim Bakker, *I Was Wrong* (Nashville: Thomas Nelson, 1997).

131. Jill Briscoe, *Running on Empty* (Wheaton: Harold Shaw, 1995), 20.

132. Ron Mehl, *The Cure for a Troubled Heart* (Questar Publishers, 1996).

133. T. H. Watkins, *National Geographic*, September 1996, 85.

134. Stephen Lee, "Tougher Buoys of Summer," *Chicago Tribune*, 12 July 1996, sec. 2, p. 1.

135. Alix M. Freedman and Suein L. Hwang, "How Seven Individuals With Diverse Motives Halted Tobacco's Wars," *Wall Street Journal*, 11 July 1997, A1.

136. Holcomb B. Noble, "W. Lain Guthrie, 84, Jet Pilot Who Refused To Dump Fuel," *New York Times*, 28 March 1997, A17.

137. Jon Van & Ron Kotulak, "Forced Exercise May Do More Harm Than Good," *Chicago Tribune*, 30 October 1997, sec. 5, p. 3.

138. Dan Schaeffer, "We're No Longer Home Alone," *Moody*, November/December 1997, 59.

140. Associated Press, "For Man Who Fell Into River, Lo, an Angel," *New York Times*, 25 December 1996, A10.

141. Fred Mitchell, "Payton Searching for Missing Super Bowl Ring," *Chicago Tribune*, 2 July 1996, sec. 4, p. 3.

142. Associated Press, "Popularity of 1996 Film Fills Shelters with Unwanted Dalmatians in 1997," *Chicago Tribune*, 10 September 1997, sec. 1, p. 11.

143. Rita Price, *Columbus Dispatch*, as seen in *Reader's Digest*, January 1996, 88.

144. Melissa Hendricks, *Johns Hopkins Magazine*; as seen in *Reader's Digest*, November 1996, 112–113.

145. Dave Goetz, *Leadership*, Spring 1996, 26.

146. Don Van Natta Jr. and Elaine Sciolino, "Body, and Tombstone of Lies, Are Removed," *New York Times*, 12 December 1997, A1, A16.

147. Ruth Ryan, *Covering Home*, (Word, 1995); as seen in *Reader's Digest*, Sept 1995, 87.

148. Skip Gray, "The Way of the Cross," *Discipleship Journal*, July/Aug 1997, 49.

149. Joe Martin, "Mister Boffo," *Universal Press Syndicate*, 1997; *Chicago Tribune*, 9 February 1997, sec. 9, p. 1.

150. Jim Williams, *Readers Digest*, August 1997, 112.

151. Patrick O'Driscoll, "Rural Areas Rustle Up Rules for City Slickers," *USAToday*, 8 August 1997, 4A.

152. Jim Mateja, "10 That Made a Difference," *Chicago Tribune*, 16 June 1996, sec. 12, pp. 1, 5–6.

153. Victor Lee, "Lee'd Stories," *Sports Spectrum*, October 1997, 5.

154. Ian Hall with Joyce Wells Booze, "They Named Him Samuel," *Pentecostal Evangel*, 11 February 1996, 18–19.

155. Paul Sullivan, "Yanks, Fan Grab Opener from Orioles," *Chicago Tribune*, 10 October 1996, sec. 4, pp. 1, 5.

156. Tim Stafford, "The Making of a Revolution," *Christianity Today*, 8 December 1997, 17–18.

157. Associated Press, "Mentally Disabled Man Gambles Away a Social Security Windfall," *Chicago Tribune*, 25 August 1997, sec. 1, p. 3.

158. Wendy Murray Zoba, "Bill Bright's Wonderful Plan for the World," *Christianity Today*, 14 July 1997, 24.

159. Brian Burrell, *Words We Live By* (S&S Trade: 1997).

160. Susan Maycinik, "Obedience or Performance?," *Discipleship Journal*, Mar/Apr 1996, 8.

161. Elaine Creasman, "A Holy Jealousy," *Discipleship Journal*, May/June 1996, 66.

162. Rogers Worthington, "Expert can't mediate his own dispute," *Chicago Tribune*, 8 July 1996, sec. 1, p. 1.

163. Glenn Collins, "The Americanization of Salsa," *New York Times*, 9 January 1997, C–1, C–4.

164. Associated Press, "Passengers Get to Airport—the Long Way," *Chicago Tribune*, 3 July 1997, sec. 1, p. 8.

165. Bernard Weinraub, "Casting Ron Howard Against Type," *New York Times*, 12 November 1996, B1, B4.

166. Elie Wiesel, *All Rivers Run to the Sea* (Knopf); as seen in *Reader's Digest*, June 1997, 156–157.

167. Jimmy Carter, *U.S. News & World Report*; as seen in *Christian Reader*, July/Aug 1997, 29.

168. Jill Briscoe, *Can a Busy Christian Develop Her Spiritual Life?* (Minneapolis: Bethany House Publishers, 1995).

169. Gordon MacDonald, "Pastor's Progress," *Leadership*, Summer 1997, 81–82.

170. Andrew Bagnato, "Good Guys Finish First (Sometimes)," *Chicago Tribune Magazine*, 1 September 1996, 15.

171. Elaine Sciolino, "A Painful Road from Vietnam to Forgiveness," *New York Times*, 12 November 1996, A–1, A–8.

172. Associated Press, "30 Million New $50 Bills Are Withheld," *Chicago Tribune*, 25 September 1997, sec. 1, p. 22.

173. Michael Lewis, "The Subversive," *New York Times Magazine*, 25 May 1997, 36–37.

174. Brother Andrew with Verne Becker, *The Calling* (Moorings); as seen in *Christian Reader*, July/Aug 1996, 107.

175. Larry Dorman, "Woods's Clubs Not Magic Wands," *New York Times*, 22 October 1996, B16.

176. Adrienne W. Fawcett, "The House That Hindman Built," *Chicago Tribune*, 16 June 1996, sec. 15, pp. 1, 6.

177. Eric Ferkenhoff, "Jet-Skier Rescued after Lake Ordeal," *Chicago Tribune*, 18 June 1997, sec. 2, p. 2.

178. Bob Verdi, "Paying for Air," *Chicago Tribune*, 13 July 1996, sec. 1, p. 1.

179. Annie Dillard, "Total Eclipse," *The Annie Dillard Reader* (New York: Harper Collins, 1994), 11–12.

180. Felix Jimenez, "Search for the Black Box," *Guideposts*, January 1997, 14–17.

181. James David Ford, "Pastoring a House Divided," *Leadership*, Fall 1996, 112.

182. Billy Graham, *How I Pray*, (Ballantine Books, 1994).

183. Tim Crothers, *Sports Illustrated*; as seen in *Reader's Digest*, December 1995, 99–100.

184. Mike Yaconelli, *The Door*; as seen in *Christian Reader*, Sept/Oct 1996, 36.

185. Verna Bowman, "Quilt of Many Promises," *Guideposts*, May 1997, 6–9.

186. Dale Alan Robbins, "When All Else Fails, It's Time to Pray," *Pentecostal Evangel*, 19 May 1996, 20–21.

187. Jim Cymbala with Dean Merrill, *Fresh Wind, Fresh Fire* (Grand Rapids: Zondervan, 1997), 16–17.

188. Bonne Steffen, "Cross-country Revival," *Christian Reader*, Sept/Oct 1995, 80.

189. Associated Press, "Nearly Half of Those Hurt by Violence Knew Assailant," *Chicago Tribune*, 25 August 1997, sec. 1, p. 4.

190. Will Norton Jr., "The Write Stuff," *Aspire*, November 1995, 55.

191. "Almost Home," *Life*, March 1996, 52. "Update: Free Willy," *Life*, January 1997, 16.

192. Reuters, *Chicago Tribune*, 24 August 1996, sec. 1, p. 20; Dan McGraw, "Human Error and a Human Tragedy," *U.S. News & World Report*, 8 January 1996, 38.

193. Daniel Q. Haney, "The Ulcer Bug," *Daily Herald*, 8 April 1996, Suburban living, p. 1.

194. Joann C. Jones, *Guideposts*; as seen in *Reader's Digest*, August 1996, 147–148.

195. Ramona Cramer Tucker, "Enough Is Enough," *Today's Christian Woman*, September/October 1996, 129.

196. Andrew C. Revkin, "Taking Lowly Pallets and Finding Treasure," *New York Times*, 5 March 1997, A13.

197. Wayne A. Lamb, *100 Meditations on Hope*; as seen in *Christianity Today*.

198. Carey Goldberg, "Windfall Sets Off a Blizzard of Bonuses for a Company," *New York Times*, 25 December 1996, A9.

199. Brenda Kearns, "The Simple Posture Trick That Can Save Your Life," *Woman's World*, 23 September, 1997, 20.

200. Ken R. Canfield, "A Child Is Crying for You," *New Man*, May 1997, 98.

201. Harold Reynolds with Roxanne Robbins, "I Couldn't Have Hand-Picked a Better Family," *Sports Spectrum*, September 1997.

202. John Schmeltzer, "Gerber Tries to Control Rumor Rerun," *Chicago Tribune*, 27 September 1997, sec. 2, p. 1.

203. Bob Condor, "At Ease," *Chicago Tribune*, 23 October 1997, sec. 5, p. 6.

204. Kathleen Donnelly, "Norma McCorvey Has Regrets, but Being the Plaintiff in Roe V. Wade Isn't One of Them," *Knight-Ridder/Tribune News Service*, 22 June 1994; Jeff Hooten, *Citizen*, February 1997. As seen in *Knight-Ridder/Tribune News Service*, 20 January 1997.

205. James Dobson, *Focus on the Family*; as seen in *Christian Reader*, Sept/Oct 1996, 36.

206. Larry Rohter, "For the Mailmen Lost in a Maze, Amazing News," *New York Times*, 15 November 1996, A6.

207. Matthew L. Wald, "Engineer in '96 Rail Crash Hid His Failing Sight From Railroad," *New York Times*, 26 March 1997, A15.

208. Kevin Dale Miller, "The Man Who Brought Pocahontas to Life," *Christian Reader*, July/August 1995, 41.

209. Alex Heard, "Your Twinn," *New York Times Magazine*, 21 December 1997, 21.

210. Associated Press, "Internet Surfer Loses Kids over Her Obsession," *Chicago Tribune*, 17 June 1997, sec. 1, p. 13.

211. Newsmakers, "Slim Fast or Else, Miss Universe Told," *Chicago Tribune*, 20 August 1996, sec. 1, p. 2; *People Weekly*, 10 February 1997, 48–49; *People Weekly*, 29 December 1997, 160.

212. Jo Thomas, "Friend Says McVeigh Wanted Bombing to Start an 'Uprising,'" *New York Times*, 13 May 1997, A1.

213. *Chicago Tribune*, "Here's One for the 'Stupid Criminals' File," 23 July 1996, sec. 1, p. 7.

214. Mitchell May, "Turn of Events: Bed of Rails," *Chicago Tribune*, 10 August 1997, sec. 2, p. 6.

215. Ed Hinton, "Asleep at the Wheel," *Sports Illustrated*, 15 September 1997, 88–89.

216. Matthew L. Wald, "Fumes Knocked Out 2 Before Plane Crash," *New York Times*, 22 January 1997, A16.

217. Henri Nouwen, *New Man*; as seen in *Christian Reader*, Nov/Dec 1996, 43–44.

219. James Barron, "Chris Farley, 33, a Versatile Comedian-Actor," *New York Times*, 19 December 1997, A21; Mark Caro and Allan Johnson, "For Farley, Comedy Was His Life," *Chicago Tribune*, 21 December 1997, sec. 1, pp. 1, 20; Steve Mills, "Drug Overdose Killed Comedian Farley," *Chicago Tribune*, 3 January 1998, sec. 1, p. 1.

220. Bob Condor, "A Gentler Workout," *Chicago Tribune*, 14 September 1995, sec. 5, p. 4.

221. Associated Press, "Gyroscopes Shut Down on Hobbled Mir," *Chicago Tribune*, 4 July 1997, sec. 1, p. 8.

222. Mark Galli, "Spiritual Disciplines: From Duty to Delight," *Discipleship Journal*, Nov/Dec 1993.

223. Richard O'Brien and Hank Hersch, "Scorecard," *Sports Illustrated*, 15 September 1997, 20.

224. William Mullen, "Right under Your Coffee, Serious Science Occurring," *Chicago Tribune*, 23 October 1997, sec. 1, p. 1.

225. John Robb with Larry Wilson, "In God's Kingdom . . . Prayer Is Social Action," *World Vision*, February-March 1997, 3–4.

226. Hugh Dellios, "Swimming Without the Sharks," *Chicago Tribune*, 6 July 1996, sec. 1, pp. 1, 12.

227. George Johnson, "Casting an Eye on Sights Unseen," *New York Times*, 12 October 1997, sec. 4, p. 5.

228. John von Rhein, "Pulling Strings," *Chicago Tribune*, 13 June 1996, sec. 5, pp. 1, 4.

229. Associated Press, "3 Teens Get 15 Years for Removing Stop Sign in Fatal Prank," *Chicago Tribune*, sec. 1, p. 16.

230. Cheryl Lavin, "The Prime Time of Bryant Gumbel," *Chicago Tribune Magazine*, 28 September 1997, 15.

231. Jane Meredith Adams, "The Man Behind Dilbert" *Chicago Tribune*, 5 February 1996, Tempo, 1.

232. Associated Press, "Agency Reports More Cases of Hair-Eating Doll," *New York Times*, 31 December 1996, A–9.

233. "Quotable," *Chicago Tribune*, 18 September 1996, sec. 4, p. 3; *Chicago Tribune*, 19 June 1997, sec. 4, p. 4.

234. *Chicago Tribune*, 29 August 1996, sec. 4, p. 10.

235. Ken Walker, "Time to Bow or Bow Out?" *Sports Spectrum*, September 1997, 22–25.

236. Charles Kuralt, *Charles Kuralt's America*, (New York: G. P. Putnam's Sons, 1995).

237. Michael Johnson, *Slaying the Dragon* (Harper Collins, 1996).

238. Uli Schmetzer, "Wanted Dead or Alive: Manila's Flies, Roaches," *Chicago Tribune*, 17 September 1996, sec. 1, p. 6.

239. Jerry Kramer, "Winning Wasn't Everything," *New York Times*, 24 January 1997, A17.

240. Robert Bryce, "Sun-B-Gone," *New York Times Magazine*, 5 October 1997, 21.

241. "Two-Minute Drill," *Chicago Tribune*, 2 September 1996, sec. 3, p. 4.

242. Randy Fitzgerald, "You Can Make a Million," *Reader's Digest*, July 1996, 28.

243. Michael Parfit, "The Essential Element of Fire," *National Geographic*, September 1996, 118–123.

244. Drew Baker, "Alternate Routes," *Sports Spectrum*, October 1997, 12–13.

245. Reuters, "Actor Is Hurt by Short-Circuit in 'Barney' Suit," *Chicago Tribune*, 17 July 1997, sec. 1, p. 12.

246. J. Mack Stiles, "Ready to Answer," *Discipleship Journal*, Mar/Apr 1997, 42–43.

247. Joel Brinkley, "It's All in the Details," *New York Times*, 3 March 1997, C1, C8.

248. Ben Patterson, "Heart & Soul," *Leadership*, Fall 1996, 130.

249. Larry Dorman, "Support from around the World Overwhelms Norman," *New York Times*, 18 April 1996, B11, 14; as seen in *Reader's Digest*, September 1996, 106.

250. Ramon Williams, "News Clips: Powerful Last Words," *Christian Reader*, July/August 1996, 81.

251. Steve Kloehn, "Fame Has Price, and Many Are Willing to Pay It," *Chicago Tribune*, 26 April 1996, sec. 1, pp. 1, 24.

252. Alan G. Artner, "Sleuthing Uncovers Hand of a Master," *Chicago Tribune*, 17 May 1996, sec. 1, p. 1.

253. Steve Wulf, "Iron Bird," *Time*, 11 September 1995, 68–74.

254. Jeffrey Kluger, "Volcanoes with an Attitude," *Time*, 24 February 1997, 58–59.

Subject Index

303

Scripture Index

12:30—133
13:21–23—59
13:22—21
13:32–37—247, 248
14:3–11—12
15:34—56

Luke
4:18—190
4:19—187
5:4–7—37
5:27–32—223
6:27–37—218
6:36—136
6:45—119
7:22—190
8:1–3—100
10:17–18—259
10:25–37—191
12:1–3—165
12:5–13—204
12:13–21—250
12:15—168, 201
12:16–21—100
12:35–40—247, 248
12:48—53, 73, 96, 262
13:6–9—96
13:22–30—122
14:12–24—190
14:15–24—70
15—159, 189
15:1–32—50, 160, 236
15:11–32—93
16:1–13—179
17:1–2—263
17:5–6—82
17:6—259
17:11–19—110
18:1–8—204
18:9–14—14, 169
18:27—259
19:1–10—160
23:43—109

John
1:3—54
1:12—46, 58, 240
1:47—135
3:1–8—51
3:3—119
3:16—22, 89, 159, 240
4:10–14—74

4:16–19—113
4:34–38—95
5:17—140
6:12—96
6:29—22
6:35—74
6:41–66—186
7:37–39—74
7:45–52—16
8:31–32—24
8:31–47—280
8:34–44—245
8:42–45—63
8:44—84
9:1–7—68
9:1–41—16
10:10—221, 245, 267
10:27–29—149, 159
11:4—211
11:25—60
12:4–8—12
12:26—126
13:8—40
13:34–35—29, 102
14:6—25, 222, 280
14:16—139
14:23–24—155, 182, 183
15:1–8—96
15:1–17—95
15:8—172
15:9–17—102
15:18–16:4—167, 198, 280
16:8—281
16:8–11—52
16:26—139
16:33—140
17—39
17:3—150
17:11–12—260
17:24—120
17:24–26—150
18:37—280
20:24–29—41
20:31—25
21:1–6—37

Acts
1:4–8—37, 202
1:8—77, 124, 172

2:1–47—37
2:17–18—175
2:42–47—43, 44, 138
4:12—25, 222
4:24—54
4:29—269
5:1–11—281
7:54–60—196, 198
7:54–8:4—167
8:26–40—77
12:1–11—176
12:1–19—64
14:22—280
15:37–38—41
16:6–10—66
17:6—153, 172
17:16–34—23
17:30–31—187
20:35—162
21:10–11—175
23:11—77

Romans
1–3—151
1:5—22
1:16—103, 199
1:18—290
1:18–3:8—112
1:22–25—74
1:29—233
2:4—160
2:4–6—290
2:5–11—126
3–4—19
3–5—105
3:9–20—188
3:10—244
3:10–12—197
3:10–23—181
3:10–26—107
3:23—51, 197, 244
3:25—56
4:1–25—107
4:25—57
5:2–5—277
5:3–4—193
5:3–5—140
5:12–14—113
5:12–21—188
6:23—60, 72, 245
7:7–25—184

315